The Survivor

THE STORY OF EDDY HUKOV

Books by the Same Author

MOVE OVER, MOUNTAIN

THE SURVIVOR: *The Story of Eddy Hukov*

The
Survivor

THE STORY OF EDDY HUKOV

By JOHN EHLE

Henry Holt and Company
New York

To Mack J. Preslar of Chapel Hill,
who first heard the story . . .

INTRODUCTION

THIS IS A BRUTAL and compassionate story, the biography of a powerful man without a country, one of the world's stateless persons, who has lived a heroic adventure on three continents; and it seems to me that the story reveals a great deal about this man, about this type of man, and about the world we live in. Most of his friends have failed to meet this world's challenges and are buried in unmarked graves in Poland, Russia, Hungary, Czechoslovakia, Belgium, Viet Nam, Burma, and North Africa. But he survives. Not only that, but he remains strong and undefeated.

He was one of the half-million Storm Troopers left alive in Hitler's Germany when the war ended. Although this period in his youth—he joined when he was seventeen—is not covered in detail in this book, we have presented his part in it frankly and, in so far as he has told us, accurately. Certainly the account does not seek either to excuse or justify his participation; in fact, his life stands as a consequence of those years. He has cut the blood mark of the SS from his arm, but he is marked by the SS to this day and is shadowed by it.

I have written the account from his point of view throughout, telling it just as he told it to me, even retaining some elements of his style and writing it in the first person. By these means I have tried to leave the intimacy and simplicity of his letters, in which he conveyed the information to me. He has read the manuscript and testifies to its truth. In addition, we have documents which establish the accuracy of much of it and indicate the accuracy of the whole.

I first heard of Eddy Hukov when a close friend, Mack Preslar, returned to Chapel Hill from abroad. Preslar, who is Assistant Director of the University of North Carolina Communication Center, had less to say about his voyage than about this one man he had met, with whom he had talked for two days—Edward Hugo, or as he prefers to be known at this time, Edward Hukov. Preslar had found that he was a man who for fifteen years had made daily decisions not so much on the basis of right or wrong as on the basis of life or death.

Believing that this life story struck close to important themes, I wrote to Hukov. We began corresponding. Back and forth across half the world the letters went. This is a tedious way for a writer to gather information for a book, but it turned out to be a good way to get to know Hukov. There was time to reflect. By the arrival of the last bulky letter in the first series of letters—each dealing with a specified segment of his life—I felt that I had experienced something of his dramatic struggle, that I had come close to knowing the same people and dangers, and that I had reacted with some of the same courage and persistence.

I felt then, as I do now, that getting to know Hukov, who had a different view of life and who had lived differently, enlarged and strengthened my own views and enriched my more limited experiences. In one moment I realized, for example, that Hukov and I lived on the same earth but in different worlds, and that each world was real and present. I was part of the protected environment of the United States, with its guaranteed freedoms, vast facilities, generous orientation to what seems to be fair and right. But Hukov was never sure what his country was; all his life he had lived among frictions, many of them pertaining to nationalities. He had existed in a flurry of papers and requirements, of bursting hatred and real fears. And when that world crumbled, he had taken a path that seemed open to him and had kept moving, unable to stop, always caught up by other new, strange worlds.

And now I can't help but wonder how many worlds there are on our planet, and which is the basic one, and how one world can justly judge another—for we are not peers. And yet we must judge.

I don't know what part of our generation's story Hukov represents. I don't know how important the Eddy Hukovs are. But certainly I have found it worthwhile to know him and to write about him in this book.

Anybody who has tried to document the experiences of one who had traveled in many countries, frequently illegally, who is now wanted for his life by one country and perhaps by two or more, and who actually has no country of his own and has never really had one, will understand the difficulties which have confronted me in recent months. Hukov's military record in the Storm Troops was either destroyed at the close of the war or is in Soviet hands. His birthplace was Lvov, sometimes called Lwow, sometimes Lemberg, now Leopol, U.S.S.R.

His record in the French Legion is unobtainable, the Legion historically refusing to release information about its personnel.

So we have had to work with bits and pieces—a publicity picture clipped from a Thailand newspaper showing him in boxing tights facing a Thai boxer; a legal document stating that he was captured in the uniform of the French Legion at the Cambodian border in 1947; evidence that his citizenship is in the confused state he says it is; a copy of an AP dispatch from Rangoon; the good memory of a sea captain, Gerry Griffin, who once befriended him; ships' records; letters Hukov has saved that he had received from businessmen who had hired him and from the German Embassy in Bangkok, as well as the German State Department offices at Koblenz; an invitation to a dinner and dance; a receipt for the repayment of a loan; letters from people who had knowledge of some phase of his journey. Some of these papers are reproduced as a part of this book.

Also we have the fact of his present legal status. We have the dozens of lengthy letters he has sent, in which he has described his adventures, and we have his answers to questions we have sent him, all of which indicate that he was where he said he was.

I have bothered many individuals and organizations during this search for documentation, and I appreciate the interest they have taken in helping me, in so far as their rules and laws permitted. I recognize with appreciation United States State Department embassies in Bonn, Moscow and Rangoon; other State Department officials in New York and Washington; the Department of the Army, Washington; the Berlin Document Center; the International Committee of the Red Cross at Waldeck, Germany; the Registrar General of Shipping and Seamen,

Llandaff, Cardiff, Wales; the Orient Steam Navigation Company Limited, London; the American-Hawaiian Steamship Company, New York; the Criminal Intelligence Division, Kuala Lumpur, Malaya; the Criminal Intelligence Division, Bangkok, Thailand; and the Rangoon, Burma, Town Police.

JOHN EHLE

New York, New York
December 30, 1957

Part I

Part I

1

ON A MISTY afternoon in the fall of 1944, we boarded the train and were soon rolling west with the hollow, sleepy rumble of the wheels. The train stopped, then crept forward a few miles, then stopped for an hour. It went on, only to stop again. Sometimes we had to wait for the track to be cleared or a bridge to be tested; other times we had to wait for another train to arrive from the west, carrying supplies to the divisions still left on the Eastern Front.

Night came. Most of the men dozed uncomfortably in the boxcars, but a few of us stayed awake, anxious for word that Germany was reached. For me it would be the first time that I would see my country. My father had often told me about it, describing each city and reading to me from an encyclopedia about populations and cathedrals. He had a map in his bedroom which had lines going to Berlin, Munich, the Ruhr, radiating out from Lvov, in southeast Poland, where I was born and reared and where he worked as an engineer in the steel mill. I knew about Germany from him and from my German schooling in Poland, but now, for the first time, I was to see it.

Just before dawn the train stopped, and the good word

3

came. "This is our Fatherland," a man said. We leaped to the ground. I knelt by the boxcars, dug my fingers into the dirt, and lifted a piece of earth. This is my Fatherland, I thought.

Weeping, I leaned over and kissed the ground.

After a while I got up and went to one side, standing between two boxcars, near the couplings, where I could be alone. From there I could see prisoners across the yard fixing the track where bombs had landed, and near the station house other prisoners were unloading a boxcar that had been left on the siding. I could see little of my country except this—prisoners at work and my own black train. But around me I knew was the broad green land with farms and cities. I could imagine it as my father had described it, for he had been to Germany several times.

"Listen," a man said.

The sound of planes came to us, high bombers crossing the arc of the sky. At the other side of the yard, some Russian prisoners dropped their shovels and picks and looked up, although the planes were out of sight behind dark clouds.

"What city will it be tonight?" a soldier asked me, his voice hushed.

I walked away from him, still trying to fix the sound of the planes, as if the sound would tell me whose they were and where they were flying. When the planes went away, the prisoners once more began to shovel refuse.

I sank down on a pile of rubble, the vibrations of the engines still in my mind. It was as it had been on the Russian front with the artillery. Sometimes it would rumble in my mind when there were no guns around. And sometimes in my mind I could even hear conversations out of the past, with the voices of men who had been in my squad. Many men had served with me while we were

4

struggling with the Russians, first moving east victoriously, then falling back until we found that the whole Sixth German Army had been annihilated—twenty-four infantry and artillery divisions, including five Panzer divisions, wiped out in one battle. That was just before the Russian soldiers recaptured Kharkov and released Leningrad. Many men had passed through my squad during this time, some to be wounded or killed, others to live, like me, charmed lives. I had not been cut a single time in all my bayonet charges, in all the action . . .

"Hey, Sergeant, what do you think of my prisoners?" A bulky guard propped a foot on the brick wall where I was sitting.

"I think the same of all prisoners. Why? Did we capture those men?"

"What outfit are you?"

"The Storm Troopers," I said. "Hitler's Bodyguard Division."

He nodded slowly, impressed by what I had told him. "You are young to be a sergeant in such a hard organization."

I smiled, remembering that I had been made a sergeant and decorated while still seventeen, and that for two years I had served in a special Panzer unit commanded personally by Lieutenant General Richard Hildebrandt. He had hurled us into any break that came into his lines, and, if the lines were safe, had sent us on patrols to scout out the enemy.

I looked at the guard. "I was brought up to fight Russians on the streets."

"Well, these are not your prisoners, for they are not Russians. They are American soldiers."

I studied him to see if he was being honest with me, then went closer to some of the prisoners, examining them from head to foot. "It is the first time that I have seen an American," I said.

The guard stuck his hands down in his pants pocket and leaned back on his heels, proud of his prisoners. "They have the best uniforms," he said. "They look smart."

I walked part way around several Americans. "So these are the ones who are now attacking us, so that we must leave the Russian threat behind. We are traveling even now to fight them."

"Yes, many trains have come through before you. It will be a big advance soon, certainly."

Other Storm Troopers had become interested in seeing the Americans, and several groups were walking among them. One from a group came near. "Why aren't there more German guards on these Americans?" he demanded.

"The Americans are good boys," the guard said. "It is not like the Russians. Also, we feed them better."

"They are bombing our cities," the man said, "killing our women and children by the millions, and you feed them well?"

"Yes. They are always getting cigarettes from the Red Cross, and some are not smokers, so they trade the cigarettes with us. Sometimes we give them food in exchange, sometimes women. They're better off than we are." He reached in his pocket and brought out a package of cigarettes. There was a picture of a camel on the wrapper, such as I had not seen. "Have a cigarette?" he asked me.

I took one and lit it from his match. We sat down on the pile of rubble and talked some more about how like gentlemen the Americans were, and about the planes, perhaps American, even then in the sky.

I sat there a long while, staring blankly into a puddle of water, thinking of all the armies crowding in around us and about Germany, which had been the home of my

6

grandparents. Now I knew it must be protected from slavery, and I was one who must do it.

Two hours later, when the train started again, I got a place at the boxcar door so that I could watch Germany unfold before me; but the entire countryside was blacked out and there was little to see. All night I waited, ignoring the rain and staring out into the darkness. At dawn we were out in the country, and the fields near the tracks and the closer hillsides came into view first, neatly spaced and marked off, fenced and cross-fenced, with a few trees near the crests of the hills and along the steeper ridges. Now we rumbled over a wooden bridge, and below us a stream gushed, filled with the night's rain.

As we rounded a bend, the outskirts of a town came into sight. The fields grew thick with houses, and then the houses fell away as the railroad yard surrounded us. Now the factories were close, with taller buildings beyond.

None of us said anything. In Russia we had seen gutted buildings. But this was my first sight of a German town, and it was badly crumbled. Sometimes we would pass a person, standing as if dazed, staring at us; and once in a while a child would come to the doorway of a house, staying back on the stoop out of the rain, and wave at us until the train was out of sight; but our welcome was disappointing for all of us.

Most of that morning we sat at a railroad siding. Later in the day we moved to the other end of the freight yard. Somebody told me the engineers were waiting for nightfall since it was safer to move at night, but I saw no sense in that, for we were fully exposed there in the yard. More likely the line was broken ahead or a train had been wrecked on the right of way.

7

"The Americans did all this to our country?" I said.

"Yes, they are very good with machines," one of my men, Brenan, said.

"So are we," I said. "We have our own machines for them."

We rolled all night. The next morning before dawn the train reached Minden, and we walked through the city to the Westfalen camp, where we were to be educated about the Americans and their weapons. I hoped there would be mail there for us, because I had not heard from my family for some months. Lvov had been captured by the Russians, I knew, but many of the people had fled, and I had no doubt my father had gotten our family away safely.

Immediately on our arrival we were given mail. I had a large stack and quickly leafed through it. There were many letters from men who had fought with me and from girls in Germany whose addresses the soldiers had given me—some introducing their sisters, others their past girl friends. But there was nothing from my family, and nothing from Linda, the German girl in Lvov who had taught me about true romance. I laid the mail aside, deeply worried about what might have happened.

Finally I opened a few letters from the girls in Germany. They told me how the people were still optimistic about winning the war. They said we should keep fighting hard. They told me much about politics and little about love, except that each one signed her letter, "With all my love."

That was the way it was now, I knew. Everything was politics, with love on the sly and the quick.

I opened a letter from Warsaw. It was from a boyhood friend who had gone to the Polish school with me in Lvov. When my father took me out of that school and sent me

8

to a German master, this boy and I remained friends, in spite of my father's objections. Now he was the only person who had lived in Lvov who had written me.

Dear Eddy,
The Almighty God in Heaven should bless you.

Many of our friends told me I must not write to you about what has happened, but I cannot sleep at night and not let you know. Now I am going to Berlin, for the war is close, but I must tell you.

Before I fled Lvov, the large American bombers were flying night and day, and when they dropped bombs on Lvov, one of them fell on your house and killed your father, your two brothers, and your young sister Bertha.

Eddy, we were at work for hours getting the dead bodies out of your house . . .

I stared down at the piece of paper in my hand, my hands trembling. I could no longer make out the words. A groan came out of me; I ripped the letter into pieces and ground them into the mud with my heels, then I stumbled into the room, where I got my pistol and started walking. Two officers saluted me but I went on. They shouted after me, I did not stop. An officer of another company came running up to me, grabbed my shoulders. "Stand where you are," he shouted.

I knocked him sprawling and walked on, anxious to get away from people before I lost complete control of myself.

But suddenly four sergeants had hold of me and snatched away the pistol. They started pulling me down the street, with private soldiers lining the way, asking what had happened. Only a minute later I was standing before my commanding officer.

He was a huge man, like my father. Since I had joined the SS, he had watched my progress with interest, but now he received me with the stern aloofness of a Prussian.

9

"Sergeant, what's the matter?" he asked. "Did you know you struck an officer?"

"Sir—I——" I shook my head, furious with my own confusion. "I don't know the truth," I said. "Is my father dead?"

Immediately he said, "No or I would have told you. I have no word about any death in your family."

"Sir, I received today a letter from a friend who was in Lvov . . ."

The captain's face clouded. I watched him as he studied his own thoughts. Then slowly he turned away, walked over to his cot, and sat down, cupping his chin in one big hand and staring at me. "Lvov?" he said softly. "Yes, you are from East Poland, aren't you, Sergeant?"

He got up, moved heavily to the door of his room, and stood looking out into the street. He began to talk in a monotone about how all of us must accept losses, even death, in fighting for our Fatherland. He told me how Germany had been broken by the war, but how she was fighting on for her freedom.

Suddenly he turned to his cot and took up several papers from a table. "I should not show you this," he said, "but after such bad news——" He selected one of the papers and handed it to me. It was an authorization for me to have the Iron Cross First Class.

"Ahhh," I said, letting the paper slide to the floor, "for me it's no use any longer for a First or Second Class Cross. I'm alone in the world from today on. Who cares what cross I have?"

"Sergeant, our country is also our family . . ."

Suddenly it was difficult for me to breathe. I tore my shirt open at the neck. "I would like to have a wooden cross for my grave." I moved to the door and supported myself on the doorpost, staring out at the sun-baked street, where the four sergeants and several private soldiers were

10

waiting. "If I could meet the Yankee pilot who killed my father," I said, "I would throw my guns aside and tear out his throat with my hands."

I stumbled out into the road and started toward an open field where I could be alone.

2 AFTER SIX WEEKS at Westfalen, we were ordered to the west to face the English and Americans. We packed up and moved out.

On the way to the front our train stopped opposite a freight train. On every car was written the word "Jews" and the cars were so crowded that nobody could sit down.

The children began asking us for bread, holding out their hands and weeping; but their parents were afraid of us. Several times I heard SS, SS, SS, SS, SS. I knew they thought we were killers and murderers.

But the children said, "Uncles, feed us. Uncles . . ."

"It is enough to break a man's heart," I said to one of my men, Zimmerman, an ugly fellow who had moles on the sides of his nose.

"Yes, but they are Jews," he said.

The guards of the train were Gestapo boys and SD. They forbade us to give bread to the children, but we ignored their orders. I had grown up in Lvov with Jews, and although my father had not liked them, he had liked them so much better than the Poles and Russians that they were almost friends. Anyway, no matter what crimes

13

the adult Jews might have done against Hitler, the children had done nothing.

But the guards did not like our feeding them. They argued with us, and after a while we beat them up and chased them away. Then we opened one car and several Jewish girls ran out. Now the most hardened of the Storm Troopers, even those who had been trained in Nazi doctrine, showed interest when they saw that girls were available. Two other cars were opened and more Jewish girls came out, until there were about fifty. One of them looked like Linda, with the same dark hair and eyes, and I liked her immediately.

By this time the local police had gathered, but those of us who had Jewish girls would not give them up. Fighting started; we gave the police a brutal beating and took the girls into our cars.

When we reached the next stop, the girls washed themselves, and this time, as the train started out, we began singing songs, most of them German army songs. The Jewish girls in my car got together and sang a slow, sad song in Hebrew, and when they were done I was deeply moved, for it was a melody not unlike one my sister Lene had sung. It had been before she had started dying, long years before, when I had been a little boy—Lene, my sister and my mother.

All that night we traveled, singing, talking, and making love, forgetful of the heavy war. At dawn the party died down to sleep or to quiet talk; so I crawled over to where my dark Jewess was. I sat near her and watched her for a while, but she remained aloof. Perhaps it was this that prompted me suddenly to say, "What are the crimes of you non-Aryans that makes the government want to kill you?"

She was startled at first, then she shook her head an-

14

grily, as if to throw the question from her. "I don't want to talk about the Nazis."

"One time an order came to the Eastern Front for the Storm Troopers to shoot every Jew or send them back to concentration camps."

She sat stiffly for a moment, then slowly her dark eyes turned on me. "How many did you shoot?"

"I haven't shot any Jews. Only Russians. I don't know how many Russians in all."

"Russian soldiers or civilians?"

"One was a civilian. He worked for the Germans; he was in charge of a prison camp for other Russians."

"Why did you shoot him?"

"You wouldn't believe me if I told you."

"Well, why was it?"

"Because he was cruel beyond any hope of salvation."

She watched me thoughtfully for a moment. "You're right. I don't believe you."

"He would break the prisoners' fingers because he enjoyed seeing pain. He wanted to hear his own people scream. So I lost my senses and shot him. And there was the strangest look of surprise that came over his face, and then when he knew he was dying, it changed to fear."

"Were you sorry when you shot him?"

"I was stunned when I realized I had shot him. And I was sorry when I found I had to go to trial. But the trial was nothing, really. I had been decorated and had a fine record, and all I had done was shoot a Russian—and, after all, that was our business. But I have not yet shot a Jew."

"Have some of these other men?" she asked, glancing about the boxcar where my men were sprawled out.

"Maybe some of them have. Occasionally a Storm Trooper unit will be sent to an execution, but they are usually recruits—men who are not ready for the fighting at the front. And more often than the Storm Troopers, the

15

SD, or Sicherheitsdienst, does that type of work, or perhaps the Gestapo."

"Would you kill me?" she said.

I touched her chin with my finger and pressed it gently, trying to make her smile. "No, I don't think so."

She pushed my hand away. "If it were a direct order, would you?"

"You are very pretty," I said, still trying to make her smile, but she was caught up in a serious mood. I did not mind though; so was I because of my family and because of the somber sound of the rolling train.

I leaned my head back against the wall of the boxcar, which was vibrating with the movement of the wheels. "Tell me now why Hitler wants to kill non-Aryians."

"I don't know. You are in the SS. You tell me that."

"Nobody in the army is ever told anything, except where to go and what to do. We Storm Troopers least of all. All we are told is to obey."

"Perhaps you were given reasons in the Nazi Youth then."

I smiled at her. "I grew up in southeast Poland—that was my youth. In fact, I grew up a German in Poland, which isn't so easy to do. Every day coming home from school, I had to fight Polish and Russian kids. They wouldn't let me go home without a fight. And when I would reach the house, Lene, my sister, would meet me to see if I had been cut. She would wash my face and hands, talking all the while about how good it was to be a German, but how I was not to hate the other kids."

"Were there no Jews in your city?" Now she was speaking calmly too, as if the sound of the train had relaxed her.

"Yes, but sometimes they were beaten, as I was, so I liked the Jews all right. But I hated the Russians and the Poles. And on the Eastern Front I have paid them back.

16

There I wasn't alone any longer; other Germans were with me, so it was a good day for me. That is what a war is, you see," I said to her. "They give you a gun and permission to shoot your enemies."

I glanced at her. She had her hands folded in her lap and her eyes were closed, as if she were praying. She reminded me of Lene and also of Linda, the girl I loved in Lvov. "But I've never killed any Jews," I said.

She nodded, but her eyes remained closed. "But you could."

I once more touched her chin with my fingers and tried to make her smile, but she remained sad. At last, however, we began to talk about the expressions on the faces of some of the sleeping men, and she smiled. We became better friends, and she asked me to help her reach the American lines.

I gave her a fifty-mark note and some advice. "When you leave the train, go to a store and buy a dress that will make you look neat. Wash well and start making contact with the Wehrmacht soldiers—some of them might help you."

She stared at me only for a moment, then her hand tightened around the money. "Thank you," she said.

The train stopped just at the first rays of dawn, and two officers pushed open the door of our boxcar and peered inside. "You can't do this!" they shouted, pointing frantically. "Now chase those girls out of here!"

The girls got up, jumped down to the ground, and scattered out as they ran through the station yard. I watched my dark Jew as she left, and silently I wished her well.

All day our train sat still. Another train arrived in midafternoon, moving on by us, stopping far down the track and waiting there. Planes hovered protectingly in the sky. One or two would leave every half hour or so, turning toward the west, there perhaps to splatter bullets at the Americans before going to the landing field; other planes would replace them.

At night our train began creeping forward again. The noise it made seemed unbearable, for all day we had been talking in whispers, as if trying not to let the Americans hear us.

"Why are you whispering?" Zimmerman demanded of me. "All day we move like criminals. This is my country; I am not a thief here."

Brenan, a huge rawboned man who had wanted to be sergeant instead of me, playfully slapped Zimmerman on top of his balding head. "You let the officers worry about such things," he said. "Who are you but a common soldier, the same as me?"

The train stopped for a while, then lurched forward again. It rolled noisily forward a mile, two miles, then once more it stopped. After a while I crawled over to Zimmerman and Brenan at the doorway and dangled my legs over the side of the car. "It is going to be a big surprise to the Americans," I said. "They have never met our division before. We will have them walking around in the ocean surf before they know what is in front of them."

"Yes," Zimmerman said, grinning. "We must send them home to their families."

"Then we can take care of the Russians," I said.

"Oh, we will win this war, Sergeant," Brenan said.

"That's what I'm saying. We will win, I think."

The train moved forward around a long bend and stopped. We waited there for several minutes, then started again, going so slowly that when Zimmerman dropped his matches, he jumped from the train and ran back for them.

"The lines are jammed up ahead," Brenan said to me. "That's all."

"Yes, that's right," I said. "The transportation system is in good shape. It's just slow tonight."

"And last night," Zimmerman said gloomily, lighting his cigarette and puffing at the tobacco. "And the night before, no doubt."

"Well, it was always slow," Brenan said, "even in peacetime. The sergeant is right; we Germans have nothing to worry about. We are strong enough to fight all our enemies."

"That's right," I said. "But there are too many enemies for me to understand it clearly. What are the Americans in this war for?"

Zimmerman shrugged. "They just get lonely," he said, staring off into the dark countryside. "They sit over there on their big island and see the other countries having a happy time cutting each other up, and they feel neglected; so they start sending over sharper knives. Then they get interested in the use of their knives, so soon the whole world is being supplied and fought by the Americans." He peered at me with calm earnestness, always his manner when he thought he had said something profound.

"No, it is because the Japanese bombed their ships, that's the reason," Brenan said.

"Why do they attack Germany and Italy because the Japanese sunk their ships?" I asked.

"Well, who wants to attack Japan?" Brenan replied.

"Yes, who gives a damn for Japan?" Zimmerman said casually.

"Even so," I said, "Germany and Italy had nothing to do with the American ships."

"Maybe Italy is on the route to Japan," Zimmerman said drily. "Maybe they are just stopping off at Italy."

"Ah, listen," I said, "here we are being pulled away from our natural enemies and moved across the whole continent to fight the Americans. And they are not in Italy

19

only, but also in France and Belgium. Nor are they on our side, but against us. And all I can find out for the reason is that the Japanese sank their ships."

"Well, they're good friends of the English," Brenan explained.

"Yes, but why are the British fighting against us?" I said. "What's wrong with these people? Why don't they help us fight the Russians?"

"What the hell do they have to fear from the Russians?" Brenan said.

"Yes, the Russians never hurt the British," Zimmerman said. "More likely the British would fight the Japanese. The British always are fighting in some far-off part of the world."

"Hell," I said angrily, "it's impossible to talk politics with you men."

Zimmerman grinned and turned his gaze back out to the trees, which were passing in slow review a few yards away from us. He took a drag on his cigarette, holding the last half-inch with the tips of his fingers. "It's a big war," he said, almost whispering. "It's a big one."

"Yes," I said, "all the world is fighting us, and we must defend ourselves."

The train was moving beside a road now, and we could see the convoy of trucks, pushing forward bit by bit, making slower time than we. A motorcycle courier, his light off, came noisily by, weaving in and out, driving part of the time on the shoulder of the road, ducking tree limbs.

We passed the truck convoy and came upon a row of tanks, parked to one side, with troops marching four abreast. Brenan glanced nervously at me and I at him; never had we seen men so tightly packed in the war zone. "Every road must be full," he said.

We passed an 88, being pulled by a giant truck, its muzzle capped with a leather case that reminded me of a feed bag for cows, such as were used in Poland. "There is a farmer managing that 88," I said to Zimmerman and Brenan. "He is ready to milk, if they give him time between shootings."

Some of the men behind us began to stir, the signs of life from outside awakening their interest. Also, we now began to see that we were not to be left alone to save our country, but that other good Germans were there, too, and that it was going to be a circus before it was over. Zimmerman slapped his pants legs, happily viewing the sights before us. Then our train cut away from the road, and we were lost again in the countryside.

3 THE FIFTH and Sixth SS Panzer and the Seventh Army as well as other Panzer brigades and units were made ready for the attack. Nine days before Christmas of 1944, shrouded in an unusually heavy fog, the great army moved, striking into the unsuspecting United States infantry divisions and hurling aside the Ninth Armored. A gap over forty miles wide at its base was torn in the line between Echternach and Monschau. General Eisenhower's jeep was captured and it was rumored Eisenhower also was a prisoner. Wild with elation, seeing victory ahead, we gave no thought to anything except moving on, conquering ground that lay between us and the Meuse River.

But the American resistance began to stiffen, especially along our flanks; and the American and British air forces, unable to fly on the opening days of the attack because of weather, were in the sky again, pounding us and our supplies, robbing us of all sleep.

On Christmas Day those of us still on our feet huddled near the tanks, shielding ourselves from the sharp wind. We sang a few carols, each one using the words he remembered, and talked about how it had been at home

23

before the war. Toward nightfall we moved out again, still going west. The terrain was poor for tanks, which were forever bogging down, so our progress was slow. Now, too, American tanks were moving into our lines.

The day after Christmas, the tenth day of the attack, we stopped our advance. We were four miles from the Meuse, but we could go no farther. There was no strength left.

Seeing that we faltered, the Allies gained spirit. Their planes were always in the air now; their artillery was a continuous rumble. Jutting out into their lines, our area no deeper than fifty miles in any direction and surrounded on three sides by the enemy, we fought as strength permitted, holding fast—as if it mattered now that we held the bit of land we had conquered. We held it anyway, too proud to surrender it, until finally our supply lines were almost pinched off. Then we pulled back, those of us left alive, leaving a quarter of a million German and Allied dead, most of them unburied—and some of them not quite dead—sprawled on a small piece of earth that was pockmarked with tanks we had ditched, assault guns left pointing to the north, to the west, to the south, planes bombed or wrecked or without fuel. But mostly it was the dead that were left.

Once more behind our old lines, we filled our days with grumblings and complaints. We told each other we hoped for another attack, this time on terrain better suited to our heavy vehicles; but the rumor started that the Sixth Panzer Army, which contained all four of the original Storm Trooper divisions, was needed on the Eastern Front and would be returned there.

"Yes, we are going east," my captain told me. "Better to stop the Russians. Think of Germany if the Russians sweep over it. Think of our country and families then."

In February, with hopelessness settling on us like a

heavy coat, we boarded trains. Everywhere I saw frustration—in the slow paces, in the bent bodies, in the eyes of Brenan and the others. Even my captain was as gray as ashes. Once alert to every movement near him, to every word spoken in his presence, now he did not hear half the questions addressed directly to him. Only Zimmerman, of the people I knew, was content. Having made peace with the war long ago, he always showed a rigidly enforced complacency.

Now, as we crossed Germany, we saw more devastation from the bombings as the dark country rose and fell before us. Twisted rails and ragged tops of brick buildings pointed into the sky; in places the ground along the tracks was covered with bits of shattered glass from nearby factories. Never was a man seen anywhere, not even an old man; and the women moved with slumped shoulders. Children picked about the rubble, finding nothing that I could see, too apathetic even to look up as we passed. One building from which a whole wall had fallen had some of the floors left, and Brenan pointed out a woman who, with her children, still was keeping house on one floor.

"Cliff dwellers," he said to me. "You see how the floor sags. If it falls, they will go down seventy feet."

"Yes," I said, "but everybody is in danger now."

Brenan nodded at my words, but Zimmerman crawled to a corner of the boxcar and stretched out sleepily. "Everything will work out in time," he said.

"In time?" I said angrily. "What has time to do with us? We are moved from one front to another, everywhere to unleash an attack. And who the hell are these damn Americans who will risk their lives for something far off from their own country? What are they—crazy men? Why don't they go home and leave us alone?"

"I wish they would go home," Brenan said.

"I don't understand them," I said. "Some of the American prisoners I talked with were born of German parents, just like me; but they said their parents were not German now, and they were not either. They were fighting us Germans and had never thought of Germany as their country. The Italians were the same way. It is as crazy as for me to be fighting for Poland. It makes no sense for a man to be of whatever country he happens to be living in. That puts too high a value on real estate."

"You think too much about silly questions," Zimmerman said. "The thing to do is to stay alive and try to be warm."

"That's right," said Brenan. "We three have seen war for a long time already, and it's important now to live to see the end of it."

"Hell, yes, I want to live," I said.

I crawled to the open door, moving among my men, some of whom were sleeping, and I sat in the doorway watching the land pass before me, thinking to myself as I saw the broken rails, torn wires, shattered poles, tree limbs on the road, homeless children with belongings packed in boxes, that here was my country and the memorial to my father.

The Russians did not know that our Storm Trooper divisions had returned to the Eastern Front, and they were unprepared for us. On the 6th of March, without any artillery preparation and without a single plane in the sky, our Sixth Panzer Army struck in Hungary, and the Russians reeled back 250 kilometers before finding a stopping place. We freed the whole territory near Lake Balaton in central Hungary.

Since I could speak Russian like a native, I was told to lead patrols and capture prisoners for interrogation. My squad, many of whom were new men, accepted this with evident enthusiasm, but Brenan and Zimmerman were more thoughtful. It was on our first mission out, after the Russians had caught a new foothold and had turned to fight us, that Brenan was killed.

It happened in a Russian bunker, which is not the burial place he would have chosen. We had just crept through open fields, under cover of night, and had approached the bunker without difficulty. I waited for my men to get into position at the door, then kicked it open. I leaped in, Brenan behind me, the others following, and shouted to the Russians to surrender. But they dived for their weapons, and the firing started.

The sound was deafening in the enclosure, but I heard Brenan shouting to me. I turned to find that three Russians had shoved him against a wall. I turned my gun on them, but they would not die. With small knives they were swiping across Brenan's stomach, and Brenan was trying to push them back with his hands. They ripped him across the intestines, which bulged out to fill up the front part of his pants.

I kept firing at them. Finally they stopped their cutting and lay in a pile of blood and flesh, propping Brenan back against the wall of the bunker, where he stood staring down at them but seeing nothing.

"Eddy," he called, looking wildly around.

"I'm here, Brenan," I said, wanting to touch him, but not wanting to touch so bloody a figure, either. Now everyone was watching him die. There was not a Russian who still wanted to fight. "What is it, Brenan?"

"They cut me, Eddy."

"Yes—you—will be all right though——"

"You better hurry out of here, Eddy."

I stared at the huge, helpless figure, bleeding great sops of blood. "All right, men, outside; and take the two prisoners," I said.

"I'm not going with you, Eddy," Brenan said piteously.

I felt tears warm my eyes and my stomach wanted to throw out everything that was in it. Here was a strong, big man, cut open in the middle, so that he could not even be carried without breaking apart.

"You live, Eddy," he said. "You and Zimmerman live."

I turned from him and went outside, where my men were holding the two Russians. I saw that Zimmerman was crying. It was the first time in a long while that the war had gotten through his thick hide. "I hope we meet some Russians on the way back," I said, my voice breaking with anger and tears.

But we did not see any for a week.

Zimmerman died in a neater way. It was a clean death, with a single bullet in his chest. It was on a morning, early, when the grass was still damp. We were coming back from a patrol and came upon a farm village in Russian territory. My men sneaked up along the ridge to peer down at it, only from curiosity, because we had prisoners and were overdue at our base.

We lay up there, shielded by rocks and trunks of trees. Zimmerman was close by. "When we moving on, Eddy?" he asked me.

"Any time you want to," I said. "Whatever you say."

He shrugged and went on puffing at his cigarette. Down below us was a main street, lined with houses, and at the far end of the street was a Studebaker truck, which had been sent to Russia by the Americans. Two Russian soldiers came out of a house and got into the front seat. We heard the truck start.

"Let me have a machine gun," I said to Zimmerman.

He passed on a machine gun from the man next to him. I got to my knees and braced the gun at my hip. Zimmerman moved a few feet farther away, so that he would be less bothered by the noise when I shot.

The truck came down the street, moving very fast. When it came to the end of the long block, I opened up with the gun and watched the windshield of the truck crack and cave inward.

The truck veered to the right and struck a tree with a crash; the engine coughed out.

Zimmerman took the cigarette from his mouth and grinned at me, nodding satisfaction with my accuracy.

Then we heard the cries, pitiful, desperate, and weak. "What is that, Zimmerman?" I said.

"Perhaps the two Russians in the truck are crying out for help."

"No," I said. "They are certainly dead. Didn't you see the bullets break through the windshield?"

The cries stopped. We waited for a while. "Zimmerman, you come with me," I said. "They sounded like German words to me."

We went down the hillside, moving behind rocks and fences, finally reaching the valley floor at the road. We moved along swiftly, coming to the cobblestones of the street, where the truck had stopped.

Our guns ready, we moved cautiously around the truck.

Chained to the back bumper by their feet were six SS men. Their hands were tied behind them. Blood was pouring from their bodies, which had been burst open by impact with the road and by the ends of the heavy chains. The brains were coming out of their heads, slipping on to the ground. A man looked at me through the blood-matted hair on his face, one eyelid was cut off and his eye was falling out. He looked at me without saying anything, then he whimpered. It was not a cry or a scream; it was a whimper, just that. And it broke my heart.

"My God in Heaven!" Zimmerman said, looking down at the mangled bodies. He snatched the machine gun from my hand, throwing his own rifle aside, and turned to

29

the street of the town. "I want one Russian to show his face!" he shouted. "I want one Russian to show his face! One!" He started stumbling down the street toward where the truck had started.

Then there was a shot, a single rifle shot, and Zimmerman stood up straight and fell backward into the dirt, the machine gun landing on his chest. He did not move.

I stood still, staring at him, then down at the blood and gut-soaked bodies before me. I moved to the truck and leaned back on the dripping radiator, which had been broken by the tree. I rested there, trying not to think about anything. I saw my men moving down the ridge toward the town and was vaguely aware that they would take revenge for Zimmerman's death.

But I wanted no revenge for myself. On that day of broken bones and teeth crushed on the streets, I wanted only to stay alive.

Back at my company I reported to my captain. I told him I had come into the German Army when I was seventeen and had been much decorated, that I had led patrols into enemy land and had never been scratched. "But I am the last man of the original squad. Only I have survived and now I don't want to go on any further."

"Yes," he said, "You are right, of course. The last man should live to tell about the others."

He made out the papers for me to be a courier and assigned me to a motorcycle. Later that day he gave me dispatches to carry the two hundred kilometers to division headquarters.

I started out, expecting to make quick time, but the roads were blasted out in many places by artillery shells, and even as I rode, shells were landing somewhere behind me. After two days of treacherous driving, I reached headquarters. I asked the major if there was something for me to carry back, and he said there was nothing. I noticed that his face looked as gray as my captain's when the Americans had begun to turn our lines on the Western Front. I asked him no questions, fearing what the answers might be, and started back for my company.

I drove until nightfall. Then, since I could not use my lights, I stopped at a nice house in a village. On the gate I wrote "One SS man," so other soldiers who might need a place to sleep would know the house was occupied. The lady of the house looked at me fearfully when I came in, glancing about as if she did not know what to expect from an SS man; but I was too tired even to set her mind at rest.

Her children helped me hide my motorcycle in the cowshed, where they had a big time covering it up with hay. The little girl, two or three years old, made a nuisance of herself pulling the hay off as fast as her two older brothers stacked it on, but neither of those two little boys laid a hand on her. Instead, they tried to reason with her, and I had a moment of relaxation listening to them, making out most of their Hungarian words. The two boys explained how the motorcycle had to be covered up to protect it from thieves; and the little girl did help them cover it for a few minutes. But when she saw she could uncover better than she could cover, she went back to doing what she did best.

Finally, however, the two boys won out, and the four of us went into the house for supper.

The mother had fixed a nice meal with a small piece of beef, canned pears and hot bread. She sat down wearily across the table from me, kitchen sweat on her face, bowed her head, as did the children, and we said a short grace for the meal. I then divided the food and poured the milk. We ate all there was, then drank a glass of water to fill our stomachs, and everybody was much happier

31

with the way the world was, although, even in that kitchen, we could hear the sound of distant artillery.

In German the woman said, "Sergeant, when will the front line pass this house?"

"Maybe not at all," I said.

"I want to know the truth."

I smiled at her, amused by the willingness of this gentle creature to face the truth about the struggle that was going on nearby. "The truth is not so good," I said. "The Russians are getting help from America, and our own factories are destroyed by bombs. The German Army is strong, but it is bleeding, and the Russians still come on in big numbers."

She studied me for a long while. Once more I was struck by the gentleness of her face and hands, the slight shoulders, the wistfulness of her. But when she spoke this time, her voice was hard, as if she were playing the part of an entirely different person in a play. "Sergeant," she said, "if the Russians come to this house, I will kill my children and then myself."

"Ahhhh," I said, caught between disbelief and awe. "You listen to me, such talk is not for women, not for mothers." Here was a woman who had been frightened of one SS man lest he touch her body, and now she was going to stick a knife into her children and her own heart.

"I will kill them," she said, looking at her sons.

The boys stared back at her, then at me, seeking a voice for their defense. I tried to think of some argument for them, but all I could think of was the little girl beside me, who was running her fingers through drops of water that had fallen onto the table.

The mother got up and took the little girl in her arms. She motioned to the two boys, and the family went up the steps to the loft. I heard her helping them get ready for bed, then she came down and cleared the table.

32

"No, I would not kill them," I said, as if there had been no intervening time. "If we die, there is nothing gained. The children have to grow up, and as for yourself, you might not be bothered by the Russians, for they cannot trouble everyone so much as they trouble a few. You are pretty and fairly young, so you might be one of the few; but perhaps not, if you make yourself less attractive, with stringy hair and clothes which do not reveal so much as the shirt you now have on. The Russians might not harm you or your children."

She kept her dark eyes on me for a moment more, testing the truth of what I said, then she went to a mirror on the kitchen door and let down her hair, so that it fell to her waist in the back. She started making it stringy with her fingers, as if to see what I meant.

"Where is your husband?" I asked.

She glanced at me, seeking a motive for the question; her fingers stopped for a moment. "He's dead for more than a year."

"I'm sorry. He left three beautiful children. You must help them live through the war and grow up to be good people." I told her about her daughter helping the sons hide my motorcycle and she smiled over that.

"I don't want to die," she said, "and I don't see how a woman can kill her children, but dying would take only a minute. How long would we have to live with the Russians if we did not die? Nobody can answer that, but it would be a long time."

"But being alive is important," I said, trying to think of something proper to say. "Let God decide your question. Maybe both of us will live all our lives fleeing danger, and never come to any answer, to any rest at all. Certainly if the Russians win, they will want me, for I am tattooed by the SS on my arm, and they would rather kill an SS man than win God's favor. But we were born to be alive, and if we survive in such times as these, maybe that is enough for a while. I don't know. But at least I am alive to ask such questions."

She smiled at me, warmly, as if we had become close friends. She turned back to the mirror, and I watched her as she wound her long hair into a bun, then leaned her head on the kitchen door, her eyes soft. "I have not had anyone to talk with for so long," she said, "except the women, and women talk strange, especially when they have to act as fathers as well as mothers."

"You let the children live," I said. "I tell you this, I have seen enough death to love the life of everybody who is not a Russian."

She sat down across from me at the table and rested her hands one on the other, before her, staring down at them contentedly. "Was it a good meal?" she asked.

"Yes. Very good."

"You will stay here tonight?"

"Yes."

"And tomorrow you will go back to the war?"

"As soon as the sun rises."

"Very well. I will fix your breakfast. There is some coffee left, although not strong. I will get the children out of bed, also, so they can say good-by to you."

I studied her for a while, thinking that here was a good mother and that she had been a good wife. I got up slowly and went around the table to stand near her. "It has been like a family here tonight," I said.

She slowly raised her face to look at me. "Very like a family," she said.

I kissed her gently on the cheek. She put her hand on my arm, and her fingers were trembling.

We went into her bedroom, and it was done with little commotion. I lay awake afterwards and thought that maybe, when the war was over, I would become the

34

father of this family. But I was not Hungarian, and it would be better for me to marry Linda, I decided. Yet my thoughts of Linda were buried now under all the thoughts the war had brought to me, and under the war's confusion. And if the war had confused my feelings, it might have twisted hers all the more, for now Linda might be a refugee somewhere in Germany, fleeing the Russians. Or perhaps she was still in Lvov, for she had Polish citizenship; it was her mother who was German. . . .

The woman beside me crawled out of bed. "I'll go up and sleep with my children now," she said. "Good night, Sergeant."

"Good night——" I could not call her by name. I did not know her name, and there was no small term of affection, such as "dear," or "sweetheart," that would do for the mother of three children. She went out, quietly closing the door, and long after she left I lay awake thinking of her, how strong she was, and yet how yielding.

I got out of bed finally and hung my burp gun over the bedpost at my head and put my pistol under the pillow. I was still thinking about the Hungarian woman when I went to sleep.

I awoke with a voice calling for me to wake up. I opened my eyes. The room was dark, but I could see a shadow near the middle of the floor. I pulled the pistol from under my pillow and pointed it in that direction. Again the voice said, "Wake up," and I recognized the mother's voice. I jumped out of bed and knelt down beside her, put my arms around her. She was on her knees, shivering with fright.

"What is it?"

"Russian soldiers," she said, pointing toward the road.

I leaped to the window. Soviet tanks were passing through the village, as were many horses and wagons, on which Red soldiers were riding. "The Russians must have broken through our lines," I said, turning to her. "You will take care of your children?—and yourself?"

"Yes," she said. "Yes, yes." Even then she took the pins from her hair, letting it fall loose.

Quickly I dressed, then loaded my gun. "If you will do something for me," I said, "go out the front door of this house and open the gate at the road, the one for wagons to go through."

"Yes, I will do that," she said.

I pushed open a back window, threw one leg over the sill. She was standing nearby, the moonlight falling on her face. "Good night," I said, then went through the window, holding the gun close to my chest so that it would not bang against the frame.

In the shed I threw the hay off my motorcyle, leaped down on the starter. In the enclosure the motor roared with a deafening sound; the cow bolted against the bars of her stall and let out long bellows. In a low gear I drove the motorcycle forward across the yard toward the opened gate. Even now the mother was walking back to her house; she would be inside and safe before I reached the road.

Suddenly four Red soldiers entered the gate, their rifles ready. I switched on my headlight so that they could not see my SS uniform and shouted at them in Russian, "Go on with the line; don't come into the house."

The soldiers stopped and were ready to salute me as I went past them and through the gate. I made the turn and headed down between the double columns of soldiers and vehicles. I switched off my headlights as a voice shouted, "German soldier."

There was a rifle shot, then several, but already I was at high speed and was passing the Russian horses and men.

"German soldier," another man shouted. Others took up the words, but my motorcycle was moving ahead of their warning. I swerved around vehicles, knifing my way between men, having no time to consider any danger.

"Stop!" A Russian officer shouted to me, standing in my path, his hand held forward at me. I aimed my motorcycle for him; he jumped out of the way just in time. A shot rang out, and another.

In a minute more there were no more Russians.

By noon I had found my company, and I was told that the Russian Army had surrounded us. That same day their iron pincers began slowly to tighten. My officers did not sleep; they watched one another eagerly, each expecting someone else to initiate an order—any order.

Finally we hurled ourselves at the wall of the Russian forces and, leaving a bloody path, broke through. The Russians attacked again. We fell back to Austria, trying to reorganize. It was there that we heard of Adolph Hitler's order: *I order you, every officer and man, to take from your uniform the SS markings; you are not worthy to be SS men.*

As I considered that, I felt defeat take hold of me. I knew we could not win the war now, that we had lost the country to our enemies.

Soon thereafter I watched what for me was the last battle of the war. It took place down on a valley floor, while I stood at an artillery position on a ridge overlooking it. Division headquarters had ordered me to deliver a message and bring a reply from an artillery officer nearby; but, when I arrived, the officer was not interested in anything except his work, so I went aside and sat down to wait for him to get around to me.

In the valley a company of Russian soldiers were rounding up the German prisoners they had captured, packing them together in the center of the highway so that they could march them behind their lines with greater ease.

37

"Why doesn't the officer order those 88s to open up on those Russians?" I asked one of the artillery men.

"They are not Russians. They are American soldiers."

I stared at him in disbelief. "This far east? This is Austria."

"Yes," he said quietly. "They have made fast progress."

"But my unit is not far from here, fighting the Russians."

"I know," he said. "The British and Americans were allowed to sweep over the whole country, for it is better to let them have Germany than the Russians."

The officer suddenly shouted an order; the artillerymen raced to their 88s and the guns were aimed. I gazed down into the valley, my mind confused with a hundred ideas about the meaning of our defeat. At the same time, I was thinking of the Americans, deployed along the road, who soon would be hugging the ground seeking protection from flying shrapnel.

The officer gave the command to fire, and I held my breath. When the explosions came, I could hardly believe my eyes. The shells did not explode near the Americans but all around the German prisoners and in their midst.

I jumped up. "Man, you are killing our own soldiers!" I shouted at the officer.

Ignoring me, he ordered another round of fire. Again the shells exploded in the road, and now the German soldiers were crawling around frantically, some of them with their arms and legs blown off, trying to find cover. They looked like ants which had been torn apart.

"They are Germans," I shouted at the officer. I started toward him. "You are a crazy man, do you hear that? I told you, they are Germans!"

"They should not have surrendered," he shouted back at me. "We have our orders, soldier." Three of his men

38

grabbed hold of me and held me back. The artillery officer calmly told his men to fire again.

"They are Germans," I said, looking on helplessly at the crawling figures on the road. "Look at them," I said. The American soldiers were running in from the surrounding area, some of them to help the German prisoners.

The 88s fired. Once again the shells exploded among the Germans. The Americans drew back, finding holes and ditches for protection. The artillery officer gave an order to bring up the horses and move off the guns.

"You fired on our own people," I said to him. "It is the end now most certainly."

Later that day I told my captain what I had seen, and he told me it was hard to believe what a people will do in defeat. "It looks as if in a few days, perhaps even tomorrow, all of us will be prisoners of the Russians. If I am alive in a week, I will consider it a miracle."

"You can escape, go home."

"No," he said. "The enemies will find all us SS men. And what will you do, Sergeant, go back to Poland, where the Russians are in charge? They will hang you in the public square; and if they do not, the Polish people will kill you in worse fashion. We made too many Poles slaves for our farms and factories."

"Then what should I do, Captain?" I asked him.

He shrugged and stared vacantly about. "I don't know. I suppose a truly wise man would kill himself."

"No," I said. "I came through this war without a scratch. There must be a reason. God must have some purpose for me up ahead in my life."

"God?" he asked, frowning at me. "You mean the same God who helps the Russians?" Angrily he walked away from me, and I remembered that once he had been a good Protestant, the same as I, but now the war had taken away his faith.

I walked about the camp, talking aimlessly about the war and our defeat. Nobody had any ideas, and everybody wanted answers. Finally, as the day lengthened, I went off by myself and tried to put together the pieces, to see what pattern they made, but soldiers sought me out. "Sergeant, what are you going to do?"

"What can we do?" I said to them. "The Russians are pushing in."

Before dark I decided on my own course of action. I went to my motorcycle and filled it with gasoline. I started it and drove out of there and onto the road toward Braunau am Inn, where Adolph Hitler was born. Somewhere on that road, I knew I would meet the United States Army.

4 IT WAS early evening when I stopped my big BMW motorcycle near an old Wehrmacht soldier, thin and almost lifeless of expression, who was looking off as if hypnotized at a huge fire about a half mile away. "Aren't those the Americans ahead?" I asked him from the motorcycle.

"Yes. Do you see the fire?"

"I see it."

"I hear that's where the Americans disarm every German soldier and burn our uniforms with gasoline."

I gazed at the fire for a long time, then turned off the motorcycle and sat down on the ground near him. "At least I'll smoke one more cigarette as a free man," I said.

He also took out a cigarette, and we smoked for a minute or two. "Why don't you go into town and try to stay free?" he asked me.

"I have no papers, and I'm an SS man. None of the SS men will escape."

"Then go into the forest and be a guerrilla."

"That would be more of a losing fight."

Many trucks were passing, and families of Hungarians, Austrians, Romanians, and even Russians were walking in the road on their way to the American side. A few had horse-drawn wagons on which supplies had been packed. Some led cows.

"I've been trying to drive my motorcycle in all this confusion," I said. "Once tonight I ran into a man with a cart. He had loaded all his possessions, even his children, in that cart and I smashed the back of it and broke his axle."

"Well, there is worse suffering today," the old man said. "I saw a man start up that hill two hours ago when it was still daylight. He was dragging one foot, as if he were lame. I timed him, and it took an hour and three minutes for him to reach this place. When he got to here I called to him, told him to come and rest in the shade of this tree for a while, but he shook his head and went on. He was too anxious to surrender, I say."

"He will reach the Americans in time, with that determination."

"Yes, he will reach them, and they will shoot him." The old man spat out into the road. "They're not so much like gentlemen as people say; they have shot many prisoners already. I think it would do just as well to surrender to the Russians."

"No," I said, "a human being cannot live in the same room with a bear." I crushed out my cigarette. "I have several medals, including the Nahkampf Spange, which I got for thirteen bayonet charges in hand-to-hand fighting against the Red Army. I know the Russians."

"Did you ever fight the Americans?"

"Yes, but not hand to hand."

He studied me, taking my measure as a man. "How old are you?"

"Twenty."

"Not even grown. And yet you fought on both fronts without injury. You are lucky."

42

"Bad grass never dies," I said. I stared off at the fire, where many men were standing, each figure a silhouette like a piece of black cardboard. "Only thirty men who started with my division were with it to the end," I said. "Thirty men out of over thirteen thousand."

I lay back on the grass, remembering hundreds of faces from that multitude, men now dead or maimed or missing. And for what? For the cause, I told myself. And what was that? Most of us had never been taught the philosophy of the Nazi party, or any philosophy at all. We had been taught one thing: to obey the orders of Hitler.

Lying there on the grass, I remembered the words of the song with which we would close every Storm Trooper meeting:

> Though all the world desert you,
> We will still be true.

Now, only a few of us were left. And we were surrendering. The world had not deserted the Führer, it had turned on him with a vengeance and had conquered him.

"What will they do to us, old man?" I said.

"What they want to do," he said. "We are powerless now."

I considered that until depression took hold of me, then I got up and brushed off my pants. "Can I give you a lift?"

"Huh?" He glanced off toward the Americans. "No. I'm going to sit here and be a free man till they get me. I'm not going to them."

As I left he was still there on the road bank, staring at the distant fire.

Because of the civilian families on the road, I had to drive slowly. Some of the women and children were sobbing, but whether from fear or illness I could not tell. As for myself, I began to think about what the old fellow had suggested, about going into a forest and fighting, or going into a town and hiding out; but I decided if I were captured in such a place, I might be sent back to Poland, where I would surely be executed. Although nothing was certain, I felt the Americans would not be so cruel as that.

"I wish I could wake up from this dream," I said aloud.

Two or three men at once said, "Yes, I, too."

I wanted to hear my father pounding at my door, telling me to get out of bed and come down to breakfast. I could see myself rubbing the sleep out of my eyes, washing my face with cold water, joking with my brother Nichol.

"I don't want to surrender to the Americans or anybody else," I said to the man beside me.

We moved on, going slower. I thought, here was the final act in the fall of the country. When I had traveled back from the western front, the stage had been set: the buildings were crumbled, the nation was laid open and bare. Now the people were on the roads and in the streets. There was no longer any hiding.

When we could make out the figures of the Americans, I pulled my motorcycle over to the shoulder of the road and sat there, trying to make up my mind what to do. The closer I came to the act of surrendering, the less I liked it. The Americans killed my family, I thought; why should I think they are not cruel?

I ripped off my gas mask, took out the poison and threw the mask off to the side of the road. The poison I put in my sock to use in case of cruel treatment, and drove on.

At the big fire two Americans, one of them a Negro, came to me with pistols ready to fire. They took my P38, searched my pockets, and ordered me to park the motorcycle to one side. I tried to talk to them in English, to ask what I was to do, but they ordered me to be quiet. Then they pointed in the direction I was to walk.

I started out and went deeper into the United States

44

lines. My heart was crying. I was thinking about not having a family and not knowing where I was going. I heard a loud-speaker, which I saw was mounted on a jeep. "Keep walking," a voice said in thick German.

I walked the whole night. In the morning, between Braunau am Inn and Munderfing, I reached a field surrounded by barbed wire. I was hungry and thirsty; the road dust had clogged my throat and my whole body was numb from weariness and fear.

"Into the field," an American soldier shouted. I went in through a crudely built gate and mingled with the thousands of German soldiers who were standing or walking around aimlessly.

"What division you from, Sergeant?" some of them called to me. When I answered, they turned away, disappointed at not having found somebody from their own outfit.

Through the morning I tried to find water. I could go without food, but not water. I told the American guard that I had to have a drink, and he told me to wait until afternoon.

That afternoon there was no water, either. "Wait till tomorrow," he said.

In spite of my hunger and thirst, I slept some that night. But the next morning, there was neither water nor food. "Never mind about food," I said to a pilot who had surrendered just after me. "But we must have water."

There was no relief for us that afternoon, and it was early evening before some Americans arrived with water, which they dipped from huge metal pots and handed through the fence in shallow dippers. Each prisoner had enough for a few swallows only, but it cleaned my mouth and throat and took some of the fire out of the inside of my cheeks and from my coarse tongue.

During the night I lay under the sky and stared up at

the stars. I thought, if I got released from there, my real problems would begin, for, if I went back to Lvov, the Poles or Russians would hang me or send me to Siberia or Tundra to be a slave till I died. But if I did not go there, I could not be with Linda.

I saw myself a movie hero, crossing forest and plains, crossing all Poland, moving only at night and talking to nobody, avoiding all soldiers and policemen, and so arriving at last at a church in Lvov, or some other safe and romantic place from which I could send for her. She would come to me, and we would embrace, crying out for joy; and I would sneak her out of Poland to a nice house in Germany where we would have seven or eight children, and I could become an engineer.

Out under the stars, thinking about her, I could see her face in the sky. From the stars I picked out eyes for her and a mouth. I counted the places where I could see her face above me.

On the third day the rumor started that the Wehrmacht and Luftwaffe soldiers would be processed and released, but that the SS men would be kept prisoners. All that day, still without food, I cursed the order of the SS that the blood mark be tattooed on every Storm Trooper's left arm, so that now, in defeat, we could not deny our outfits and go free.

On the fourth day, we of the SS and Luftwaffe were sent to another camp. There we were told by the guards that the SS men would never be released because of our vicious fighting on the western front, but that the Luftwaffe officers, and then the Luftwaffe men, would be released soon. Still we were without food. I was so hungry I thought of eating grass, but my complaints to the guards won me nothing. "We have no supplies for you," one young guard said. "The whole German Army dumped itself on us. What do you expect?"

"For four days . . ." I said.

"Four days, five days, ten days, what do you expect? We didn't start this damned war."

"No, and I sure as hell didn't send you an invitation to enter it!" I shouted at him.

"Well, we're here, and you're there; and as for myself, I wouldn't give you enough barbed wire to choke yourself with." He made a big fuss until one of the American officers came up and led him away.

To a Luftwaffe pilot I said, "Why didn't you boys fly more and teach these Americans manners?"

He grunted and sank down weakly to the ground. "Gasoline," he said.

"Hell," I said, "is everything gasoline? Did we lose the whole war because of gasoline?"

"Gasoline and oil," he said.

I sat down beside him and scratched the insect bites on my legs. "I wish we had a chance to fight this war over. I didn't think the American boys would ever try to starve us Germans."

On the fourth night, I went among the sleeping prisoners seeking food to steal. In one man's bag I found bread, about a quarter of a loaf. I knew that, if the man woke up, he would try to kill me, so I looked at him carefully to judge his size, and I saw that he was a small man, and much older than I. It was clear he was not much of a soldier. Suddenly I was unable to steal from him. I knew it was foolish, but I could not steal from a man who, even if he awoke to find me eating his bread, could do nothing about it. So I tore off only a small piece and put the rest back in his baggage.

The bread was sweet and clean in my mouth. It was as if I had a new sense of taste. I determined to hold the

47

bread on my tongue for an hour, but I found I had to move it around in my mouth to keep the taste coming to me, and finally it was dissolved. When I swallowed, there was nothing to swallow except saliva. Then I became ill. My stomach tried to throw up the bread but could not, and there was nothing else there.

On the fifth day the loud-speakers on the jeeps started calling for men from the battalions and companies of the Totenkopf Division. "At last they have reached the SS," I said, "but if they call out the Totenkopf by companies, they'll never get to my outfit. I tell you, there's just one hope, and that's to escape from this camp."

"From here?" another SS man said, pushing himself to a sitting position on the ground. "The American guards are alert. They'll shoot you like an animal."

"It's better than dying a prisoner."

"And where can you go? We're marked; they'll find all SS men."

"Look, stop talking nonsense," I told him. "Do you have a shaving knife?"

"Yes," he said.

I removed my shirt and with two fingers pulled out the skin on the inner side of my left arm, where the blood mark was tattooed. "Cut this damn thing off."

He stared at me for a moment, then turned his eyes away.

"God," I said angrily. "What a kind SS man you are! Because of such men as you we lost the war!"

Another SS man came over and asked what was happening. I told him, and immediately he took out his shaving knife. "All right," he said, "I'll do it."

I pulled out the skin, and he cut it off. I threw away the small piece of raw skin, on which was marked the letter "A," and put on my shirt and jacket. I was bleeding; after

48

a while my whole shirt and jacket were in blood. I was in blood and very hungry.

"I'll get out of here tomorrow," I said to the two SS men. "I'll get out and steal papers. I'll go to Poland and get my girl, and then I'll go to—somewhere. . . ."

I sank down to the ground. "Better to be captured by the Russians," I said.

"Oh, death won't be so bad, after all," one of them said. "I feel like an old man, anyway, and have nothing ahead in sight."

I began praying after a while. I told God that if He would get me out of that camp I would consider becoming a priest. But even in my aching, dizzy mind I realized He would know I was lying, so I said, "God, I won't be a priest, but I'll be a farmer, which is almost the same, and I'll go to church and rear my children as good Christians, and if one of them is suitable, I'll make him a priest."

I told God that I also wanted Him to take care of Linda, because she was all I had left in the world. "You watch her, God, and if a Russian soldier comes close to her, kill him, Father."

But even as I said that, I knew God would not do it. Yes, I thought, here He was with all the power to protect people from evil, and He would not. I could not ask Him to protect this innocent girl from the Russians. "Why is it that You let the Communists win the war, anyway?" I asked. "I talked with Russian parents whose sons were taken away and never heard from again. The Communists will send a man to Siberia just for breathing, and You let them live on the same earth with everybody else."

I decided God was not listening to such talk, so I tried to determine what my sister Lene would pray and decided her subject would be the people who were in worse condition than she.

But my arm was bleeding, and my body was tight with

a five-day hunger; I could think of nobody worse off than I. So, in honesty, I prayed for myself. "Help me escape from prison, God. Help me escape, and don't make me have to kill an American guard, for then it will all end in a bad way. Just let me get through the barbed wire and out of this camp. You'll have to help me or I'll die in this place. God, help me. And help Linda. Help my dead father, who believed in You until You took my mother, who was a beautiful woman and he loved her, and You left him with children and no way to care for them. But he did believe in You before that and when my sister Lene died he prayed to You. If he had known the bomb was falling, he would have prayed to You for that one second, too, and now I pray for him, who believed most of his life. I am praying for my brothers and for my little sister Bertha, too, for their souls. And I pray for Lene. Bless Lene, God. And protect Linda, God . . ."

I prayed for a long time, repeating myself over and over. Finally I had said everything I had to say to God. Then I tried to get some sleep. But I was too tired to sleep, and too hungry and thirsty. I feared I would choke on dust, and I had no spit to swallow.

To occupy myself, I began to think about women I had known and about the differences in their bodies, their voices, the ways they walked and moved and smiled and made love. I thought of the faces of the women I had known, trying to recall exactly how they had looked, even the little girl in Prague who took me to her room and stole all my money while I slept. I could remember her thighs and breasts and body, but I had seen her face only for a moment in a dim street.

I lay there on the ground and thought of my whole life past, starting in Lvov where I would play in the streets with the Polish and Russian children, marking out towns with our fingers or with sticks, drawing houses and

50

schools, churches and roads. Even now I let my fingers trail along through the soft dirt, as if I were a child.

I thought of my father, angrily denouncing all Poles and Russians, praising Germany, no matter what she might do; and my sister Lene telling me, "Don't listen to him, Eddy. He'll lead you astray." My father would grin at her, almost foolishly, as if he were unsure how to come to grips with such impertinence. Then he would lead me out on the porch and talk to me about the way the world was organized and what changes needed to be made, Lene all the while standing in the doorway listening, shaking her head at me. But when I was old enough to need to be told such things, it was she who said, "Eddy, listen, you must not fall in love with a Polish or Russian girl; your father would be killed by it. Promise me that, Eddy."

So I promised and went out and fell in love with two Polish girls in one month.

But when I really fell in love it was with a German girl named Linda. There was no other girl in Lvov so pretty as Linda, and that was everybody's word on the subject. She had dark hair and eyes, light skin, smooth as cloth, and her face could change expressions in a twinkle; but in her happy face there was some sadness, and in her sad face there was very little sadness. Soon I was not sleeping or eating, but was thinking only of Linda. The motors in the garage where I worked after school sounded loud and harsh; I lost interest in everything except her.

But when I had gone with Linda only two weeks—or perhaps longer, for time went by without my knowing it—a Russian blacksmith came into the garage to see me. He laid his hand on my shoulder and turned me around roughly. I was frightened, because he was a grown man of twenty-five and I was sixteen. Also he had shoulders even wider than mine, and I could tell by the feel of his hand that his fist would be like iron.

51

He pointed toward the door at the back of the building. "Come outside."

I followed him. My friends hung back, watching. We stopped near a big tree and again he laid his hands on my shoulder.

"For six months I went with a girl," he said, "and now for two weeks I can hardly see her. So let me tell you, I am in love with this girl and will do anything for her, and you keep away, or I will give you a beating you will remember!"

I said nothing. He tightened his hand on my shoulder and said, "Do you understand?"

"Yes. I heard everything you said."

"Do you understand my full meaning?"

"Yes, but I will see her often, if I want to; no one will tell me what to do."

He drew his hands from my shoulder and folded his arms across his chest. "Your friends are nearby, so you are brave."

"Yes," I said, "but if you fight me, my friends will watch."

He glanced over at the garage door where my friends were gathered, then back at me, his arms still folded. "I've given you a fair warning, Hugo."

"Whatever you say," I said.

He waited a few seconds more, undecided as to what to do, then abruptly turned on his heels and walked off, his big shoulders rolling with the long strides of his legs.

I went back to my work. When the others asked what he had wanted, I told them nothing. With me, all matters pertaining to Linda were close and personal.

When work was over, about five o'clock, I left the garage and started home. I walked only a short distance when a car stopped in front of me and four men jumped out. They grabbed me and pulled me inside. As we drove off they began to beat me in the face. Outside the town they stopped the car, threw me out, and continued hammering on me. I resisted as best I could, but soon I was down on the ground. The men went on beating and kicking me until I lost consciousness.

The next morning I could not see from one eye because of swelling, and my lips were double normal size. For three days they were like that. Friends from the garage came by to see how I was, and my father and brothers questioned them, but they did not know what men might have beaten me up. "We'll go with you and get them," they told my brothers, "if you can find out who they were."

On the fourth day my face was in shape, but I stayed in the house, getting my strength back and thinking about that blacksmith and how to handle him.

On the sixth day I told Lene I was going down to the store for some food, but I went past the store to the blacksmith's shop. I called out and he came to the door, a hammer in his hand.

"Coward," I said, almost choking on my disgust for him.

He came toward me. I ducked under his hammer swing and brought my left fist in against his face with all my power. He stopped stock still, his eyes glazed. I hit him again. He stepped back half a step and blinked his eyes. I hit him again, and he went down like a bellows folding.

In my hands I brought water from the trough and dumped it on his face. He rolled his head back and forth, turned his body over. He got to his knees and was almost standing when I hit him.

I got more water and sprinkled him and told him, as he slept, that I was a priest and was going to make him a holy man of God.

When he got up this time, I hit him again. This third time he could not get up.

53

"Where are those four men?" I asked him.

"You go to hell," he said.

I kicked his ribs. "Where are they?"

"You German son of a bitch," he said. He got to his hands and knees. "You bastard, I can't get up, but if I could I'd kill you."

I threw him the bell rope attached to a large brass dinner bell mounted near the door of his shop. "Grab that and pull yourself up."

Painfully he hauled himself erect, and he held to the rope while I hit him. I hit him a dozen times, the bell clanging out all through that part of town. Each time I hit him I asked him where to find his four friends. He would not tell me. All he would do is curse me for being German. Finally I laid him down on the street with a single blow, then I threw the end of the bell rope over the bell brace, so that he would have to lie there until he found a friend to help him from the gutter; and if he had no friend, then he could stay there. All I knew was that he was not dead; I left him still alive.

Now I chuckled deep inside myself, finding pleasure in thinking about a defeated Russian. Other experiences came rising from my past, tumbling over one another in my mind. It would be well to go back beyond the start of the war, I thought, and not let the war happen at all, and not lose anything.

I remembered how my father, when he was worried, would sometimes walk the three or four kilometers from our house on Trudowa Street to the lake at Mlekarna. One afternoon he took me there in order to explain privately about sex, for now that I was dating Linda, Lene felt that I should be informed. All afternoon I waited expectantly for him to begin, but he found other subjects, such as the weather and the color of the water.

54

We were walking back toward home when finally he said, "Eddy, this is important, what I tell you now. Eddy, by God, you listen to this." He was speaking in a husky voice and so low I could hardly hear him, and all the while the muscles of his face and neck were working. "Eddy, there are differences between men and women, and it's time you knew something about them. I don't want to end up with a problem on my hand, so I'll give you the true facts and we'll see. Perhaps you've already found out that there's a difference, have you?" He peered at me hopefully.

"Yes, sir," I said.

"Good," he said, beaming. "By God, that's fortunate." He darkened again. "Now, Eddy, I don't mean the style of the hair or the way they dress or anything superficial, do you understand me?"

"Yes, sir," I said.

"Fine." But he darkened again. "And I don't mean the tenor of voice or anything like that, Eddy, or in the shape of the face, or anything like that, do you follow me?"

"Yes, sir," I said.

"I knew you would," he said. I watched him as he concentrated, his shoulders hunched over, his forehead wrinkled. Suddenly he cut his eyes at me. "Where the hell did you learn the differences?"

"Sir?"

"Where did you learn them?"

"Well, sir, I'm—not sure I have learned them exactly." I hesitated to tell him I had dated two Polish girls.

"I thought you said you knew."

"Yes, sir, I—well, sir, I don't know anything about it. Nothing at all, sir."

"My God," he said, his face pouting. "Well, I'm not asking you how you know; but do you know, Eddy?"

I hesitated. "Yes, sir," I said.

"Children in the school talked, did they, boy?" He peered at me suspiciously. "Well, that's all right. Can't stop them from talking. Is that where you found out, Eddy?"

"Well, yes, sir," I said slowly.

"I suppose they told you everything, did they?"

"I—uh—yes, sir."

"Good for them," he said. "By God, that's fine."

When we reached home, he pointedly ignored my sister Lene's questioning stare and, evading her, went upstairs. I was about to follow him when she said, "No, Eddy, wait. Come in and sit down for a minute."

I followed her into the living room and sat down, ill at ease.

"Eddy, I don't know what your father might have said to you, and this—isn't a subject I know a great deal about, because, as you know, I—have no boy friends and have sought none——"

"Yes, Lene," I said, wondering why this was so. She was a large, strong woman, pretty, with my mother's face. Several men had come to call and had dated her, but she had shown little interest in them.

"But, Eddy—I want to say that—respect is a factor one doesn't need wide experience to understand; and I know it applies in such matters as this. Being loved by a man is —very meaningful to a woman, I believe, and perhaps more so than it is to a man. A man goes around with conquest on his mind, and perhaps he likes to run up something of a score; but a woman is seeking someone to love her, protect her, hold her dear. I mean, Eddy, this is in every woman's heart, I think, although some seek it carefully, protecting themselves from hurt; and some seek it promiscuously, hoping that numbers will reveal a whole solution; and some have given up, forfeiting the notion of romance. I suppose if we were

56

wise, we would see that every woman is different, and the advice that might do well for one would be poor for another."

"Yes, Lene."

"Advice to a man is—is easier to give; and all I want to say to you is to respect, insofar as you can, every woman, believing that whatever course she takes, a good motivation may be driving her. And remember that loving a woman should be beautiful, as a natural part of life in the sense of birth and growth and fulfillment. If you lose sight of that, you are the loser. And when we lose an ideal, it's difficult to get it back, Eddy. Far better to hold to it, even in spite of evidence, and seek other evidence to support the ideal."

I looked at her somber face, beautiful to me, and felt in my heart the warmth and courage of her, my sister and my mother. I said nothing. I could not speak, but in my face she saw that I had heard all she said.

"Well," she said abruptly, "I'm sorry that, without your even asking, I've opened my mind to you."

"Lene, thank you, Lene . . ."

"It helps to talk together, I think. And I want you to learn sympathy, Eddy, because you're so strong. Those who are strong must learn to be gentle. Your brothers have done that; I've watched them mature, and now they are self-contained. They're not quick to fight now. They think and try to understand. But you are young yet, and I won't be here to help you, Eddy."

I did not know what she meant about not being there, but it was a painful thought. All my life I had been with Lene, had depended on her; I had loved her and had known that she loved me. She got up suddenly, wiping a sleeve across her eyes. She went out quickly, closing the door, leaving me there in the big, heavily furnished room, fighting back my tears.

But it was later that year, when my young sister Bertha and my brother Nichol went up country for the summer, that I shed my wild tears for her. One morning, when my father, Edmund, and I came down to breakfast, she was not there. The stove was cold. I ran up to her room. "Lene," I said, "wake up." She was difficult to awaken, and when she did awake and tried to get out of bed, I had to help her. I felt that perhaps a fierce pain was gnawing at her even while I was there.

"Don't—mention this to Father," she told me. "He—doesn't like—weakness. . . ." She sat for a moment on the edge of the bed, breathing long, shallow breaths, then nodded that she was all right.

The next morning she had breakfast waiting for us, and so she did all that week and the next. But another morning came when she was not up. I ran to her room and threw open the door. "Lene, come quickly."

She awoke groggily. I put my arm around her shoulders to help her up, but when she was part of the way out of bed her body sagged in my arm and she slumped back. I stepped away, stunned. Then I put my mouth close to her ear. "Lene, hurry before Father gets here," I whispered. "Please get up, Lene."

She made no move. "Lene, please, Lene."

She opened her eyes. Her breathing was labored and raspy. "Call Father," she said, "then lift my legs onto the bed."

Father came upstairs loudly announcing to the household that Lene was pretending to be sick, his strongest child pretending, in order to gain sympathy for herself. When he found that this brought no response, he claimed she was pretending in order to get out of work.

But when he saw that she was really ill, his big frame trembled with fear and sorrow. He sank down beside her

58

bed, took her hand in his two hands. "Lene, sweet, what's the matter?" he said.

I backed up into the corner of the room and stared at them, not wanting to intrude, but knowing I would not leave her.

"Sweet, baby, what is it?" he said.

Lene shook her head slowly, breathing deeply. "I'm sorry," she said.

"No, no, not if you're sick. I'll get the best German doctors; you'll be all right. When your mother was sick, I trusted God more than the doctors, and she died; but I'll put my whole trust in medicine, Lene. I can't lose your mother and you, too. I can't lose both my darlings."

I had never heard him talk like that to anyone. He was always brusk or joking; and now he was calling Lene his darling, and I was watching it.

Three doctors came, examined Lene. They took my father to one side, and the four of them whispered together for five minutes. Before they left, the doctors gave a final glance at Lene.

My father came over to Lene's bed, pulled up a chair beside it. "You're—going to be—all right. Did you hear me, Lene?"

"Yes, Father."

"You believe me, Lene? I never lied to you, honey."

"I believe you, Father," she said quietly.

"Yes, you're going to be all right," he said, tears coming to his eyes.

Ill and in pain she lay for a month, the doctors frequent visitors, my father's laughter shrouded, the house hushed and dark. I stayed by her side, anxious for her to ask me to do some favor.

"Eddy," she would say, "let me feel your hand."

I would put my hand in hers. She would press my fingers. "Now press my hand, Eddy." I would do that. "Gently, Eddy, gently. That's the way to do it."

Linda would come by in the afternoon and sit in a chair near the bedroom door. We would talk softly of the happenings of the town, for Linda was my only outside contact during that time. Frequently Lene would be awake and would talk with us. "The world has a place for everyone," she would say, "and a warm place for you two." She would tell us about the family we would have, the happy moments of birth and the sad moments of sickness and death, of the deep meanings of life. Each time she spoke I could think of nothing except: this is Lene's life; this is the way the world was to be for her, but the world refuses to do it, so Lene will give her place to me and bless the world for its kindness.

One morning she called my father, Edmund, and me to her bed. She said, "I had a dream last night. I dreamed that tonight at five minutes till eleven I will die."

"Ah," my father said, "Lene, the doctor says you'll be all right. You're going to be well in a few days now."

"At five minutes till eleven," she said.

He went downstairs. I could hear him pacing the living room. He came back after a while and said, "Lene, I've been praying to God for you."

A smile came to her face. Gratefully she reached out her hand to him. He took it. "I—I prayed to God for you, Lene."

"Yes, Father. It is right for you and God to make peace."

Two doctors came in that day and examined her, but she gave neither of them a sign of recognition. They went away without saying anything to her or me. When Linda came, Lene tried to speak to her, perhaps to say good-by, but the words clogged in her throat. Linda went away so quietly I could not hear her footsteps on the

60

stairs. Later that day she returned, but now Lene did not recognize her.

All through that day my father came and went, unable to keep his big body still. Sometimes his lips would move, but soundlessly.

At a quarter till eleven that evening, while Lene slept, he came in and felt her pulse. He went out again, only to come back a minute later. In my mind I could hear a clock ticking, although there was no clock in the room.

At five minutes till eleven he felt her pulse. He laid her arm by her side, stood there for a minute. "Edmund," he called.

My brother did not answer.

I said, "Father, is she all right?"

"Yes," he said. "She's dead."

I stood in the corner of the room, stiff and weak, Linda came to the doorway of the room. Tears were in her eyes. "Eddy," she said, almost a whisper.

"Ah, God," I said. Anguish flooded me. I ran to my sister's bed, fell on my knees. I began to weep and pray. Linda sank down beside me, putting her arm around my shoulders.

I began to pray aloud. "God," I prayed, "love Lene! God, love Lene," I cried.

Now on the dry ground of the internment camp I prayed for her once more and tried to talk with her.

Then I remembered the ghost which had come to me in my father's house before I had left home for the German Army. It had been Lene's ghost, I knew, and my brother Edmund, who had been in the room with me, saw it, too, and also told my father it was Lene come back to wish me well on my long trip and in the fighting. So I felt she was there, even in the American camp. I listened for her voice and watched for her, but there was no response.

61

"Don't you leave me, too, Lene," I whispered. "Please stay with me."

The night passed in agony, my dry mouth seeming to crack at the walls, and my throat tore itself with each breath I took. The blood, dripping down my arm, made puddles at my elbow on the ground; my shirt sleeve was soaked and dark red. By the time morning came, I had lost much strength.

"What—what about water?" I asked one of the other prisoners.

"No," he said, his mouth forming the words slowly, "they are letting us die here."

Just as he said that, the loud-speaker on a jeep began: "Attention, attention, every man who belongs to the First Battalion of the Adolph Hitler Division, come to the building."

"Ah!" I cried out. And to myself I said, Thank you, Lene. It is enough now that you have done for me.

I lay there on the ground, gathering my strength, then I pushed myself to my feet and made my way down to the gate.

The Americans counted us off into groups of ten. In my group I was the only one with a sergeant's rank, so I came under questioning before a captain. "Sit down," he said in German. "Your name and rank?"

"Edward Hugo. SS Untersharführer."

"Give me your military book."

I handed it to him. He studied the picture in the book and looked at me. "Yes, this is correct," he said. "Do you know that you will be executed today?"

"As you say."

He stared at me, idly tapping his pencil on the table top. "I was joking," he said and turned over the paper on which he had written my name. "Which army did you serve?"

62

"I served in the Panzer Artillery, First Battalion of the Adolph Hitler Storm Regiment. I was under command of General Sepp Dietrich and was attached to the Sixth New German Army."

He wrote that down on the paper. "Where were you born?"

"In Poland. Lvov," I said.

A startled smile broke on his face. He laid the pencil down and stared at me for a moment, then he spoke a few words in Polish, and I answered him. We began to talk in Polish, I answering his questions about my life. Finally he smiled at me. "Boy, you are my countryman," he said. Then in Polish he told me about having immigrated to America as a boy and how it had been with him there. We talked for half an hour, then suddenly he threw away the sheet of paper on which he had written my name, and my military book he threw in a fire. "Come along," he said.

He led me to a private room and called a soldier there. "Go get some food."

The soldier hurried out, and the captain examined my wound. He cleaned and bandaged it, using long heavy pieces of gauze. Then he took civilian clothes from a foot locker. I was dressed in my new outfit by the time the soldier returned, carrying a mess kit full of food and a cup of milk, which he left on the table.

I ate ravenously, devouring huge bitefuls, not even noticing what the food was. It made little difference; my body was hungry for strength.

When I finished the captain gave me a cigarette. I smoked most of it and began to feel much better.

"Now let's see what we must do," he said. "I will get you out of this camp today. There's nothing to be gained by keeping a million men in prison. But you'll be picked up again unless you stop speaking German. Forget that

63

language, Hugo. Speak only Polish or Russian. And your nationality is not German, either, but Polish, understand?"

"Yes, sir," I said.

"Very well. Now I have to go to Salzburg, and you might as well come along." He took me outside the building and started down the road toward the motor pool. "You walk like a sick man, Eddy," he said.

"I feel better every minute now."

When he stopped his jeep at the gate, the guards did not seem to notice me. No one asked questions. As we drove away, we passed several German soldiers trudging along the road, some of them going toward the camp, where, no doubt, they would surrender.

The captain, on the way south to Salzburg, talked a great deal about the war. He was a man of strange contrast. He was doing me a favor, perhaps keeping me from being shipped to the Russians; but at the same time he wanted to talk about how much he disliked the Storm Troopers.

"You boys were ruthless," he told me. "Where did the Germans get their idea that they could take over the whole world and destroy everybody and everything they didn't like?"

I was too tired to say much, and when I tried to speak, my words came out as if from an old person.

"Well, now that it's over," he said to me finally, "I guess we might as well try to put the pieces back together."

In Salzburg, as he dropped me off, he said, "Eddy, I'm driving to Munich in the morning. If you are here at this spot about 6:00 A.M., I'll give you a lift. It'll be a help for you to cross the Austrian border into Germany with an American captain."

With that he was off in a cloud of dust.

That night I stayed in the house of an elderly couple,

64

who moaned in low voices about the war and the great mistakes. I ate dinner with them, then they told me to use their bed, and they would hear no argument. So I bathed in steaming water and lay in the deep mattress like a child, thinking what a strange bag of tricks the world carries, for on one night a man might sleep on the ground and be hungry and in pain, and the next night be in a feather bed, have a full stomach, and be on his way to Munich in the morning.

At dawn I had breakfast with that nice family, and at six I met the captain and drove to Munich. "Now stay low for a month, two months, for as long as you can. Then buy a ticket for Hamburg with this, you hear?" He handed me an American ten-dollar bill. "There are many American ships there. You might stow away on one of them and go to the States." He shook hands with me and wished me luck.

Then, before I could speak, his jeep moved on.

I watched it, wondering what kind of strange person this was who would do so much for a man whom he had fought but a few days before. Then we had been shooting at each other; but now, because we had talked together about our lives, he had freed me from jail and carried me to another city, had given me money, and had not even waited for me to thank him.

I thought of my helping the Jews on the train and was grateful to him for his help to me, in the same way.

Thinking of this I did not at once realize where I was. Now I looked about and found myself in a strange, large city. The feeling of loneliness came down on me like a hot wind. I stared at the faces of the people shuffling by, some of them still wearing the uniforms of the Wehrmacht soldiers. Everybody kept his eyes on the ground; nobody questioned another person, even with a look.

65

I knew not one person in that city. No one knew me. And no one must know me, even that I was German, or that I had fought for Germany. Certainly nobody must know that I had been a member of Hitler's SS.

5

IN THE NEXT six months I faced several desperate decisions, the last of which changed my entire course of action and sent me away from Germany, perhaps forever; yet none of these decisions was solely my own to make. Many of us were like corks tossed on the ocean, subject to the currents and tides. And from the beginning it was a swift, treacherous current which held me.

That was true even in those first several weeks. First I went to Frankfurt and hid on nearby farms. Hundreds of us were roaming the countryside, some going hungry for days at a time, begging or stealing what we could, staying together in order to defend ourselves from the slave laborers. One out of every five persons in Germany was a released slave laborer. Almost ten million of them had been brought into the country during the latter years of the war—Russians, French, Poles, Italians, Czechs, Belgians, Dutch, Scandinavians, and Balts. They had been forced to work on farms and in factories. Now the gates of their camps had been opened; they were free. And ill with hatred of their German masters, they sought revenge.

Thousands of Germans were hounded by fear and hunger from one place to another. They would stay on a farm

67

for a week or two, then move on, hoping to find something safer. In the woods there always were many people, including children, who had been taught not to speak, not to laugh, not to cry or make any other sound.

I stayed near Frankfurt until my wound healed, then I took a train to Hamburg, climbing up to the roof of the car so that I could flee more easily should the police ask questions. As the train went along, I saw that poverty was a problem everywhere. At every station throngs of people, dragging children and possessions, were trying to get aboard. Everyone was going; yet nobody was arriving.

At a small station named Radbruch, a pretty girl, who had a quaint, alert way about her, tried to force her way into the overcrowded car below. Failing in that, she tried to climb onto the roof.

I helped her up. "It's good for a man to climb high alone," I said, "but not for a girl."

Though light of hair and skin, she reminded me of Linda, and I was attracted to her at once. She told me her name was Erika, and that she had spent most of the war years with an aunt, but now she was returning to her parents in Hamburg. At first we talked about the hard times and the overwhelming loss of our country and members of our families; but after a while we talked of lighter subjects and began to laugh freely, so that the forty kilometers to Hamburg passed happily.

In the Hamburg station I helped Erika down and we said good-by for a time, she going to her parents' home and I making my way to the Polish refugee camp, Camp A and Camp B, which was near the American military headquarters.

I had no trouble gaining admittance. When the director asked my name and birthplace, I told him the truth. Only when I told him I had spent the war years working as a

68

slave laborer did I lie. But he accepted all the information and wrote out my papers.

In the camp the English guards and Polish residents did everything they could to make me comfortable, giving me three good meals a day, six American cigarettes supplied by the Red Cross, and coffee and cakes in the evening. Frequently they came around to the rooms for talk or gambling. But I was never at ease. There was always the danger that they would discover the truth about me, that they would use me to revenge themselves on Germany or send me to the Russians. Over and over they repeated the stories of grim persecution, both in Poland and in the slave labor camps. A few of them had been at Buchenwald and Dachau.

When I tired of their stories, I would go to the harbor to seek a ship, although this soon became an obvious waste of time, or to the market places to trade cigarettes for money. Sometimes I bought gifts for Erika and her parents. Their house was in a nearby middle-class section of Hamburg, and usually I would walk there, starting in late afternoon and stopping occasionally to talk with other strangers about their work, or about their ideas for the future. Everybody had a story to tell and wanted a listener.

Sometimes I would see soldiers coming home for the first time since the war, walking with the slow, steady pace of men who had traveled day after day. On one occasion I saw a returning soldier reunited with his wife and two sons. I watched them, the man and woman weeping and holding to each other on the front stoop of their house, while the boys stood back and watched fearfully, not sure about this strange man who was clutching at their mother. Another time I talked with a soldier who had gone to his old family house, only to find it demolished. The neighbors had given him the new address of his family, and he had gone there, only to be sent on again and again. Now he had come to his fifth address, and still had to go on to another one.

I would spend much time on these walks watching the work of rebuilding. There were few machines, so most of the work had to be done by hand. Frequently Erika and I would go down to a corner in her neighborhood and help a man and his wife who were clearing their property. On many a hot summer afternoon we worked with him, breaking the clinging bits of mortar from the brick before stacking them, and throwing into a pile the broken beams and splintered boards, saving the others. Later we helped lay a foundation for their new house.

"Soon they will move in and start a family," Erika told me, speaking wistfully. "The war never stops love for long, Eddy."

Most often she joked as the work was done, and never did she permit anybody to talk about the shortage of building materials, the coming of cold weather, or any other deterrent.

I spent much of my day watching Germany start to rebuild, but in late evening, when I returned to the Polish camp, I would hear the groaning insults to my country and her efforts. I would lie awake listening, asking myself what my father would think if he found me living as a Pole and accepting silently such opinions. No doubt he would order me out into the streets, even without papers, to take my chances with the police and find food where I could.

Yet I much preferred the camp to creeping through the countryside, begging or stealing; and I would have stayed there until Germany had healed her broken parts if it had not been for Erika's father and his farm.

The farm was in a community near Hamburg and consisted at this time of acreage only, which he customarily rented out. He suggested that I might like farm life as much as Erika did, and that I might settle down in the farm town in which he had grown up.

"Eddy, the ships here are guarded against stowaways," he told me, "so tell me what you think about farming, Eddy?" He watched me eagerly, as did Erika, waiting for the slightest flicker of interest. "Have you thought about having a farm where you could be the master?" he asked. "Listen, I was born on a farm. It is better than the city. Farmers see the planes go over, but there are no bombs. The cities fight the wars, not the farms; and the cities start the wars, also. On a farm every man has his own land and means of support; it is between him and God, not between man and man, or between countries, either. Go to the country. You will see." He studied me for a while, waiting for an answer. Erika glanced at me, then away, as if afraid to look at me directly.

When finally I told him I would visit his town, he beamed happily. "Yes, you go to the country, Eddy," he said.

That night, walking back to the Polish camp, I thought that Erika had seemed confused, and I wondered if perhaps she and her father had planned my future. Certainly I could not complain, even if it were so, for I could hardly do better at any time, much less in a time of danger and loneliness, unless I could go to Linda and my home city. But Lvov was behind the Russian wall. If Linda was not there, then she too was lost among the throngs of refugees.

The next morning I sold my day's food ticket to a Pole and waited in line at the office of the Polish camp for a travel permit. Then I bought train passage to the farm village. As we left Hamburg, the train moved slowly down lines of piled-up rubble, past windowless buildings, the strewn wreckage of factories and houses. But when the country came into view, the land, even in autumn, was full of promise. There was hardly a sign that the war had been fought. Here the seasons would always come, I thought, crops would be planted in spring to be harvested later, and young would be born to the animals.

As the train rolled along, picking up speed now, I allowed the idea of the land to settle on me. Although I had never farmed, I knew it would not be more difficult than working with motors; and now with my past shattered, as the city was shattered, I wanted a quiet life.

I left the train at the small home village of Erika's father and strolled down the street to find the burgomaster. I was whistling happily, contentedly noticing the solid workmanship evident everywhere in the houses and barns, the sturdy gates and fences. I walked half a block before realizing that the town was deserted. The only sound was of a cow mooing, as if in pain.

I waited for a long while, but nobody put in an appearance. I took courage and shouted out.

A muffled voice answered from far away. A moment later eight or ten men came out of the farmyard gate of the last house on the left.

"I'm glad to see you," I called to them. "I thought this was a ghost town."

The men laughed, but nobody said anything.

"Where is the burgomaster?" I shouted.

One man staggered a few steps toward me, moving drunkenly. "In this village there is no burgomaster. We're the masters here. We threw all the Germans out, the same as they did to us in Poland. Now is the time to pay it back."

"Good," I said. "I am Polish, too. You are doing fine work here." I backed off, then hurried away, ignoring their invitations to come and drink with them.

In a nearby town the displaced German villagers

72

eagerly told me how the Poles had arrived the day before, waving rifles and even a panzerfaust, its bazooka-type shell in place. They ordered the German citizens into the street, where they insulted the men, almost all of whom were old or crippled, and humiliated the women before their children.

Then the villagers were ordered away. They left at once, thankful to escape with their lives.

But now their cowardly action puzzled them. They were as irritated by that as they were by thoughts of the Poles. Also the stock needed to be tended, the cows milked, and as the day lengthened the farmers grew increasingly annoyed.

"Something must be done," an old man, perhaps eighty, said. "We must recapture the town."

"Yes," another said, and others joined in. Soon everybody was encouraging everybody else to take part, and asking their hosts there in this neighboring village to take part, too. The enthusiasm mounted, so that by midafternoon weapons were brought from the houses. Men and women armed themselves with anything at hand—a shot gun, a shovel, a club. A single-barreled shotgun was offered me, and I noticed that several people were watching to see what I would do. I took the gun, examined it, wondering if it would be wise to take part. At last I decided to go with them.

But I had many fears. I knew that the Poles were not only fanatical in their hatred, but also heavily armed; and the thought of what might happen should a drunken Pole fire the panzerfaust shook my confidence in the venture. There was, however, no discouraging either the men or the women. The women were particularly anxious to begin the march, and even the cautious suggestion which I made, that perhaps we should wait until dark and take the Poles by surprise, brought the answer that the attack must begin right away if they were to hope to have supper in their own kitchens that night.

Only a handful of the older women lagged behind with the children. The rest of us marched the three kilometers in under an hour and entered the town in full strength.

Down at the far end of the street, a drunken Pole, who had been dousing his head in a horses' trough, let out a startled roar. Without losing a step we bore down on him. He backed away and roared again.

From a window another Pole ordered us to halt.

We came on, the women's faces stern and determined, as if chiseled from stone. The chickens were cackling as they ran here and there across the road, and several dogs began to bay. The cows mooed louder than before.

The drunken Poles poured out of the houses and advanced on us, firing pistols into the air and waving their dangerous panzerfaust. But the women did not hesitate, nor did many of the old men. The two armies approached one another. My shotgun was loaded, but I could not bring myself to fire.

The armies met, the battle was joined, and I was in the midst of it. I used the gun as a club, driving the stock against the head and shoulders of the Poles. Two men went down before me, both immediately falling victim to the women's trampling feet. The other six Poles were finding spades and clubs poked at them wherever they turned. One Pole, seeing the fight was turning against his side, yanked the safety pin from the panzerfaust; but a large woman struck the side of his head with a frying pan.

I started to laugh and took a swing at him because he still had the panzerfaust, but I was laughing so hard I missed him. Then a farm woman crowned him with a shovel and that made him drop the weapon. An old man scooped it up, hobbled with it to the creek, and dropped it in.

74

At once, the Poles began their retreat, nursing their bruises and wounds.

That night the farm women were so pleased with the performance that they outdid themselves in making bread and cake, cooking beef and pork, opening cans of pears and turning out lumps of butter from the churns. Wine came up from the cellars and whisky from the cabinets. A record player was placed in an open window, and we danced in a courtyard. Soon fiddles were brought out; the music rose. It was well after 1:00 A.M. when the town decided it would settle for the day.

My help in the battle placed me in high standing with the community, and although I now realized farm villages had their parts to play in wars, as well as cities, I began to think Erika's father had been right about this town being a good place for me. Soon I went back to Hamburg considering the many good, safe years I might spend there, and wondering if God, after all, were not trying to give me a special blessing. Now with Erika I might have a home again.

I entered the Polish camp with these happy thoughts, but instantly they were shattered. No sooner was I inside the gate than I came face to face with two of the Poles who had fought in the farm village. I went on, trying to act as if I had not seen them.

I left the camp quickly and took a taxi to Erika's house, all the while wondering what I should do. Now it was likely that I would be recognized as a German, and if the Poles found out further that I had a scar on my left arm, my punishment most certainly would be death or transfer to the Russians, since I was from Poland.

I glanced out the rear window of the taxi to see if they were following. The street was empty. I knew, however, they could find Erika's address from my visiting permits or from two letters in my footlocker; but it was unlikely

75

they would move against me until I returned to the camp.

Erika embraced me warmly. Then she and her mother took the leftovers from the icebox and spread a meal for me. They and the papa sat down at the round dining-room table to watch me eat and hear the story of my visit to the farm town. The old man took delight in the story. Often he would slap his open palm on the table top, so that the china rattled in the safe, and bellow out his laughter. "That's my town, all right," he would cry. "You were in my town, boy."

I had to repeat the story in full before the mother finally managed to lead him upstairs, and Erika and I were left alone.

"Come along," she said abruptly, rising and holding out her hand to me. She led me into the living room and there lit a fire in the grate. Sitting down on the rug in front of it, she drew me down beside her. "You made the visit to Papa's town seem very light and funny, Eddy, but I could tell you were worried about something. What is it?"

I smiled at her. "You know me very well, don't you? Actually I was wondering what would happen if the Poles found out I was in the SS."

"Ah, don't worry about those impossibilities," she said. Never would she permit anybody to worry about anything, if she could help it.

I smiled at her, wondering for a moment if she had any idea of the cruel notions in the minds of the Poles and what might happen to me.

"Eddy," she said, "dear Eddy, what's the matter? Are you at the end of a rope?"

"No, dear. I don't feel a noose yet."

"And you won't. You know why? You are too strong and quick. You will escape everything, I know. In all this world you could escape everything."

I laughed and slipped an arm around her waist.

76

"But, Eddy, if you ever do feel the end of the rope, will you come to me?"

"Yes, dear," I said. "But if you were wise you would leave me alone. I don't know what will become of me, but there can't be much good in it for anyone as gentle as you."

"You are gentle, too."

"Ah, I hardly know what you mean."

She smiled wistfully. "Eddy, stay here tonight. Stay with me, will you? Don't go back to camp tonight."

"If you like." I kissed her. As I did, her hand closed on the back of my neck. I felt her move as she pushed off one shoe and then the other. One foot touched my leg. "Erika," I said, "I will stay with you . . ."

She chuckled deep inside her throat. "I'm glad for love," she said. "I don't think I could stand thinking about war another minute."

I ran my hand gently along the curve of her back. "One minute, dear," I said, "and each of us will forget everything except the other."

6

THE NEXT MORNING the mother gave me breakfast. With a wink, the father assured me I was welcome to remain in their house for a time, and I thanked him for that but told him it was important for me to return to the Polish camp, in order not to lose my papers.

I ate the fried eggs the mother had fixed and the biscuits with jam that she and Erika had made. I was still talking with Erika an hour later, long after the father had gone to work and the mother had left the kitchen, when there came a sharp knock on the front door. Since Erika was washing the dishes, I started for the door to answer it, but through the glass I saw one of the two Poles standing there.

I stepped back quickly, returning to the kitchen, my mind reeling with half-formed thoughts. Other knocks sounded from the front door.

"Who is it, Eddy? Did you go to the door?"

"No, I . . ." I was so confused I could not think. Suddenly I pulled her close to me and whispered, "Listen, go to the door, and no matter what the man asks, don't tell him I've been here."

"But . . ."

"Hurry."

She ran from the kitchen and through the dining room. I heard the front door latch turn and the door open. "Did you want something?" she called, as if the man had left the door and was walking away.

I could not hear the answer, but after a moment Erika said, "Well, I have not seen him and care nothing for your threats!" She slammed the door and came back into the kitchen, deeply troubled.

"You're a good girl, you know that?" I said, kissing her and trying to act unafraid.

"Eddy, there were two of them, both strong men. I think they would be willing to kill you."

"Yes, that may be." I pushed her aside and started to leave.

"No, don't go, please," she said, "not if those two are in your camp."

"Don't worry, dear," I said. "Only at night does a Polish game get dangerous."

I went out the back door and ran down the lane of back yards to a main street, where I caught a ride on a truck that was going uptown. A few minutes later I was at the gate of the Polish camp, debating whether to go in or not. In spite of my doubts and fears, I finally decided it would be better to try to bluff my way through, for if I left the camp I would be a fugitive again.

I sauntered into the barracks area, trying to act as if I had not a care in the world. Some of the Poles who were lounging about in the sun nodded and I nodded back. Neither the Poles nor the English guards said anything to me.

Inside the barracks I went to my bunk and got out my razor and towel, whistling a Polish tune all the while. Everything was well thus far. When I turned to go to the

80

shower room, however, I found eight men standing in front of me, blocking the aisle.

"Well," I said, "what can I do for you?"

Not one of them spoke. It was as if nobody wanted to be the leader.

I took out a pack of cigarettes and lit one. "Anybody want a smoke?" Still no one said anything. I stuck the pack back in my pocket.

"Hugo, where are you from in Poland?" asked a man with big bunchy shoulders.

"Lvov."

"What are the names of the main streets in that city?"

I stared at him, as if amazed by his question. "Why would anybody care for names of streets?"

The man's expression did not waver. "Don't you know the names of the streets?"

I nodded emphatically. "But first I want a reason."

Another Pole ran his hands down in his pockets, wiping his palms as if he had sweat on them. "We want to be sure Lvov is your home town, that's the reason."

"Why would I lie?" I asked, puffing at my cigarette. "And if I were to name a hundred streets in Lvov, which one of you would know if I were telling the truth?"

Once more they looked uncomfortably at one another. The oldest among them, who was about fifty, suddenly jerked his head at a young fellow. "Go find somebody who knows Lvov," he said.

The young man ran off, happy that he had an important assignment; and the Poles whispered among themselves about whether to wait or proceed.

"Who are these men who accuse me of not being from Lvov?" I asked.

"There are two men who say you injured their friend," the oldest Pole said. "Their friend has a broken shoulder

81

blade and will have to have medical treatment for many months. They blame this on you."

"It was a battle in a farm village," another Pole added, "They say you led the Germans against them."

"What village?" I said angrily. "What Germans? I've been here in Hamburg."

"Not in this camp you haven't. Not yesterday."

"I was living with a girl yesterday."

"Which girl? What's her name?"

I hesitated, then shook my head slowly. "After what I've just told you about her character, I can't tell you her name."

The men glared at me. "Don't joke with us, Hugo," the oldest one said.

"No," I answered. "I am not joking, believe me."

A lanky Pole spat on the floor to show his irritation with the way the questioning was going. Then suddenly the two Poles who had been looking for me at Erika's house came through the door. They saw me at once, and both of them let out a bellow. "That's him! God, God, God!" one of them screamed, almost stuttering. "You damned bastard, you come to this Polish camp!"

"God damned Gestapo German," the other man said wildly.

Instantly I charged the two men, and they fell back, stumbling and falling over each other trying to get away from me. I realized then that they were cowards, and so were more dangerous than ordinary men.

When they had retreated a fair distance from the rest of the group, I went back to my bunk and snatched my towel and razor again. I turned to leave, but once more the men closed in at the aisle. They had the same cold, stony faces.

"Hugo," said the one with the big shoulders, "at what slave camp did you work for the Germans?"

82

"One near Frankfurt," I answered evasively.

"And the name of it?"

I knew the name of a slave camp in that area, and was trying to recall it when the lad who had been sent as a messenger brought in an old man from Lvov.

"Here we'll get the truth," he shouted. "We'll prove he is not from Poland."

"Yes," one of my two accusers said, approaching the group with confidence, "and also if you'll look on his arm, you'll find he has been tattooed with a German SS blood mark."

One of the calmer Poles said, "Let's get this done in order. First the matter of his birth."

The old fellow from Lvov tilted up on his toes, peering at me as if trying to identify me. "I don't remember you," he said.

"It's a large city," I answered.

"Just the same," he said. "I would have seen you. I never forget anyone, even though I am an old man." He stared at me a moment longer, then he began questioning me, asking for names of churches and streets, of squares and factories. I answered everything correctly, which seemed only to irritate him and make him more demanding.

"Well, that market is well known throughout Europe," he would say. "It proves nothing that you know its name. But tell me this, if you are truly from Lvov, what are the names of the four principal streets that serve that market?"

"No, old man," I said, exasperated, "you name me those four streets, and I'll see whether you know Lvov or are fooling these honest men."

The old fellow laughed at my challenge, but when he saw I was serious, he became frightened at once. He had

83

bragged about his memory, but now was afraid to put it to the test.

"What are those four streets, old man?"

He glanced about, uttering wild profanities and seeking support from the group.

"Well this is strange," I said to them. "Here you have put me on trial, but I know more than the judge. All of you know I am Polish and that a German could never come into a Polish camp and live without detection."

A low murmur of agreement went through the group. Taking quick advantage of it, I pushed my way through, and this time not a person tried to stop me. But even as I stepped through the door of the barracks, I could feel their eyes on me, staring at my back. I knew they were not done with their questioning, and that my hope of staying in that camp was in vain, after all.

Once outside the gate, I wandered about the streets, trying to think of some solution to my problems. I wanted a safe life where I could work and love and rear a family, but now that future seemed to be fading from me.

And around me was the corpse of Germany, divided among her captors. Much of her land and millions of her people had been annexed permanently to Russia and Poland, and one-quarter of the remaining land and sixteen million Germans were under Russian rule, where they lived in terror. The Russians shipped the young men to Russia to work as slaves in the mines and factories, while they packed women and old people into trains and sent them to the west, to be dumped as refuse.

Even in the sections ruled by England, France, and America, factories were being sacked. All foreign possessions had been taken, all money was in foreign hands. The captors said Germany would never rise, her people would not know a high standard of living again. Even now her people were hungry, and it was a hunger of the body and the spirit. General Hildebrandt, himself, whom I had served, was in prison. On the Eastern Front, he had sometimes talked with me about the war and how it was going. Whenever he saw me, he called me "son." Now he was in prison, perhaps to serve the rest of his life there. All the leaders were gone, and the cause was lost.

In a dark corner of a tavern, I thought about this, and I tried to figure out what I should do. If I went back to the Polish camp, the Poles might know before many nights that I had been in the SS. If I went to Erika's house, they would find me and perhaps would take out their revenge on her and her family, as well. If I tried to hide in the farm village, I would be found.

And if I tried to make my way to Hamburg or some other part of Germany, I might be picked up without papers and turned over to the Poles and Russians.

I drank a bottle of wine. I started another one and was half through it when a huge fellow, clutching an overcoat around him as if he were chilly, came in, peering about in the dark place. He approached my table and sat down.

"I'm looking for boys who are in trouble," he said, smiling; but the smile seemed to be out of place on his rough face. "You want a job?"

"Yes."

"Can you fight? I mean, are you a real fighter? I pay tough boys only."

"What's the job?"

He picked up a scrap of paper from the litter on the floor and wrote out an address. "Come to this house," he said, rising, "and bring this note. It's a two-story brick house."

"Yes, but what is the job?"

Without another word he turned and went out.

85

I tossed the paper to the floor and got up, stretched some of the drunkenness out of my body and made my way out into the bright street. Then I went to the harbor, about a four-kilometer walk. There I asked several men how I could stow away on a ship.

"No way," they said.

"But listen, I don't care what ship or where it's going. I just have to get out of Hamburg for a while."

"We know," one of them, an unshaven man, said. "That's our purpose, too; but there are no ships you can get on. I've tried four times to get on ships, but now I've given it up."

"Well, what are you going to do?"

He shrugged. "Crime is all that's open right now."

I thanked them and went back into town. I walked around the streets for a long time, going in one shop after another seeking work; but nobody had work. Few shops even had merchandise.

Finally I returned to the Polish camp. I stayed there for a while longer, but every day and night brought terror to me. When I could not stand it any longer, I took from my footlocker my cigarettes and razor, a bar of soap, and a towel. Knowing I had little time, I wrote a message as quickly as I could.

Dear Erika,

I am marked for death if I stay here, for I am wanted by everybody. The Poles, English, French, Russians, Americans, all want SS man. Now I can feel the end of the rope, but I will not come to your house. I will only bring bad things to those around me. I am marked by God Himself, I think, and I don't know yet how I can escape His punishment.

I must leave this camp and I will have no papers, but do not worry too much about me, for I have been in tight places before, and even now have a solution in mind.

Dear Erika, I love you, and in my love for you I hold for you all kind thoughts.

E<small>DDY</small>

I addressed an envelope, put the letter in it, and left the barracks at once.

Outside several Poles were waiting for me, watching me with deep, vacant eyes.

I walked to the post office and mailed the letter. Then I went to the café where I had had the wine. I told the waiter of my experience, of the note the stranger had given me, and asked if he knew how I could find that man again.

"I don't know," he said, "but I have a note. You can have mine." He took it from his pocket and handed it to me.

"Well—what is this address, do you know?"

"Yes, of course," he said. "It's the French Foreign Legion."

Part II

7

THE FRENCHMAN filled a glass with wine and pushed it across the table to me. He pulled a thin stack of forms before him and began to fill in the blanks, pressing down heavily so that the carbons would be clear. "The term is five years," he said, speaking in tight, thick German. "We are not interested in your past, unless you were a prominent Nazi or a member of the SS. We do not accept either in the Legion."

I said nothing.

"At the end of the five-year enlistment, you may re-enlist. Also, when you have served one term, you may apply for French citizenship."

I glanced around at the room, which was large and bare of furniture, except for the table and chairs we were using. On the walls were pictures showing smiling Legionnaires chatting with Arabs and refreshing themselves with cool drinks.

"I don't believe these pictures," I said abruptly.

"Oh, now, the Legion's not too tough for you, is it?" he said.

"If it's like these pictures, it's not too tough for anybody."

He smiled. "Yes, very well. Now, what's your name?"

"Hugo. Eddy Hugo."

"Nationality?"

"German. Polish, that is."

He smiled. "You seem to be confused, Mr. Hukov."

"Hugo," I said, correcting him. "I'm not so confused I don't know my own name."

"No, of course not."

He asked me nothing more, but he was filling in all the blanks on the form.

"From now on," he said, "you are Edward Hukov, a Yugoslav born in Belgrade. Remember. Also I have to tell you that today, October 25, 1945, you start your five-year term with the French Foreign Legion. From today on, if you do not obey orders, you will be jailed, and if you desert, you will be caught and shot."

He pushed the paper toward me. Slowly I wrote out my new name—Eddy Hukov.

I was taken to a room in which were several cots and there was issued two blankets and a handbook. I stretched out on one of the cots and started to read.

"The Legion is your new country," I read, "and you will always keep in your heart this motto: *Legio Patria Nostra.*"

I heard a man in another part of the house singing, as if to himself as he worked.

> Mein Regiment, mein Hiematland,
> Meine Mutter, habe ich nie gekannt,
> Mein Vater starb schon fruh im Feld, im Feld,
> Ich bin allein auf dieser Welt.

I thought over his meaning: my regiment is my homeland; I never knew my mother; my father died young in war; and I am all alone in the world.

The next day I was sent to Saarbrucken with several

other new Legionnaires. On our arrival we were treated well, and the situation began to look reasonably acceptable. Sometimes I would think of Erika, or I would fall into depression considering Linda or almost any other subject connected with my past life. But now that I was in the Legion, with even a different name, different birthplace, and still another nationality, I saw the past as someone else's story, having nothing to do with my present or future.

Most of the men in my group were Germans, but there were some Poles, Russians, Hungarians, Romanians. Everything but Frenchmen. As someone said that first night in the barracks, "The Frenchmen don't have the stomach for fighting."

"That's so," a tall German named Reinhold said. "I fought the French and will agree to that."

"They like their wine too much," another soldier said, "and their women."

"I like their women too," Reinhold said.

Many of these men had come into the Legion in order to escape trial for various crimes, some of them murder. Reinhold was in because the French in a prisoner-of-war camp had tortured him until he signed up. Many of the men were already talking about escaping.

Also there were several who had been as discouraged as I by the fall of Germany and the breaking apart of everything, so they had chosen the Legion as the only way out. Some of us were sitting around the barracks one night talking about the desperate condition in Europe, when a big fellow named Himmler, who could have washed if he had wanted to but evidently preferred his filth, punched me in the shoulder and said, "How you talk so big about the way the war was? What were you, a friend of Adolph Hitler?"

"I was an army sergeant," I said.

He belched out a groan. "A sergeant? You wasn't no damn sergeant!"

"I appreciate your interest in my case," I said angrily, "but it makes no difference to you, does it?"

"Stand up," he said.

I stood up.

"You're not within three inches of being as large as me in any direction. Not in my outfit would you have been a . . ."

I hit him one blow, and he went back ten feet and slid down a wall.

"Now how tall are you?" I said.

He sat there staring at me, his face twisted in rage and humiliation, then pushed himself up from the floor and staggered away, mumbling vague threats about my future.

A few days later, we were sent to Strassburg. The camp there was encircled with stakes topped with barbed wire and was well guarded. Here our old French officers left us, and we came under new officers and stricter orders. Right off we were lined up for roll call, about a hundred and fifty of us, and were ordered to take everything out of our pockets. Then they searched us. The man who searched me took all my money and cigarettes and walked away.

"Come back here," I shouted at him. Others bellowed that they were being robbed.

"Order in the ranks," the French officers said. "You're in the Legion."

We were dismissed from ranks late in the afternoon and sat around on the ground grumbling about our losses and waiting for roll call and supper. Roll call came just at sundown. The French called us by name and asked each of us his nationality.

"Eddy Hukov," the sergeant shouted.

I did not immediately recognize my new name and hesitated a split second before yelling out.

"You bastard, are you deaf? Your nationality?" he shouted.

"Polish," I answered, confused for a moment.

"No, God damn you, you're a Yugoslav! Guards, jail Hukov without food for three days!"

For one reason or another, every third or fourth man was taken out of line to be thrown in prison. After three days in that stinking hole, I began to sense the true quality of the Legion.

From Strassburg we went to Paris, and there about three hundred of us had to walk through the city in order to reach another railway station. Most of the recruits were still in German Army uniforms, although about sixty of us were in civilian clothes. The German soldiers marched in front, the civilians behind. As we went through the streets, the French women and children dropped flower pots on the Germans and shouted, "Tiny, diny, haily, lailo, haila, ha, ha, ha, ha." Several men were injured.

When we reached the train, I had a long discussion with myself about the walk through Paris. They were hurling objects to break our heads, and at the same time we were supposed to fight for their country. I had told lies to get into the Legion, but now the lie was on their side.

A whistle sounded; we climbed into the cars. The train began to roll. "Where are we going?" I asked the car leader.

"To Troa," he said, "if it matters where you go."

"When do we eat?"

"Eat?" he said, and took a sandwich out of his pocket and began to chew on it, smiling at me. He was a Frenchman, a sergeant named Leger, and a tough-looking man. "You like to smell my sandwich, soldier?" he said.

He winked at the big man, Himmler, whom I had knocked down. Some of the other Germans had made friendly gestures toward Leger, and they, too, thought it funny about the sandwich. But I noticed that they had no food either.

At a small junction on the way to Troa, our train stopped opposite another which had its doors locked. Leger and Himmler broke the lock on one car and entered. When they appeared again, they were carrying two leather suitcases. Nobody said anything to them or cared about the theft. A French sergeant was stealing from a French train, and nobody gave a damn.

As we entered the gate of the camp at Troa, however, the guards searched our bags and pockets. And they opened the stolen suitcases, which the sergeant had set to one side. Inside they found a uniform and other belongings of a high French naval officer in Marseilles.

The guard turned angrily to my group. "Where did you get this?"

Nobody answered.

"Whose bag is this?"

I thought our sergeant, Leger, would speak up with a lie, but he said nothing.

An officer came on the run. When he saw the uniform he turned to my platoon. "Sergeant, take all twenty-five of your men and lock them up until one of them confesses."

No sooner had he said this than a police car pulled up at the gate, and two French policemen jumped out. They told the officer that a theft had been committed while the Legion was underway. While we stood at attention, the officer explained that the Legion was already investigating and that an admiral's clothing had been recovered. "Soon we will know which man is guilty," he said.

As we were being marched down to the guard house, Leger said just loud enough for our group to hear: "I once knew a man who opened his mouth, but when he tried to talk, his tongue was cut out." He repeated this over and over.

No sooner was the jail door closed than the sergeant and Himmler and two other Germans went into conference. The rest of us sat around on the floor, sullen and angry because of being locked up for doing nothing, and frightened, because there was no telling what was ahead for us. I was so disgusted that I was paying no attention to the sergeant, until Reinhold came over and sat down beside me.

"I think you might be in trouble," he said.

I glanced up to see that Leger and Himmler were watching me as they carried on their conference. The sergeant straightened, glaring at me. "Hukov," he said, "somebody must take the blame for this, or we will be tortured."

Complete silence fell on the room. Trying to act calm, I rose from my seat on the floor and leaned back against the wall. "Well, let me call the officer, and you can confess."

Reinhold also stood now and leaned back beside me.

"No, what we want is the truth," the sergeant said. He came closer to me, and Himmler and two of their friends closed in behind him. Some of the other Legionnaires edged away from our part of the room.

"Hukov," Leger said, "why did you steal that suitcase?" Nervous sweat had coated his face, the beads standing out like sores.

"You filthy bastard, you remember one thing," I said. "Touch me with one hand and you'll——"

Suddenly Reinhold pushed himself out from the wall and walked away from me. I was too surprised to go on speaking. Now I was alone facing four men.

"What did you say?" Leger asked quietly. "Something

97

about touching you?" He put out his hand and laid it on my shoulder.

My left fist swung into Leger's belly and my right slammed into his face, leaving him stunned. But he gave me a blow in return that knocked my head against the stone wall. He struck again and my eyes blurred, then he brought his knee up into my groin. A rolling pain pushed through me, but, seeing the sergeant's three buddies moving in, I forced myself to straighten and was prepared to fight them with my last strength.

Then a body hurled itself from the sidelines and knocked all three of them to the floor. Reinhold leaped up and was close by me again, grinning.

With a roar, the sergeant charged at us, but knowing that I had help gave me power and I unleashed a blow that left him staring at the wall. Reinhold and I then went to work on Himmler and the two others as they tried to get up, kicking their bodies and heads with our boots.

But Leger had gotten his bearings and charged me once more. I saw the glitter of a knife blade sticking out of his hand. I had a mental picture of Brenan with the Russians cutting at him, and anger overcame me.

"You drop that knife," I shouted, almost incoherently. "You drop that knife," I said again, staring at the blade, which was waving slightly at waist level. I moved to a table and with one shove turned it over and with another pulled a leg free.

The sergeant made a false lunge, and I caught him beside the head with the table leg. His eyes closed for a moment, he almost dropped to his knees. I grabbed his wrist and twirled him, so that he stumbled over one of his partners. While he was on the floor, I stomped on his wrist. He released the knife.

I kicked it out of the way and tightened my hold on the

98

table leg. "Reinhold, you want a club?" I said, pulling another one loose. Thus armed, we moved in on the three remaining fighters, and were making short work of them when the sergeant managed to get hold of my ankle with one hand. I kicked his face, but he held on. Two of his men came in on me and took away the club.

I jerked free and went for the table to get another club, but the two men were charging again. I grabbed hold of a table leg and, using it to swing the table, sailed the heavy piece of furniture into the two fighters. They toppled backward, their cries caught in their throats.

Reinhold waded among them, picked up the table, swung it at Himmler. The table flattened him.

Now everybody was on the floor, and nobody seemed to want to get up. Reinhold and I had had our clothes half torn off. Both of us were bleeding from the face and body. We grinned at each other and enjoyed the victory.

Then I slumped down on the floor beside the sergeant. "Now," I said, "do you still want to cut somebody with a knife?"

"No," he said. "I've had enough."

"Well, call the guard, and tell him who stole the suitcases."

"Hukov, I'm a sergeant in the Legion. I'll lose my rank and be sent to prison."

"Call the guard," I said.

Leger shook his head, so Reinhold kicked him in the stomach. He bellowed out and continued bellowing, until the guards came and took him and Himmler away.

"We'll not see them again," Reinhold said, almost fondly.

"Just as well," I said. "They were too rough to be good friends of ours."

"Somebody is always trying to make the Legion rough,"

he said, grinning over at me, "while the rest of us are trying to make it like home."

In that camp we had little to eat, and there was much bartering for the small amount of food and cigarettes available. During our month's stay in Troa, I lost over thirty pounds.

Then we were taken to Marseilles and put in a Legion camp with high walls. Nobody could escape over those walls. The first announcement they made there was that we would be given a medical examination. At once I thought of my SS scar and desperately tried to figure out a way to get around the doctors, but there was no escape.

A gray-haired Frenchman examined my chest and listened to my heartbeat. "Lift your arms," he said.

I did that. He stared at the scar on my left arm for a moment. "SS?" he asked.

"No, sir," I said in French.

"Guard," he said, "this man is SS."

Two armed men grabbed hold of me and led me into a cellar room, where several boys had already been taken. As I sat down on the damp, cold floor, I noticed that the two guards made a secret sign to one of the prisoners.

Soon this prisoner came over and sat down close to me. "What's your name?" he said in German.

I shook my head as if I could not understand him.

"Which SS division were you in?"

I shook my head.

There were about eighteen men in the room, talking in German. Some of these men also had cut off the SS mark, but their conversation revealed that they were truly SS. But I said not one German word, no matter who spoke to me or what was said.

That night an officer came with four Legionnaires and took me out. They tied a rope to my wrists and pulled up

Photostat of the paper Hukov carries which permits him to live in Thailand. Translated, it reads as follows: February 23, 1947. Edward Hukov, a Polish national, was captured by the Thailand police on the border of Indochina, a French Legionnaire, and this paper is given to him for his release and temporary identification in Thailand.

(Signed) **C.I.D. Police Chief**

Hukov and Mr. Waldemar Gottlieb, the
German who fled Communist China and
for whom Hukov worked as a bodyguard.

Eddy Hukov, photograph taken in Bangkok in January, 1957.

the rope with a pulley, so that I was standing on my toes, my weight on the rope above my head. A whip slashed into my skin; the blood began to run down my back.

"What division were you in?" the officer asked.

I said nothing. The whip slashed into me again, and again, and again . . .

I regained consciousness back in the cell. I had a fever. My lips were moving, as if uttering a prayer, but even though I tried, I could not speak out.

I dozed fitfully that night. The next day I could not move my body without fire burning through me. And again that night they took me to the same place. As they began to beat me on the open wounds, I cried out in Polish, "No, it will do you no good!"

"What did you say?" the officer asked me in German.

"I don't understand you," I said, still in Polish.

"Stop," the officer ordered. "We might be beating the wrong man. Take him down and we'll question him."

A Polish member of the Legion, in the company of this officer, asked me a hundred questions about Poland and Lvov, and about my days as a Polish worker under the Germans. "And you say you worked in the fields near Frankfurt? What did you do there?"

"I did all types of jobs," I said, "but when gasoline became scarce and we could not run the tractor, the labor became very hard, and the German in charge became cruel to us. Sometimes he would make us work from before dawn to after sunset without food, cutting wood, gathering beans from the plants—and this is tedious work. I tell you your back begins to ache by noon, and by seven o'clock at night, when you've not had any food at all, and with this cruel man standing over you——"

"All right," he said, interrupting, "keep your answers short. Where did you live on this farm?"

"In the barn. All twenty of us lived there, and among

101

us were three women. But all of us stayed in two stalls which had been cattle stalls before we came, but we spent one day—that was all we were given—to clean them up and make a better partition, so the women would have some privacy, so——"

"Yes, so you slept in the barn," the interviewer said, staring at the far wall. "Well, that very well might be." He looked over at the officer. "He speaks good Polish," he said, "and he knows Lvov. I think also he might have been a Polish worker."

The French officer came up before me. "Maybe. But, Hukov, how did you get the scar on your arm?"

I looked at the officer and did not say a word, for he had addressed me in German.

The interpreter asked me the same question in Polish.

"I was cut with a sickle," I told him.

"How could you cut yourself on the left arm with a sickle?"

"While I was kneeling down. I was working in the field cutting hay, and there were all eight of us out there, each with a sickle, and I was being careful that nobody else's sickle cut into me. They were little sickles, for the German farmer had only two professional sickles, and the rest of the sickles we made for ourselves. My sickle I made out of a length of metal which I sharpened at night. It took me almost a week to make it. Everybody had a crude sickle like that, and there was no telling when a man would get cut. Also I was being careful for rock, because I did not want to dent the metal, for I would have to spend more nights straightening it. Also I might lose my sickle in the rocks. Then, too, I didn't want to stick anybody else with it, and also I wanted to be careful of snakes, which might be in the field—and we were all kneeling down, you see, and there would be no way for me to avoid their bite. Then, and this is important, the man who ran that farm had told us the hay must be cut no more than one inch from the ground. Now this is very close to the ground to be cutting anything, much less hay with a homemade sickle, when you do not know about rocks and snakes and you are afraid of sticking somebody else or being stuck by somebody else's sickle, so I stuck the damn thing in my own arm."

The Polish interviewer stood up and crashed his fist down on the table. "He's a Pole," he said. "Nobody can talk like that but a Pole."

"Well, what did he say?" the French officer asked him.

"He said he cut his arm with a sickle."

The officer waited for a moment. "Is that all he said, in that long speech?"

"That's all, sir. That's the way it is with Poles. I think he's a real Pole and not an SS man."

"Very well," the officer said. "I was right. Take him back to the Legion. Tell them he's not an SS man."

Back in my camp I could not sleep that night or the next, and I did not speak German, not even with Reinhold.

8

ON THE 22nd of December we finally received uniforms. My pants were so tight I could not get into them, so I slashed the legs open with a knife. I told the boys, "Even if we are half naked, at least all of us Yugoslavs are now officially in the French Legion."

On the same day I was attached to the Thirteenth DBLE, the personal division of DeGaulle. And by the end of December, 1945, I left with a French battleship for North Africa, arriving on the 7th of January in Bizerta.

As I went down from the ship and stepped to the earth, I spoke again in German for the first time. "Boys," I said, "we have arrived in a new world and to a new life."

"Ah," Reinhold shouted, laughing. "Hukov can speak German again! Hukov has remembered his German, boys!" All of us laughed, but when the officers asked what we were laughing at, nobody answered.

At the barracks there was no more barbed wire, only white-capped Legionnaires standing guard at the gate.

"It's better now," I said hopefully to Reinhold. "I think perhaps this will be all right."

"Yes," he said, looking about the camp. "We will do better here than in France."

Each day Bizerta added to my hopes for a better life; it was my lucky city. One morning at roll call, for example, my company commander said he needed a man to represent the company in a boxing match, and at once the men began calling my name.

The captain asked me if I had boxed, and I told him I had had some fights as a boy.

"Look here, then, you must beat the Second Company's boxer tomorrow night, and he's tough. I've seen him, and he's taller than you and heavier."

I was pleased that the men had chosen me to represent them, but I was nervous, too, particularly on the next night. Our whole battalion was out to see the fight.

In the first round I tried to learn my opponent's tricks, so I did not try to hit him hard. But in the second round I moved in and knocked him out. For the victory I received seven hundred francs in prize money and a wrist watch, which I sold to a French officer for five hundred francs more. Also I received the congratulations of my captain and the acclaim of the whole company.

But our good days in Bizerta did not last. We received orders to go to Sidi-bel-Abbes, a march of several hundred kilometers over the hot sand. Our company of 120 men started out.

All of our officers were French; but the soldiers came from every nation in Europe. Thrown together in this manner in Bizerta, we had gotten along well; but out on the march, where everything was strange and we did not know what lay ahead, every Legionnaire began to try to find his countrymen in order to have united strength should trouble start.

Germans and Austrians were one group; Poles, Russians, Czechs, Bulgars, and Yugoslavs were another; Italians, French, and Spaniards were a third; Hungarians, Romanians, and Greeks were a fourth.

106

If there was a man from another country, he had to join one of the four groups or else he would not be safe. I refused to join any group.

The corporal of my squad was much concerned about this. "Hukov, you think you can stay free of groups and survive in the Legion? Why don't you join the group with us Yugoslavs?"

"I'm not a good Yugoslav," I said.

"Well, what group suits you?"

"None. I wish each man would stand on his own feet. I am tired of groups." I also told other representatives that I would not join, and that I thought it would be better for us if we had less organization.

On the second day of our march, I was proved right. We had gone only fifty kilometers through the orange plantations and sand fields when, toward nightfall, we reached a pond of water about one hundred yards long. Nearly all of us were bathing when suddenly some of the men began to run excitedly toward the camp.

"What's happening, Kraft?" I called to one of them, a blond fellow born in Karlsruhe, who was generally secretive and unresponsive, but who had taken a liking to me.

"There's a fight. Come on."

As we moved nearer we heard an officer shouting: "Don't interfere. Let those two men go on till they stop themselves." We pushed through to where we could see.

One fighter was a Spaniard, the other a Scot. Both of them were strong boys, patient fighters, given to much maneuvering. For twenty minutes they fought, then the Scot landed a hard flurry of blows, and the Spaniard grabbed a knife and stabbed him.

The officer stepped in at once and was about to separate the two men and bring about order, when suddenly an Austrian leaped forward and shouted, "The Scot is our man!" meaning that the Scot had joined the group with the Austrians and Germans. Instantly the whole of this group rose. The terrified Spaniard shouted for his group, which included Spaniards, Italians, and Frenchmen.

Now in several languages the excited shouting started, and the officer, caught in the milling throng, broke free and rushed away just as the first battle began. I heard the sounds of bone on flesh, hollow thuds and cries. The officer began shouting for order, but there was no order in that fight. I went to one side, as did the members of the two other groups, and watched it. Reinhold was in there fighting, and I wondered just what he was fighting for.

Officers came running down the hill. Corporals made their way into the group, ordering men back. Finally the fight was broken up. Six men had been stabbed, several had broken heads, but the victory belonged to nobody.

Down at the water hole, the men washed off the blood and dirt. Silence settled on them, but after a while an Italian began to sing, and soon others were singing with him, including Germans and Austrians. But when the song ended, the men began staring uneasily at one another again, and soon the groups re-formed.

I swam off to myself and listened to their different languages, wondering if ever in the world, no matter where a man might go, he could be welcomed by every people as a friend.

Sidi-bel-Abbes was headquarters for the Legion, a modern city of fifty thousand which the Legion had planted with flowers and trees. There were four gates in the old city wall, and from these led the two main streets, north-south and east-west, which were broad and partially shaded. But the Legionnaries were not liked by the Europeans who lived there, and they did not want the Legionnaires to use these avenues. For us were left the small alleys, where the Arabs lived, keeping their filthy, dingy shops, and selling bad wine. Or we could go to the entertainment center kept by the Legion, where women stayed—from all nations and in all conditions and ages.

The Legion camp was outside the wall, a huge settlement of yellow buildings, where Legionnaires stood guard in strict discipline, their kepis shining in the blazing sun. To each barracks room, twelve men were assigned, including a strong man and a corporal. When either of these two gave orders, the others had to obey. I was made the strong man in my room.

Each morning we would rise early and do calisthenics. Then we would march. Some days we would march forty kilometers in the hot sand—and one good step in the sand became only half a step after the sliding had stopped.

In our fourth week at Sidi-bel-Abbes, the commandant said he was looking for some tough boys. Kraft and I were among the six he selected. We received sub-machine guns and provisions, and jeeps came to pick us up.

We were taken to a big prison, and as we entered through the fifteen-foot-high walls, a heavy iron gate closed behind us. "What the hell are we doing here?" I said.

A sergeant came out of the dark interior of a building, blinking his eyes in the glare of the outdoors. His head was shaved, his face gaunt and deathly-looking. He studied us, as if measuring us against a task, then said, "Last night two prisoners killed a guard, so you see it is a tough group in here. Tomorrow morning we will take fifteen of the toughest, we will chain one to another, and we will lead them fifteen hundred kilometers to an outpost prison on Sahara desert." All of us had heard about Colomb-Béchar, the main prison at Sahara, and the other more remote places for punishment.

On the next day the six of us and the sergeant marched the prisoners to the train and saw them into the boxcar.

109

We were to go by rail into Sahara; but much of the way we would go by foot.

After the train was underway, I asked one of the prisoners why he was being sent to prison.

"To build roads in the desert," he said sullenly.

"Yes, but for what reason are you being sent to prison?"

"Theft," he said. The man next to him said theft, also. In the Legion a man who loses one piece of his uniform or equipment is sent to prison for theft. Two men said they had deserted the Legion.

"I thought a man was killed for deserting," I said.

"Yes, we'll die at Sahara," one answered. "It can be done with a bullet or with the sun."

The man closest to me, on one end of the chain, was more reserved than the others, and I thought I recognized in him the hard self-control of the SS. I asked him if he had been a Storm Trooper, but he denied it, although he admitted having been in the German Army.

He told me about his life since the war, part of it spent as a prisoner of the Russians, where he had been tortured and almost starved. "They would burn our flesh and ask if we felt pain," he said. "When I heard we were to be shipped to Russia, I killed the guard over me and escaped."

"Why are you being sent to Sahara?" I asked him.

"I struck an officer with a wine bottle."

Both of us had to smile at that, even though we knew he might die at Sahara. "I wish I could help you," I said.

Quietly he said, "If you want to help me, take off the chains." He lifted his pants leg and I saw the raw, ragged flesh, half burying the shackle.

I turned away, unable to look at it. As we rode on, all I could think about was the sight of that man's leg. Finally I spoke out to the sergeant. "How about letting them free of the chains?"

110

The sergeant, who was sitting on the floor near the open door, peered up at me sharply. "Stay away from them."

"The chains have cut into . . ."

"Shut up and sit down, or I'll lock you up with them."

"Ah, Sergeant, look here——" I patted the sub-machine gun hanging around my neck. "You plan to lock me in chains?"

He rose menacingly, but finding he could not bluff me, he sat back down, sighing heavily as if he were disappointed in me. "We have three days on this cattle car," he said, "and they will wear chains every minute, no matter how loud you talk."

"Sergeant, we should take off the chains," I said again.

Without a word the other guards pulled back across the floor, so that nobody was near me or the sergeant.

"Those chains have cut into their legs," I said, "and they're in pain. We're not gaining anything for ourselves this way."

He glanced at me, then out the door of the boxcar, as if annoyed. Two of the prisoners, anxious to win his good graces, laughed. One of them, a Yugoslav, said, "Lock him up with the chains, Sergeant, and let me go free."

The sergeant smiled at the prisoner, nodded to him encouragingly.

The prisoner began again. "I promise you I won't try to escape, Sergeant, and I won't give you any trouble, either, not like that German son of ——"

I struck the man in the face with the butt of my sub-machine gun. He fell back against the wall, blood raining down his cheeks. I stepped back until I felt the wall, watching the sergeant, ready to fight; but he did not move from his place. He was looking out the open door of the boxcar as if nothing had happened.

111

A few minutes later he seemed to remember me again. He beckoned me toward him.

I obeyed. He motioned for me to sit down beside him. I sat down, my hands still on the sub-machine gun.

We rode on a long way, then he said, "When I came into the Legion I had two lessons to learn before I could be a good Legionnaire. Do you know what they were?"

"No," I said, keeping careful watch on him.

"One was pity," he said slowly. "I had to learn pity, for a man has to have pity if he is to live in the midst of cruelty. Don't you agree?"

"Yes," I said.

"And the other thing I had to learn," he said, "was cruelty."

I was stunned.

"Without cruelty, what could I do with pity? So I learned cruelty, then I was a Legionnaire. And waiting to use one or the other, I discovered patience. I'm a very patient man."

"I see what you mean, Sergeant. So now you are a son of a bitch."

"So now," he said, smiling, "I am a son of a bitch. And also I'm a sergeant in the Legion."

I saw his point and had to laugh. "Well, I don't want to be a sergeant, then."

"Why not? You have both qualities already. You have pity and cruelty. The blow to that man's head was neatly done."

"No," I said, "not cruelty."

"We'll see. Legionnaires are made in the Legion." Once more he looked out through the open door.

He said nothing else that night. The next morning he talked to me again, but there was little point in what he said. I decided he just wanted to say something that day.

So we traveled south in that vast loneliness, the prison-

112

ers still in their chains and I now a friend of this strange sergeant.

The morning of the fourth day the train stopped at a small station. "Everybody out," the sergeant said. "The train stops here now, and we must walk 400 kilometers to the prison camp."

While the donkeys and our two camels were being loaded, I walked around to the other side of the train to see what was there, and as far as I could see was desert.

9

BY EARLY AFTERNOON we were ready to march, but the prisoners refused to get up from the ground. "Kill us," they said, "kill us or take off the chains."

The sergeant singled me out and told me to shoot one of them. I refused at once. He glared at me for a moment, then said, "One of you other guards shoot a prisoner."

The other guards fell back one by one, except Kraft, who fingered the trigger on his rifle, lost in thought. Coldly he looked over the sixteen men, one at a time, as they watched him. But soon all of us realized that he did not have courage enough to fire.

"Well, God damn," the sergeant said, "I've got a pack of holy guards."

"You ought to look at the prisoners' legs," one guard said. "They can't walk five kilometers, much less four hundred. Not one of them will reach the prison."

"That's true," I said. "We have to open their chains."

The sergeant glared at me, then at the prisoners and guards. "All right." A smile came over his rough face. "But I want you to agree to a hard rule. I set the pace, and if one prisoner lags behind on the march, we shoot him."

115

Out on the desert not a sound was heard. I spoke up finally. "That's fair. If you will take off their chains."

He fished a key from his pocket and unlocked the chains. The prisoners were so happy some of them began to weep. That afternoon, however, the sergeant set such a pace we did thirty kilometers before the sun set.

We chained the prisoners for the night, to make guarding them easier. My duty was from twelve to two.

Standing guard there in the desert of Sahara, I got a strange feeling. Not one house, not even a small bush or tree was around us. Nothing except land and heaven. I thought of what my father might say about the great expanses. No doubt he would long for Germany, as I did.

So the thoughts went through my mind as I looked out over the desert, and then I came back to check my prisoners. They were asleep, every one except the German who I had thought was an SS man. He lay with his head resting on his hands, his eyes looking straight toward Heaven.

I sat down near him. "What are you thinking about?"

"Horses," he said.

"Horses? What of horses?"

"Horses and a bull. My father's horses and bull. Good stock, and the bull was the only one of his kind on my father's farm, so he thought he was a horse."

I laughed. "You're a liar."

"He thought he was a horse, I'm telling you. He would insist on being let out with the horses, and he would try to run like the colts and fillies. He would nuzzle up to the feed trough with them and generally make a fool of himself. Good stock, too."

"Well," I said, "I don't know much about bulls."

"Oh, it's the same with people." He reflected on that for a while, then nodded his head several times. "Someday, maybe soon, you will be like the bald sergeant."

116

I gave him a cigarette. "Not I. You have the wrong man, believe me."

"You can't fight the Legion," he said.

We smoked, enjoying the endless, clean silence. "It's a comfort to a man, this place," I said.

He laughed. "Not for me, not tonight. Beyond here I have no hope. Tonight I must escape."

After a long while, he went on. "I've been waiting for you to come on guard. When I first saw you, I thought I recognized you from home. I knew you would help me."

I dug my shoe into the sand and wondered what I was going to say.

"Free of here, I could get back to the rail line," he said. "I might snag onto a train tomorrow. I could get back to the coast, and there I could hide out. I've killed one guard and would kill another if it would get me aboard a ship."

"Where are you going? You can't go home."

He sighed heavily. "I can go home somehow."

"And if I let you go, I'll be killed."

"You can come with me. Look, help me, will you? I'm in pain."

"In pain and crippled, and talking about catching a train on the desert and getting a ship if you can, and getting home if you can. And you can't. But it's a good dream."

Once more he groaned. After a while he said, "It's a fine dream."

"It is. Maybe God could do it for you, but He won't."

We had another smoke together. When it was two o'clock, I called my relief and went to sleep.

The next day we began our serious traveling again. The sand seemed to want to suck us down and smother us. All day the desert brooded, and near evening a strong wind rose. It rumbled, as if big trees were in the way. The sand

117

began to move, cutting our skin till blood flowed. Each man covered himself as best he could.

The donkeys began crying. Sand was in my ears and eyes; I was swallowing and breathing sand.

Then, as suddenly as it had come on, the storm left us, and the sand settled again. The desert was calm and peaceful. One of the prisoners, who had been nearly nude when the storm broke, lay in the sand, bleeding all over and weeping. The sergeant ordered him to get into line.

"All right," the sergeant said, "we must make up for lost time." He started out, moving with giant strides.

That night after we chained the prisoners, they began to cry out for help.

"The men are thirsty," I said to the sergeant.

"Let them spit and swallow it."

"Also the donkeys," I said, for they had begun their plaintive song.

"Never mind about them," he said. "Each day we have less supplies and need fewer donkeys."

The next morning we passed a caravan, and that noon another. They came from far and were going far, crossing the Sahara.

"Why is it nobody uses trucks?" I asked the sergeant.

"Soft sand would suck them up," he answered. "Only the camel can't be buried. He will carry his 400 pounds fifty kilometers a day."

"The donkeys also carry their load."

"It's not the same. The camels always live through a journey." He ran his hand through a camel's thick hair. "No sand can get through that," he said, "nor sun rays, either. A camel can close his nose to keep out the sand, and his brows will protect his eyes from the hardest storm. He can walk for nearly two weeks without water or food.

118

The camels always survive. They were born for it. But the donkeys sometimes die."

When we stopped near the middle of the afternoon, I tried to make friends with one of the camels, and we got along well until I tried to make him budge from the ground. I punched him lightly on the chest. No response. I kicked him. No response. But when I started to kick him again, he got up, and as he did, he spat squarely into my face, so much spit that my face was covered with it. I could not wipe it off, even to see what I was doing. When I did, all I could see was Kraft, sitting on the ground, laughing at me, and the camel, standing above me, looking off at the horizon.

We moved on at the same fast pace, the sergeant pushing us to the end of our strength. Some of the prisoners were broken, pitiful sights, and now in the sky we saw big birds, like eagles. They followed us each time we began to march. "What do they want?" I asked the sergeant.

"They want that donkey," he said, pointing to one. "He's getting lame." The sergeant peered up at the big birds. "And I have no doubt they'll get him."

The next day he shot the donkey, and we moved on. We did not see a single bird for three hours, then they were back in the sky, following us. "What do they want now?" I asked.

"One of us," he said.

Several of the prisoners showed signs of falling out, and the sergeant set an even stiffer pace through the burning desert. Also he gave us less water. Now the sand was getting inside me, filling up my body, so that I walked heavy. My footsteps became like lead. The sun baked me, so that I could not think or move quickly, while out in front the sergeant went on, stopping occasionally to look back.

I thought that should one of the men fall out, he would

ease the march for the rest of us. And I felt, too, the sun would soon take one of them, or the sand.

We plodded on, every man mindful of the weaknesses of his neighbor, taking pride in his own strength. But in late afternoon, when I turned to see how the men were doing, one man had fallen far behind.

Quickly I went on, walking as if I had seen nothing. But I began wondering if it were not better to go back and shoot him than to let him die alone in the sun.

Soon the sergeant turned to survey the group. Instantly he started running back along the straggly line, counting aloud. At the end of the column, finding one man missing, he mounted a dune and peered back behind us. Turning, he shouted, "Kraft!"

Trembling, Kraft moved past me and double-timed back to where the sergeant was standing on top of the dune, perhaps two hundred feet from me. The sergeant put his hand on Kraft's shoulder and pointed toward the man. We watched as Kraft raised his gun. Even from two hundred feet I knew he was trembling, that the sergeant was steadying him. I thought, perhaps, also, that the sergeant was talking to him in a low voice, explaining how we had made a promise, and everything was just.

We waited, expecting to hear the shot, but none came. Instead Kraft lowered the gun and began waving frantically toward the prisoner who had fallen behind. I started running toward where Kraft and the sergeant stood. As I drew near, I saw that the prisoner was trying to run in order to catch up. But he was staggering like a drunken man over the face of the desert, blinded by the sun and his fatigue.

"Shoot him," the sergeant said. But Kraft shouted out to the prisoner, directing him to come toward the sound of his voice.

The prisoner fell. He got up, pushing himself painfully

120

from the ground, and came on until, about forty feet from me, he fell again.

"Shoot him," the sergeant said, taking out his own pistol.

I ran to the prisoner, as did Kraft, and the two of us helped him to his feet. "Come along," I said.

I could feel his bones under my hands. There was not much flesh on him. He was panting like a wounded animal.

Kraft and I helped him back to the waiting group. Not till we reached there, did I glance back. The sergeant was walking slowly toward us.

He moved past Kraft and me and took his place at the front of the column. Then he started walking fast again, now faster than ever before. I helped the prisoner for a while, then I turned him over to Kraft, who soon turned him over to one of the other prisoners.

The birds were low in the sky. But all of us were standing and present when sunset came and the day was finished.

After that day I had no sense of time or pain, only of heat and dryness. Never had I known such marching. The prisoners' ankles bled freely now, the blood washing away the sand from their feet, and they moaned and wept as they walked. The sand coated us inside and out. It was in our mouths, our throats, our stomachs. The sergeant gave the guards a little water, but he gave the prisoners almost none.

That next day was a nightmare of heat, and glaring light, and weariness. However, nobody fell behind. And the day following, in the low sun of early morning, we saw barracks in the distance. "There," a man shouted, pointing.

The sergeant seemed not to notice that our destination

121

was in sight. Some of the men began to sob with happiness.

But as we walked through the morning, the buildings seemed to come no closer. "This is a mirage," I told the sergeant.

"Yes, I know it is," he said.

My body was crying out for rest. When next I looked up, the buildings were closer. "No, it's the prison," I said.

"Yes," the sergeant answered, "I know. A desert outpost always looks like a mirage."

Prisoners were clinging to one another, trying to stay on their feet.

"All right," the sergeant shouted, "let's arrive in style."

With that he began to double-time toward the camp. The bleeding prisoners began to move faster, then to run. I ran as best I could. I gasped for air, but all I breathed was heat.

The buildings looked close. At last we arrived.

I sank down on the hot ground. A guard brought me a sip of water. I drank it and stared about at the camp which stretched endlessly, for there were no outside walls. The desert was the high wall that no prisoner could cross.

The canteen housed the guards and officers, and a wall surrounded it, protecting the attendants from the prisoners. Inside I found a paradise, with the best French wines, whisky, food, water, magazines, books, girls. "Where does all this come from?" I asked my guide.

"A caravan comes every two months to bring supplies and exchange girls," he said, "and planes drop small supplies and mail."

In one barracks were rooms for rent. "Sometimes tourists come here," he said. "It's quiet and restful."

I saw that it would be as restful as death. I felt that if

122

I shouted one word the sound would carry out, as if drawn by the ever-extending distance, and I would not even hear my own voice.

"How long do the prisoners stay here?" I asked.

"Two years. Even if a man is sent up for fifteen years, he serves his full term by staying here two. But of every hundred men who come here, thirty die, and nobody leaves without taking the marks of the desert on his body."

I wondered, on seeing the prisoners, whether this estimate of survival was not generous. They were fed only water and carrot soup, and they were worked in the desert sun, building camps, making roads, digging wells. Even as they moved, they looked like dead men. Their skulls were shaven; their skin was a dark, brown leather drawn tightly over their bones. Not one of them ever would be a well man again.

Many of the guards were Arabs, and I could imagine what tortures took place in the dark cells. Arabs hated Europeans, and they believed that Allah rewarded them if they tortured a Christian.

Late in the afternoon I bathed in a pan of water, the water tingling every nerve in my skin, and at seven o'clock I ate a good dinner. Afterward, no sooner had I entered the lounge when a girl approached me, one much too pretty for such a place. I knew immediately she would have a sad story to tell about why she was there, so I tried to avoid her, but she said, "You're from Sidi-bel-Abbes and arrived this afternoon." She plopped herself down on a sofa, leaving enough room on either side of her for me. "Sit down a minute with me."

I sat down. She began talking and laughing, and soon I was caught up in her spell.

I bought a bottle of wine, and she led me up to the roof

123

of the canteen. There we found a private corner and stretched out on our backs. Looking up at the full moon and a sky full of stars, I asked myself if this were true, or if I were dreaming of magic.

I reached out my left hand and the wine was there. I reached out my right and the girl was there. The night was true enough.

"When I saw you downstairs, I thought you were a sad person," I told her.

"No. Why be unhappy here? This is a better place than one room in a bombed-out building in France."

"Well, I don't know about that," I said.

"Look at the sky, that's the ceiling of my room here, and the walls are the horizon."

I opened the wine and poured two glasses. We drank under the stars.

A beautiful girl, I thought, looking at her.

I stretched, then put my hands behind my head and studied the sky, as if it were a big map. The map of my life, I thought. It was full of stars, and there was no pattern to them. Once I had made out the face of Linda in the stars, but now I could not do it, perhaps because this girl was by my side, perhaps because Linda was so far away in my mind now. Through the distance in time and space that had grown between us, I could not remember her expressions; I could not see how it was that her face would go from happy to almost sad in a slow fading, as if the face were sighing.

"You'll go home soon?" I asked the girl.

"One day, when I have money and find a husband, I'll go back to France and settle down where I was born."

"Look, I would make a good husband for you," I said. "We could get married and you could live in Sidi-bel-Abbes."

124

"With you?"

"Yes. What's wrong with that?"

"No, I don't want to marry now. Now is the time to make money. When I am seventy years old, I'll marry."

We laughed and I poured more wine. "Tell me about yourself," she said.

"Oh hell, I have no story. I'm a German born in Poland."

"Is that all?"

"That's the start of it, and tonight is the end of it for now. In between is a bad dream, in which I lost my family and my country, and since then I have not found anything again. Nothing is as strong and warm and safe as were my family and my country, but they are all blown away in the war." I sat up, nervousness increasing in me. "Ah, I don't want to talk about it."

"No, tell me."

"No. If I told you what has happened to me, you would want to tell me what a hard life you have had, and before long we would be sad."

I lay back on the deck beside her. "I want to think happy thoughts, and perhaps laugh."

She giggled like a child. "You've a very serious voice to be talking of laughing."

I poured more wine and drank it down in a swallow.

"I also was in Germany during the war," she said.

"You are French and were in Germany during the war?"

"What's wrong with that?"

"Well," I said, "go on and tell me your story."

"No, not if it would make you sad."

Already I was getting sad just thinking of my life, and there under that big sky I was wanting to be sad for a little while with this girl. "Go on, give me the details."

"No details. In Germany I met a Pole, and we became

125

engaged. He promised to marry me after the war, but I got word that he was killed. My family was dead so I had nobody, and I decided not to care about anything and to make a great deal of money."

I propped myself up on one elbow and looked down at her face. "Please don't make much money off of me, dear girl," I said, "because I am a Polish boy myself."

She smiled up at me and closed her eyes.

"Did you realize I was that same Polish boy?"

"No," she said, smiling.

I touched her face with my hand and kissed her. She put her arm around me.

"If you are to be that Polish boy, who am I to be?"

"Well, you are one of two people. I don't know which one. But your hair is dark so I think perhaps you are Linda."

"Was she pretty?"

"The most beautiful girl in Lvov, and very pure."

"I don't want to be too pure," she said. "Who is the other girl?"

"Erika. A girl I knew for a short time in Hamburg."

"I would rather be her." She moved closer to me. "I'll be Erika," she said, "if you want me to be."

"And I'll be that Polish boy."

"No, it will mean too much to me . . ."

"I will be that Polish boy, because I want to be a Polish boy again and nothing else; and I want to forget everything that has come between me and the Polish boy, and not be sad."

"No, not sad till we're seventy."

"Then we'll be sad. Then we'll be what we are, but for now I want to be what I almost was. And you are the girl I love."

Her arms tightened around me. I felt her close against

126

me and ran my hand over her body and through her hair. "Erika," I said, "let's not be sad."

Tears came to my own eyes, and under my hands I felt her crying as she held to me.

10

ON MY RETURN to Sidi-bel-Abbes, I was sent to Sousse, Tunisia, a two-day journey to the east, where my battalion had been transferred. There I was attached to the Thirteenth DBLE, First Battalion, Third Company, and given training with an American tripod machine gun.

At once I mastered the gun, and the lieutenant, impressed by my ability, made arrangements for me to be sent to the noncom school, there to be trained in the ways of the Foreign Legion.

I should have been pleased, of course. Noncommissioned officers had higher pay, separate quarters, their own cooks, tailor-made uniforms. Whatever order a noncom gave, the men obeyed. Every sergeant had his personal orderly. In no army in Europe was the noncom given such privileges; in the Legion they were practically in full command, because the commissioned officers never came around, except in time of war.

But I told the officer I was not interested in being a noncom in the Legion. Already I had had enough of the Legion, and certainly I did not want six more months of training on the desert in the noncom school, in order to be

129

more a part of it than I already was. I had seen brutality on the Eastern Front, and nothing in the Legion, even with its perverts and severe punishments, surpassed that; but on the Eastern Front we had been fighting for our lives and our country. In the Legion, brutality was simply the accepted way of life.

Not long after I turned down the lieutenant, however, I wondered if I had not made a mistake. We heard rumors that we would be shipped to the jungles of Indochina, where rebel uprisings were reported. Soon the rumors materialized in an order to board ship.

We were going to Asia, to the other side of the earth.

At Bizerta, in mid-February, 1946, twenty-five hundred of us boarded a British ship, the *Ormonde*. The sun shone down on us, as if it would say *bon voyage*, and I felt a kinship with it. In my journeys, I found that people changed, as did places and sights, but the sun always was the same.

The loud-speaker ordered everyone to his station, so I went into the hold and hurried to my section. Forty Legionnaires were to stay in one cabin with one officer. Our officer told us to get a hammock each and hang it on hooks, which we did. I stretched out in mine, and it was as fine as any bed. Also I found that I could scratch my back without turning over. I lay there for a while, scratching myself through the canvas and laughing about how it felt, so that other Legionnaires tried the same system.

Then the ship's engines grew noisy; somebody said we were ready to leave. One of the boys pulled out a bottle of whisky and we drank toasts to Africa. We finished that bottle and were wondering where to get another when a British seaman came to our cabin with a bottle which he was offering for sale.

"How much?" I asked him in English.

130

"One hundred francs."

A Legionnaire took the bottle from him and opened it. "Have a drink, boys," he said. "A toast for this generous British seaman."

He handed the confused Englishman fifty francs.

When the ship began to move out, I went up to the deck and waved to the people on the dock who had come to see us off. There were many girls—Arabian, European, and Negro—and civilians of all countries. As the ship pulled away, I watched them and Africa disappear.

On our first day aboard, the commander of the Legion and the British captain organized a police force, which would be armed and placed in charge of law and order, a total of one hundred men to oversee twenty-five hundred Legionnaires. I was one of the hundred. But such a small group could not handle so many Legionnaires both night and day. Legionnaires began to snoop in every corner of the ship's cabins. Every minute somebody was opening an officer's door, stealing goods. Also there was much drinking aboard, which made it even more difficult to keep order. My hours on duty were filled with problems.

But off duty I was free. Often I would stand on deck and watch the big ships pass, and also the fishing boats and other craft which sailed the Mediterranean. I would spend my hours thinking of the bloody past of that water and of the men who had spent their lives on it, all the way back to the deep history when the boats were small, up to the time when I could stand on a steel deck and look at water sloshing far below me. I had liked the idea of the sea since childhood and had once told my father that I would like to live on the ocean and die in the ocean, too. He had laughed and said, "Dear Eddy, probably you were a pirate in another life and lost your life that way. That's why you like the sea."

I spent hours on the deck, dreaming of such magic. And

always I told myself I must remember the way I was going, for I would have to come back again. I tried to convince myself that it didn't matter that I was leaving Europe and going to Asia. But when I would stand on the stern of the ship and look out at the churning water below and then back at the sea we had crossed, I saw that there was no track, no path home.

I told myself that there would be a path, somehow, and that now I was only on a journey about which, in my old age, I would tell my children, off there somewhere in a nice house in my country.

We entered the Suez canal as part of a large convoy. I was on deck when we started through, watching the canal unfold like a snake warming itself in the sun. The wind was blowing against my face and body and I braced myself into it, paying attention to no one until a man I knew but slightly came up close to me and whispered: "Hukov, let's jump overboard and desert to the English. They will treat us well."

I laughed at the idea, because I knew the English would turn deserters over to the French. My laughter made the man angry, and he went away, cursing me. I looked after him, wondering how the human mind could be so foolish.

But soon his idea began to creep into my thinking. At least it offered a chance to stay closer to Europe. Even at that moment we were moving through the neck of the continents, and beyond that neck lay the whole body of the East, in which a man could wander forever, going from nation to nation. Beyond the canal were the unknown countries, spread out around the oceans. If I did not desert now, perhaps I would never see Europe again.

Suddenly I also wanted to jump over the side of the ship and try to start back toward Europe; but before I was certain what I ought to do, the ship's alarm system went off.

"All men back in their hatches," the loud-speaker said. "Military police will see that all men go back into their hatches."

"What happened?" I shouted to an officer.

"Overboard," he said. "Seven Legionnaires over the side."

I ran to the rail. My acquaintance was down there with six others, trying to swim the two hundred or so feet to the bank, and having a time of it because he was a poor swimmer and had not taken off his boots. I thought for a minute that this weak fellow would be sucked into the propeller of the ship, but he managed to stay clear.

"Are they stopping the ship for them, sir?" I asked a lieutenant.

He shook his head. "If we were to stop, we might lose a hundred men."

We members of the police, who were permitted on deck, stood at the fantail and waved to the seven deserting Legionnaires as they helped each other out of the canal, shaking water out of their hair and clothes. They waved back, all of them laughing like crazy men they were so happy. I watched them sadly, wondering if I had passed up a golden opportunity.

Beyond the canal, the military police received instructions to look for a French corporal. Every loud-speaker called his name in every cabin and corridor, and we searched in vain in all the lavatories, cabins, on all decks. "It's too bad about him," I told Reinhold. "I suppose he got seasick and leaned too far over the side of the ship."

"He didn't go over quite that way, Hukov," Reinhold said. "And I wouldn't waste time looking for him if I were you. He's at the bottom of the sea." Reinhold then told me about a new organization aboard, started by the Nazis,

133

which planned to take over the ship and force the captain to take them to a place of their own choosing, where they hoped to start a new country. The French corporal was the first casualty. "The French officers know about the movement now," Reinhold said. "I know this because not a one of them will come out of his cabin at night, or even open his door. Also the English crewmen go two or three to a group. So we'll have to wait and see what the French and English come up with."

What came up, and very quickly, was a second movement, not among the French officers and British crewmen, as we had thought, but among the Legionnaires who were not Germans. The Poles, Czechs, Bulgars and Yugoslavs began to organize their own party, and to this party the crew and officers gave their encouragement. I favored the Slavic group, also, but I kept my opinion to myself.

Fights began breaking out on the ship. Each day they grew bigger. There were broken heads of all nationalities. It was dangerous to be standing guard, for no one knew when he might be attacked and carried off. All authority was taken from the police and turned over to the leaders of the two groups. The laws of the ship became the laws of the Slavs and the Nazis.

Then abruptly, like the storm over the desert, the war was over. There were no more fights.

"It's a stalemate," Reinhold told me. "The Nazis see they cannot take over the ship, so now it's all off."

"So the Nazis have learned to stop fighting when they see they can't win," I said.

"Yes," he said, "it's a good lesson for them; one they could have used two years ago."

11

WE ARRIVED at Trincomali, Ceylon, on March 3rd. All of us wanted to see what an Asiatic city was like, but the French would not allow us to go ashore. During the two days we were there, three motor-boats manned with machine gunners patrolled our ship, in case one of us should try to desert.

The air in Trincomali was so heavy that it weighted down the lungs. Even when we left that harbor and started east, there was no breeze, no escape from the sickening heat. March is one of the hottest months in the South China Sea.

On the 12th of March, we arrived at the mouth of the Saigon River, in the province of Cochin China, in South Indochina, and the bothersome loud-speakers began talking continuously. "In case our ship strikes a Jap free-floating mine, keep proper order," they said. "Jump into the sea and wait for help."

"Good Lord in Heaven," a huge Romanian said, "how can you keep proper order if you have to jump into the sea?"

"What are Jap mines doing here?" I asked my sergeant.

135

"This territory was occupied by Japan in the war," he said. "Their army is still here, waiting to go home."

Our French officer, Lieutenant Pilsoner, came into our cabin. He was a young man, but deep lines already were in his face, so that he looked strange and old. "Don't go on deck," he said. "We have to move up the river to Saigon harbor, and there are Communist rebels and Japanese deserters along the banks. They'll shoot if they see a target."

He left and we drank a toast to the Japanese and Communist rebels out in the night, waiting to see our ship pass.

I became drunk and wanted to go to sleep, but the men would not put out the lights in the cabin, so I lay in my hammock and listened to the babble of words from half a dozen languages and thought about the natives out in the jungle along the banks of that wide river. I wondered if they could breathe with comfort the air of their country, and what they would think about Germany, if I could take them there and show them the sights. Also, I wondered who they were and why it was they had kicked up such a fuss that a big European nation had sent its Legion to fight them.

When the whisky gave out in our cabin, the men either went to the hammocks or stumbled off to a cabin where drinking was still going on. Finally the light was put out and I went to sleep.

The next day, the 13th of March, 1946, the great anchor of the ship was dropped into the harbor at Saigon. Behind us another ship, tanks and artillery pieces lashed to its deck, wet its anchor. We were happy to have ended the voyage; but an idea came to me as I looked at the watching faces of my friends. I thought, here we have arrived; after the long journey, we have reached the end; but not a man has come home.

136

We waited only a few minutes before the loud-speaker began blaring out orders. "First Battalion, First Company, down the gangplank!"

Ten minutes later the order was, "First Battalion, Second Company!"

Finally the loud-speaker said, "First Battalion, Third Company!" That was my company, and the 120 of us hurried to solid ground.

All three battalions were marched to an open field near the dock for roll call, after which we were told not to wander off, although we could sit down and smoke. We were in this open field for several hours. Most of us became ill because of the heat, and a few men collapsed.

In early evening, sixty trucks arrived. We boarded them and the convoy began rolling through the Saigon harbor district.

Normally Saigon was the largest and busiest city in Indochina, but now the shops and restaurants were closed, windows were broken and boarded over.

"What does this mean?" I asked Leman, a rifleman in my squad.

"I don't know." He also was staring at the near-deserted streets. "But it's a poor reception. I don't even see a rickshaw to make me feel we are in Asia."

When we passed Europeans, they would wave at us; but there were few natives, and those that we saw were sullen.

It was dark before we reached the countryside, where our trucks moved at high speed. After a short while, the lead trucks stopped; the convoy halted. Ahead we saw a bridge with Legionnaires guarding it. The word came back for us to load our guns and stay on the alert.

Our captain shouted to the company. "Now we will cross the bridge and go thirty kilometers more till we reach Thu Doc. This is dangerous territory. If the rebels fire, fire back."

We crossed the bridge. I looked at my watch: it was midnight. Then we heard rifle shots from the guerrillas. We did not fire back, and the drivers did not stop the trucks. We kept on rolling, moving into dense jungle until we arrived deep in Cochin China at a military outpost occupied by the regular French Army.

"All right," our captain shouted, "Third Company is assigned here."

We jumped down. I wanted to kiss the Indochina dirt; I was that glad to be at the very end of the journey. I thanked God in my heart for a safe arrival.

"This is where we're to be stationed," the old man said. "All sergeants to the front for instructions."

While we private soldiers waited, several of the French Army men struck up conversations with us. One of them told me that three companies had been stationed there, but now our one company was to occupy the fort alone.

"One company replaces three?" I asked him.

"Yes, the Legion is a tough organization."

The sergeant of my platoon began to read off orders. My orders were to take over the machine-gun post at one corner of the compound, which I did, relieving the French soldier who was on duty. "Do the guerrillas attack every night?" I asked him.

"No. About every other night."

"Are there many of them?"

"A few thousand native rebels and a few hundred Japanese soldiers who deserted their army. How many men are you, one hundred twenty?"

"One hundred twenty," I said, nodding.

He took his machine gun from the tripod. I screwed my own gun in place and shouted to Leman to bring me ammunition. While I waited I looked out at the dark jungle.

138

It was as endless as the ocean or the desert. As a boy I had always thought the world was made up of cities, since that was what I knew, and on my travels it was always surprising to find that most of the world was controlled not by man but by nature.

The Frenchman was still standing nearby, nursing his machine gun. "What is this war about?" I asked him.

He shifted the gun to his shoulder and began talking in a tired monotone. "When France fell to the Nazis, the Japanese came into Indochina. They taught the natives to read and told them they should be free. So the natives began to rule, and the French colonists were out of office."

"Now the French want back in, is that it?" I said.

"Yes. When my unit arrived six months ago, the colonists went wild with happiness, and here in the South they threw out the Vietnamese rulers. The next day the Vietnamese struck back. In Saigon the lights went out, the water was cut off, then fires were set, and shooting started. French women and children fled to the Hotel Continental and filled it until they were crowding the halls. The rebels captured many men, women, and children, however, and carried them off. Almost all the natives, even those we had thought were loyal, left the city. Saigon became a ghost town."

From the center of the compound came an order for the French troops to board the trucks. "I wish you luck," I said to the young Frenchman as he moved away. An hour later the trucks left, the sound of their motors rumbling through the jungle, gradually fading out, leaving us with an unfriendly silence.

A Legionnaire sneaked across the compound as if afraid to let anyone know he was there. Two men crept over to my corner and peered out. One of them whispered to me, "Do you see anything, Hukov?"

We had arrived and were in place, but we did not know

139

what to expect. If this were the Eastern Front, I would know, because there had been a pattern to the Russian tactics. I would know what British or American soldiers might be expected to do. But this was jungle, and natives were here, perhaps even now peering out at us from the thick undergrowth.

Half an hour went by. Suddenly there was a shout, "Banzai!" Two rebels leaped over the barbed wire and raced toward my corner of the compound, hundreds of others rising up behind them. I could not get my thinking straight; my movements were slow.

At last I heard the rapping of my American light-machine gun. I stayed on the trigger. It was very dark, and I could see only the light on the end of my gun. I aimed low, firing at the ground, so that no rebels could move under my fire, even though they crept along the ground.

Lieutenant Pilsoner hammered me on the shoulder with his pistol and pointed toward where a Japanese machine gun was firing on us. I changed the band in my weapon and laid a long burst into their position. There was no more fire from them.

Once more my lieutenant hammered me on the shoulder and pointed to an area where twenty rebels were almost to the north walls. I fired three long bursts at them. When I looked back at the lieutenant, a grin was on his face. "Very good, Nazi," he said. "Excellent."

"Sir, what makes you call me a Nazi?" I said. Always before he had referred to me by name. "Why Nazi?" I asked.

"Ah," he said, then laughed. "Ah, why indeed?"

A few minutes later the attacks ceased. At 6:00 A.M. we could see the narrow field around us. The lieutenant pointed out the dead "Banzais." He told me to come with him and have a look at them. I counted eighteen dead bodies, some Japanese. We confiscated their guns and

140

brought them back to the camp. Then ten of us took the bodies of the two dead Legionnaires and carried them to the burial ground. Many soldiers had been buried there before, each marked by a small mound of dirt.

I helped dig down in the soil. We buried our dead properly. A Swede, a small man with a kind face, volunteered to say a prayer, which he did, but in Swedish, so I did not know what he said. No doubt it was a prayer for men far off from home who had been killed by men they did not know for a country that was not their own.

I tapped the soil into place on one of the graves. It was dark, like the soil of Poland.

We had no other attacks for two weeks, but we spent much time scouting the countryside, looking for rebels. It was hard, unprofitable work. As we passed through, the countryside appeared to be deserted. Off in the distance we might see a cluster of Vietnamese repairing the dikes in the rice paddies, but never did we see a soldier.

Yet if one Legionnaire left the post, especially if he was unarmed, he might later be found along the roadside, dead and cut to pieces.

Seeing such atrocities committed on our friends, we came to hate the rebels and spent more time than ever seeking them out. We found that sometimes their soldiers would hide in the water in the klongs and rice paddies, breathing through reeds when our patrols came by. It was almost impossible to spot them, but, on one occasion, we found three at one place, two at another.

We had arrived at the beginning of the rainy season. Each day the rain came down in such drenching outpours that it seemed God had emptied a huge bucket on us. And no sooner had the ground begun to soak up the puddles of water than the sky opened again for another flood.

For six months it was to rain. The ground would never be dry. The heat and the dampness would soak into our

141

bodies. Metal would sweat, leather would turn green, and food would quickly rot.

But nature thrived. Even in the first month of rain, we saw that trees and bushes grew at fantastic rates, some of them ten times as fast as in Europe; and the world around us became a sparkling, emerald green.

The rebels were less active in the rainy season, although we had a few other attacks from them before we were pulled out of that post and sent to other posts in northeast Cochin China. During these several weeks, we began to gain a better understanding of the war. We were told that, shortly after Japan surrendered, the Allies occupied the country, the northern half being taken over by Chiang Kai-shek's Chinese, the southern half by the British, who landed with both British and Indian troops. But there were not enough troops in the South, so instead of disarming the defeated Japanese Army, the British ordered them to stand guard, also.

The French were disgraced before the Vietnamese. They had few troops on hand and no authority. The Japanese had locked up their small army. Much of it was at the citadel at Hanoi, in the far north; and the Chinese left it locked up; they would not release it.

At last French troops arrived from Marseilles, but even after their arrival, the French had only 15,000 soldiers in the southern part of the colony.

In March a tentative peace was negotiated between the French and the Vietnamese leaders in north Viet Nam, but in the south, the fighting never stopped.

It was a new type of warfare for me. Here there were few, if any, planes, few tanks. It was a battle of small units. In fact, our company soon was broken up into its platoons and they were sent to different posts. My platoon of forty men was sent to an outpost near Lai Thieu.

There, on the fourth or fifth day, we were engaged in

142

a skirmish which indoctrinated us into the ways of that section.

About 10:00 A.M. a young native came to our camp and told us in fluent French that he knew where the leader of the local rebels was resting. Lieutenant Pilsoner asked him how far this was.

"Not more than four kilometers," he said.

"And how many men guard him?" the lieutenant said.

"Only two or three men."

The lieutenant asked many other questions, all of which the young Vietnamese answered readily. Finally the lieutenant ordered the second squad, of which I was a member, to move out and capture this rebel leader.

The twelve of us followed the native informer for eight kilometers, then our sergeant asked him how much farther it was. He told us it was one kilometer more, so we followed on. But after four kilometers more, the sergeant grasped the informer around the neck and demanded that he tell us the truth.

"There it is," he gasped, pointing toward a jungle house.

We encircled the house and moved in. We found an old woman of seventy living there, and that was all.

The native informer explained that the rebel leader had already left and that, as a matter of fact, he had to leave too. But the sergeant ordered him to return to camp with us.

At this point, thirteen kilometers from our base, we knew one of two things had happened. Either the rebels were attacking the base, and had used this young Vietnamese to lead us away, or they were planning an ambush for us.

As we walked back along the narrow road of the jungle, the young native tried several times to leave us, so Leman tied his hands and led him with a rope. We were very

143

tired, and because of that we were walking far from each other, perhaps fifteen yards.

After eight kilometers we reached a place where a small rice field had recently been cleared and left for the water buffalo to graze. A few pineapple trees were left standing, and around the edges were thick bushes and clumps of bamboo. As the first scout reached the other side of the field, I was just entering it; and it was at this moment that the first shot went off, followed by bursts from either two or three rebel machine-guns and many shots from several dozen rifles. The rebels were firing at us from across the field.

Leman was hit and went down. The others of us took cover and returned the fire, but five men of our eleven turned not to the open field, but to the bushes, in order to protect the rest of us should rebels leap out from there. The guerrillas had a habit of doing this, descending with their big "coop-coop" knives and cutting off European heads.

I did not see the young native informer killed, but at a lull in the firing, I noticed his body was stretched out near the Yugoslav. His head had been bashed in, and his face was now covered with insects as well as blood.

We fought the rebels for about four hours and it was evident that we soon would be out of ammunition. I crawled to Leman's body and turned him over. He was dead, the bullet having torn out part of his spine.

I took eighty rounds from his ammunition belts.

When I got back to my gun, a Hungarian, who had been a top track man in his country, crawled over to me. "Hukov, I am going for help."

"Don't be a fool," I said. "The rebels will get you. And if they don't it's at least five kilometers to the outpost, and it will take you an hour to run that far. Stay here."

But he did not listen to me. He leaped to his feet and

144

rushed along the boundary of the open field. I knew at any moment he would be hit, but he reached the jungle.

After his escape, the rebels began to shorten their fire. Sensing that they were weakening, we opened fire from every gun. Because of our show of strength, the rebels lost courage and ran, a few of them even throwing their rifles away.

We picked up Leman's body and, changing our course, we, too, ran as fast as we could.

One kilometer from camp, we heard distant fire from machine guns, so we knew our fort was under attack. Our sergeant ordered us to attack the rebels from behind, using the remainder of our ammunition. "This will be our last chance," he said. "When every man has fired his last round, he will be on his own. He can escape as best he can."

The sergeant deployed us on either side of the road and told us to hold our fire until he gave word, because he wanted the few remaining rounds to be fired close together, in order to fool the rebels into thinking we were a large force. We moved down the road, walking close together now, until we came within sight of our camp, at which point our two brother squads opened fire on us, believing us to be rebels. The sergeant ordered us into the jungle, which was so thick we could not get more than two yards from the road.

"God damn it," he shouted, "what a hell of a damn war! I wish I had a French son of a bitch in this squad. I would send him out with a message!"

The men in the outpost continued firing along the road, so there was nothing to be done except stay in cover. But the sergeant grew more angry as he waited. "When I give the word," he shouted, "everybody open up on the damn tree tops. Blast out the tree tops, so the men in the camp will hear our guns."

145

It was true our guns sounded different than the Japanese weapons, so we opened fire, and almost immediately the men in the camp stopped shooting at us. We flooded into the road again and moved quickly to the clearing around the outpost, where we expected to find the rebels ready to fire at us, but instead we saw them fleeing. The men in the outpost shouted for us to come on in, that our firing had frightened them away.

Two weeks later, the French gave me the Croix de Guerre with Bronze Star. To celebrate, several of us stole a jeep from another company and took it to Saigon. Reinhold and Kraft were along, and a Hollander and a Swede completed the party.

Nobody had money. Legion pay was equivalent to three United States dollars a month, and we spent that on gambling, whisky, and cigarettes. We did not have a cent, but we went to Mama San's place and got some girls, even though we could not pay them. The five of us then went off in our jeep and made a tour of the town. Then in late evening, we stopped at a restaurant on the Rue Catinat, where only officers and civilians were eating. We ordered wine and the best food, and it was a big treat for us. Back at the camp our cook could boil eggs well, and that was all. There we usually had buffalo meat with rice bread and vegetables. Only occasionally did we have a pig, and it was rare, indeed, when we had a chicken or duck. Now we could order what we pleased.

After we were full, Kraft ordered two bottles of whisky and the check. When the waiter returned, he took the whisky out to the jeep and left the four of us with the check.

When I heard the jeep's motor and knew Kraft was

ready to go, I told the waiter to bring us a pencil. Here he fooled me, because he did not leave our table, but dug a pencil out of his pocket and handed it to me. I did not know what to do at that point, so I checked over the figures on the bill, then I wrote across the bottom, "General de Gaulle will pay," and off we started.

The waiter tried to stop us, so Reinhold knocked him to one side and we hurried on.

But, just as we were all in the jeep and ready to leave, a military policeman's jeep stopped in front of us, barring our way. Two policemen came up to us and asked for our papers. Immediately three of us knocked them down, took possession of both jeeps and made off up the street. Two blocks away we parked their jeep, and all joined in the same party.

"Well, Hukov," Reinhold said, whisky drooling from the corners of his mouth, "it was a fine celebration you gave us."

"Thank you," I said. "Next time I will be your guest."

Kraft, sitting in the driver's seat, said, "Hukov, you entertain like an officer. It's a pleasure to know such a man."

"I've been decorated," I told him, "so I have had to learn good manners."

We laughed and drank as much whisky as we wanted and when we got our jeep back to camp, invited the other men in our squad to join us. Before we finished the second bottle, however, the lieutenant broke up the party. "You must keep clear heads," he said. "This war is not going any too well as it is."

That was the attitude of all the officers. A harried, sullen expression had come to their faces. We Legionnaires won our battles in Viet Nam, but the victories only inflamed the rebels all the more. There were twenty-five

147

million natives in Indochina, almost all of them in Viet Nam, so the rebel army had plenty of replacements. The angrier the natives became, the more willing they were to join in the war.

And the more aggressive they became, the more brutal was the action of the French officers toward them. Across the Saigon river, about thirty kilometers west of our fort, was a long bridge, and on that bridge not hundreds, but thousands of rebel prisoners were executed and thrown into the swift stream below. Twice I was ordered to take part in executions there. Once our squad shot about forty Japanese and Vietnamese of the Viet Minh. The second time we shot about a dozen. It was done with dispatch. In Viet Nam, as on the Eastern Front two years before, no quarters were asked or shown by either side.

But sometimes I wondered what it gained the French to fight. We cleared the plantations, but no Frenchman was safe on them. French men and women were even captured by the Viet Minh on the streets of Saigon and carried off. They lived behind bolted doors, in many cases armed with pointed sticks, for there were not enough weapons; and they prayed they would be protected by the Legion, which was composed of the cast-off peoples of every nation in Europe, with only a few from France.

Knowing that the Legion was thus composed, the rebels sometimes sent us propaganda leaflets.

Every European fighting for the French, whom the French sent here to die, has one chance.
Surrender to us and we will treat you well.
Legionnaire privates can become rebel officers, and the payment is good.

I laughed at the few men who considered the leaflets seriously. "With honey you catch only flies," I told them. I pointed out that we Germans had done the same thing

148

in Russia, and when the Russians surrendered with their propaganda leaflets in hand, they were shot or left to starve to death. "This is a hard war," I said to my friends, "and it might kill all of us, unless we escape. But the escape must be from both the rebels and the Legion."

12

12

IN A FEW DAYS my platoon was transferred to Thu Dau Mot, near the Saigon river, in which we would sometimes swim. On the street of a nearby village one afternoon, I saw a Vietnamese girl of about twenty-four, who was strikingly beautiful. She had the bronze skin of the Vietnamese, with shiny dark hair and flashing dark eyes; and she was tall, almost as tall as I. She wore clothes which evidently had been imported from France.

A shopkeeper told me she taught in the school. "She studied in French universities," he said, "and knows everything."

I could not think of a proper way to approach her, but I knew if I waited until the next day, other men in my platoon would see her, too, and competition would set in. So I ran after her. "Lady," I said, coming up to her, "lady, excuse me, but it has been a long time since I have heard a woman speak a single word in a European language, for here I am in this strange country."

She smiled at my awkwardness. "Where are you from?" She spoke a perfect, lilting French and was even more beautiful than I had at first thought.

151

"Lvov, Poland," I said. "I would like to tell you about my life sometime."

She was still smiling. "My parents' home is down this road. Will you come with me and have a cup of tea or coffee?"

I went with her and met her parents, but all the time I drank my coffee, I looked at her only.

After that, as often as Lieutenant Pilsoner would permit, I went to her house. Soon I was living so that I could visit her. Only one characteristic bothered me, and that was her interest in politics.

With her I wanted to think about love and nothing else, but sometimes she would start talking about the war and the French. "They allowed some of us to go to the French universities," she said. "There we came to realize that the French have been in Viet Nam for almost a hundred years, and the people are worse off than they were when the French arrived. The same is true with much of Asia, but now Asia is rising. In Burma, Malaya, Indonesia, the people are also demanding their freedom."

"Yes, it is a big revolt," I answered, "but here we are alone under the heavens, and time is passing." Frequently when I saw her, I had to listen to her talk of politics before we made love.

Her name was Kugy, or so I pronounced it, and she shared her personal secrets with me. Also her parents took me into their family circle. Her mother was a kind lady who watched the servants carefully, prepared much of the food herself, and had it served with great care. She rarely voiced an opinion and sometimes appeared to be embarrassed by the outspoken views of her daughter.

Kugy's father was a mild, friendly man who had big rice fields and pineapple and coconut groves. His huge plantation gave him many problems, but he laughed often, always with a big voice, and was serious only when the

152

war was mentioned. Then pain would flicker across his face, his smile would die away. "The natives have to fight," he said, "but now the Communists are taking over the revolt and where will that lead?"

I told him of my own hatred for the Communists in Russia.

"Eddy," he said, "they have a trick of taking over. Several months ago there was a famine in the Tonkinese delta. Perhaps it was the fault of the Viet Minh, perhaps of the French. Certainly some plan should have been made months before to get rice to that area. In the famine, Eddy, death struck fiercely. The French admit 600,-000 people starved. The Viet Minh say 2,000,000 starved. Can you imagine 600,000 people starving to death in one small area? Corpses rotted in the streets of Hanoi. And for years past, every year before the crop comes in, the people are hungry, living on one meal a day, and that only a thin soup. They boil rice until it is a paste, and once a day each person has a bowl of it. This is the way it is there almost every year, and what is the solution?"

Not since leaving the Eastern Front had I heard of such misery, but I saw in his honest eyes that he was not lying to me.

"The French have no answer," he said. "They say this is the way it always has been. But the Communists insist this is not right. They tell the people that changes must be made, and they work to bring these changes about. And that, you see, is the trick of the Communists; they take over the cause. It is a good cause, and they are there first with a solution. This revolution starts, so they come up first with leaders and say follow us. The people are not Communists themselves but they will follow the Communists. Now, where will it end? Where will they lead us?"

I enjoyed talking to this man. He could see both sides

153

of the problem, and its many facets. "All Asia takes hope, now that the United States has given the Filipinos their freedom," he told me one night. "But where is the United States now in Viet Nam?"

Often I went to Kugy's home; sometimes I ate there, sometimes sat around in the evening and drank beer with her father. He told me he hoped I would marry Kugy, and I told him I would when my term in the Legion was over.

One night after dinner at her house, Kugy took my hand and led me to her room. "I have a secret to tell you," she said. She took me to a picture of Jesus hanging on the wall and lit a candle before it. "Swear to Jesus Christ that you will not harm me," she said.

I do not like to swear to God, but this girl was my nearest friend, so I swore to God for her.

She began to cry and I took out my handkerchief and wiped the tears from her face.

"Dear Eddy, I love you and so do my parents. They are your father and mother now. You have no one except us. You are part of our family."

"I am. I thank you and I am."

"So you must learn about our country. It's your country, too, now, Eddy."

I sat down on the bed in her room and stared at the floor. "Well, as you say," I said.

"And it's being crushed. The French squeeze our people; they take anything they want. You have been here long enough to see this."

"Yes," I said. "What you say may be true."

"Even animals fight for their homes and for some rights, and so do we. Eddy, my older brother is a rebel officer, and he fights for his country and for our family."

I was moved by what she said. I knew what she wanted and could see myself fighting beside her brother and helping to clear the land of the French. I could see myself

154

coming to her house, which was my house, too, and to her family, and being received as a hero. In every village soon they would know my name—Hukov, Hukov, Hukov, like a burning flame through the jungle.

"Eddy, why are you silent?"

"Kugy, I'm not a man of politics, and you're not a girl of politics. If we become people involved in the thoughts of countries . . ."

"In Viet Nam, Eddy, there's no escape from that."

"My dear, I love you and your family, but I can't fight my own people."

"We are your people now."

"You are my people, here in this house; but I can't fight the Legionnaires. And many of the rebels fighting with your brother are Communists. A few Communists go a long way, Kugy. It's dangerous to fight with Communists."

"But how can you fight for France?"

"I can't fight for France. I fight for my friends in the Legion. We are attacked and we must fight. I don't want to see my friends die. I can't fight against my friends, and I can't fight for Communism."

"Even for your new home? Even for your love for me?"

"My dear, if you make love a thing of politics, you must find someone else to love you. I'm sick to my soul of politics."

She began to weep piteously. "I'm tired of life," she wept. "My country is torn apart. The French torture us."

I put my arms around her. "You're educated, far better than I, so don't say you're tired of life. That makes no sense."

"Education! What good is that at such a time?"

"Now stop this nonsense. You offered a fair bargain, and I turned you down. I won't fight with the rebels, so you tell your brother that. And you tell him, also, that when my term is up, I'm going to marry you, politics or no politics, and take you to Europe."

She seemed to be cheered by that but still she said we should go into the jungle and fight for our country.

That night I could not sleep. My mind was troubled because I knew I had failed her. I opened the mosquito netting around my bed and looked out. I could see the dim shapes of the other nets, hanging like silk shrouds. I thought: How could I make myself kill you, boys? How could I turn a gun on you? Maybe another man could do it, but he would not be of my blood. I have seen the countries, and now all I know to be loyal to are my friends.

If any doubts remained in my mind about the proper course for me, they were dispelled two days later. An old Chinese lady came to our camp and said something in Chinese, which nobody could understand. She pointed up the road and grabbed us by the arm, trying to persuade us to follow her. Our sergeant said it was just another native trick, but Lieutenant Pilsoner ordered our squad to see.

Not far from camp, on the river side, we came to her house. One of our men stayed with her and the rest of us surrounded the house and closed in. We found a European lying on the floor, wounded in his leg; he was almost dead.

We carried him to our camp, and Lieutenant Pilsoner gave the old lady one hundred piasters for her kindness. She stood to one side and watched as we bandaged the man's leg and gave him an injection. When he came to, the lieutenant asked him who he was.

In a weak, thin voice he told us, "I am a German Legionnaire, a deserter. I was a member of the Second Battalion of the Thirteenth DBLE but, with four friends, I decided to desert, and we joined the rebels. On the first day they took our guns and treated us very bad. For the past three months they have sent us from one camp to an-

156

other, and each time they transferred us, they covered our eyes with a piece of cloth, so that we could not see where we were going. Yesterday morning they brought us to a large Japanese camp. Last evening, the officer led us to a wooden house and said, 'Please sit down and I will order you food.'

"We sat down and the officer left. Then several guns opened fire on the house. Quickly I jumped out the window and ran toward a klong. The canal was not deep and was full of grass. I covered my face with a leaf, so that no one could see me.

"Then I found I was wounded. In the water I tried to stop the blood with my hands.

"Suddenly lights were shining over the klong. The Japanese began to search and dived into the water, but they did not find me. After two hours they stopped and I moved under water to the other side of the klong and made my way into the jungle. I came to a field of sugar cane. I crossed the field and came to a big river. I was almost out of strength, but I started swimming for the other side. Several times I went down in the water. Each time I managed to get my head above the surface, I shouted for help. I kept going down and fighting back to the surface and shouting out, until at last an old lady came with a boat and helped me to shore. I don't remember anything after that."

We carried him to a jeep and took him to the headquarters of the Thirteenth DBLE. I thought they would shoot him, because he had deserted the Legion. Instead, on that same day, they ordered him to lead three battalions to the Japanese camp. Two thousand Legionnaires gathered near where the Chinese lady had found him. We moved through the cane field and through the jungle to the klong. It was nearly evening when we found the camp.

Half of the guerrillas had already left; we attacked the

157

rest. The rebels counterattacked and we lost heavily in dead and wounded. But after three hours, we captured several hundred Japanese and native guerrillas. Many others had been killed.

We captured hundreds of rifles, approximately fifteen tons of munitions, and two Japanese-made tanks. Hundreds of women were at the camp, it being their job to prepare food and care for the wounded, and these we captured also.

Then we entered the house from which the German Legionnaire had escaped. The four dead deserters were there. The Legionnaire began to weep for his friends.

"You see what it means to desert to the rebels?" a captain said to him. "You deserted the Legion and should be put to death. But you have led us here, so we will not kill you. You have been brave and have helped us capture a battalion."

But the man, looking down at his friends, continued to weep.

I knew I should take this man's experience up with Kugy, since she had asked me to desert to the rebels. When next I went to her house, she came running out to greet me, as always, and I took her in my arms and kissed her, but only on the forehead because her mother was watching. I started to tell her about it right then, but her mother came out to the road and told us to come in to dinner.

After dinner Kugy and I went out into the orange garden, where only the moon was watching us, and there I told her what happened to Europeans who wanted to fight with the rebels. "I have seen one of them and the bodies of the other four," I told her. "I know black from white when I see them with my own eyes, and now nobody can tell me grandmother tales. If I had taken your advice, I would have been murdered."

158

She stood stiff and silent, unsure what to say. "I—I love you," she said at last. "I didn't know about that. Please believe me."

I could not help suspecting her any more than I could help loving her.

She began to weep. "Please—I didn't know that."

I took her in my arms. She was trembling. "It's all right," I told her. "I know you wouldn't sacrifice me for politics."

"No," she said. "No, no." Her arms closed around me and soon we forgot everything but love.

Later, stretched out on a patch of green leaves watching the stars, she said, "Eddy, why is it like this, that you have come from Europe and met me here in this village, and I have given my heart to you?"

"Our stars are directing our lives and God's angels are keeping us on the right way."

"Angels?" she said, smiling.

"We can't see them, but they're with us all the time. The angels are protecting us from bullets, and sickness, and evil people. If a man believes in good and does his best for humanity, God gives him the power of His angels."

She laughed. "Eddy, you should have been a priest instead of a Legionnaire."

"No, but I've believed in Jesus and God in my heart since the night I saw my sister's ghost."

Kugy had to know about that, so I told her.

"You didn't see a thing in that hall, Eddy, except perhaps shadows of a curtain."

"Well, it led me to God, and I think it was Lene, not a curtain. But it wasn't real enough to make me want to be a priest, I'll admit."

She laughed and kissed me. "Eddy, what do you think our first baby will be, a boy or a girl?"

159

"Look here," I said, "when we mix our Asian and European bloods, whatever sex it has, that little devil will jump from one banana tree to another."

She began to laugh so much her parents came out from the house to see what was the matter with her.

At ten o'clock, Legionnaires had to be in camp, so I left her house at a quarter to ten, which gave me just enough time to get there. As I was nearing the camp a huge black cat ran out over the road. I grabbed a stone and threw it after her. "Damn you," I said, "you're blackening the night." But there was nothing else I could do.

It was exactly ten o'clock when I reached the camp, and Lieutenant Pilsoner had just started to snoop inside each mosquito net to make sure everyone was in. I crawled under my own net.

"Legionnaire Hukov, come out here," he said.

I got out. "Yes, sir?"

"Is your light machine gun in order?"

"I cleaned it this afternoon."

"Well, I want you to take the heavy machine gun." He pointed to a black object nearby. "The sergeant brought it here for you. Mount it tomorrow."

He went on down the line of cots, peering into each mosquito net on the way, and I climbed back into bed and quickly fell asleep.

I awoke when the four guards on duty opened fire. I leaped up and ran toward my corner of the compound, but a Legionnaire, coming from that direction shouted, "Go back, Hukov. The rebels are already inside!" He had hardly spoken the last word before the rebels, with their knives flashing, descended on us. I had no weapon, so I quickly fell back into the barracks. Although the rebels had broken through only in my corner of the compound, I feared there was nothing we could do to push them back. Every Legionnaire was in a panic.

160

Inside the barracks, I tore at the mosquito netting, trying to find some sort of weapon, and finally stumbled over the heavy machine gun. Quickly I loaded it with a belt.

From that position I could see only the walls of the barracks, but I turned the heavy machine gun in the direction of the rebels. A few Legionnaires were out there, too, perhaps, engaged in hand-to-hand fighting, but men were dying all around me and something had to be done. I opened up the heavy gun, firing bursts through cases where our provisions were stacked, and through the barracks wall. There were many explosive bullets in the ammo belt and they shattered wherever they touched the beds, wall, or even the netting, but the machine gun made such a noise it was impossible to think of danger. I could think only of how loud the gun was.

Then some of my bullets hit a reserve supply of munition, and they began to explode. I crawled as fast as I could to the barracks door. Outside, the lieutenant was shouting orders for the Legionnaires to advance toward the corner I had cleared.

We poured into the corner and found the last rebel leaving over the wall, retreating so fast they left my light machine gun in place at the corner.

One minute later the fort was in our hands, as secure as on the day it was first used. "I tell you," the lieutenant said to my sergeant, "we could not have done it. This fort was lost, we were all dead, and then Hukov started riding that bastard gun. Hukov, you're a crazy man."

"Yes, sir," I said. "Well, I didn't realize it would make so much noise." I was still in a daze from the heavy sound.

The sergeant of my squad, beside himself with happiness at still being alive, came out of the barracks, a bottle of wine in each hand, proposing a toast to me and the heavy machine gun. We passed the bottles around,

161

everybody taking a drink; but our celebration was interrupted by another rebel attack. The natives came out of the jungle, screaming like men cheated, seeking revenge; but we beat them back easily this time, now that we were awake and armed. They attacked a third time and kept up their attacks until just before dawn.

When the sun came out we found fifty dead rebels on the field. Six Legionnaires were dead or dying, and six were wounded, a heavy loss for our platoon of fewer than forty men.

One of the dying was Kraft. He had a machete cut across his stomach, and he had been shot through the right side of his chest. The medic for our outfit only shook his head each time he examined him and moved to another man.

About noon, out of his pain, Kraft said to me, "Hukov, look in that bag there, the one with the leather fold in the side."

I opened the bag. Inside were his personal possessions.

"You see the small kit, a brown one?"

"Yes, I see it." I took it out and opened it. Inside were needles and thick cord.

"Listen, Hukov, you do what I tell you now. I studied medicine once and know what I'm saying. You have to sew up my stomach."

"You're too sick to think about that."

"Now just do what I say."

He told me every step to take and I took it, piercing his skin with the needle and drawing it through, but as he talked his voice became more husky, until it was not clear what he was saying. Then, as if forcing himself to wake up, he came out of his delirium and spoke coherently again.

I followed his orders as the lieutenant looked on. My fingers were trembling so much I could scarcely force the

162

needle through his skin, and my stomach became sick; but I kept thinking that this was all I could do to help him.

When I was halfway across the cut, he suddenly sat erect in bed. He stared straight at the wall for a moment, then fell back on the pillows with a gasp. He was dead.

I stood frozen in terror for a long while, then I took the needle out of his body, cleaned it, and returned it to its case. I wondered if I should gather his personal belongings for his family, for his mother still lived in West Germany. But I decided it would be up to the lieutenant to decide what to do about that.

I was leaving his bed when the Yugoslav in our squad came up to me and said, "You dirty bastard, you killed my friend with that machine gun. You shot among the Legionnaires and killed him."

I did not know whom he meant, until he pointed at Kraft's body. When I started explaining, he turned away. I went after him, but Lieutenant Pilsoner grabbed my arm. "Don't mind what he said. You saved all of us."

But I was deep in sorrow about what this man had told me. I knew that in firing the gun I had been right, but something in my heart made me ill.

Because of this one night of fighting, I was made a corporal, the other machine gunners were made First Class Legionnaires, and the lieutenant received the French Cross.

This recognition came three weeks after the battles, just before we were replaced by French troops and ordered to Lai Thieu, about one hundred kilometers northeast of Saigon. Our whole company of 120 men was there, and we were sent on patrols through the jungle every day. Many of the boys caught malaria, and even the quinine did not seem to help them. Conditions grew worse until there were only ninety men who could fight if attacked.

One day our company received orders from Battalion

163

to find boats and move down river. We went through the jungle to a river and borrowed the natives' fishing boats, promising to return them the next morning. When we had enough boats for our men and supplies, we loaded them and started paddling downstream.

We had about fifteen boats and in each six to ten Legionnaires. At midday, by accident, we passed a rebel camp, and they opened fire from both sides of the river. Many Legionnaires leaped into the water and lost their guns. They floundered about, some of them being shot even before they could strike out for shore. The rest of us started firing at the rebels, but I saw that my boat was sinking, and the feeling came to me that I would die there.

I jumped into the water. My machine gun carried me to the bottom, but luckily the river was not deep. In the dirty water I could see nothing, but I started walking along the bottom.

Finally I came to some tall grass. I got my head above water there and breathed at last. I could see no other Legionnaires, except a few still firing from the sinking boats. Many of them, I knew, could not swim.

Slowly I raised my gun above the surface and emptied the barrel of water. I crept through the grass toward the bank. I knew I would die, so it made no difference to me about the danger. All of us would die. Near the bank I steadied myself, then stood and pulled the trigger.

The gun fired. I swung the muzzle toward the machine gun that was shooting at the Legionnaires. With two bursts I killed the three Japanese who manned it. I opened fire on the guerrilla riflemen while other Legionnaires swam ashore. Some of them had lost their weapons, but two men turned the Japanese machine gun on the rebels, and with that gun and mine, the position was soon taken for the Legion.

164

Captain Rossie of my company shook my hand. "Hukov, I have never seen the equal of what you did." Right then he promised me the rank of sergeant and Croix de Guerre with Silver Star.

But even as he spoke, my courage began to leave me. I began to wonder why it was that I had been the one who had landed first, had opened fire from the grass, had knocked out the machine gun and saved my company. I asked myself how much longer I could hope to live through such engagements, and why I was fighting.

That morning my company made its way out of the jungle and reported our engagement to battalion. The First and Second Companies were sent in to bring out our dead and the weapons which had been lost in the river.

Then, without a chance for rest, our platoon was sent out in three trucks on a long patrol. But, fortunately, it was to take us near Kugy's house, so I welcomed the assignment. One evening when we were parked at Thu Dau Mot, I asked Lieutenant Pilsoner for permission to visit her.

"You love this girl very much?" he asked me, smiling. "Do you love her more than any other woman?"

"Sir, I've loved many women and all of them differently. Now I feel my age coming on, and I think I will settle for a girl I love enough."

"Your age!" he said, laughing. "You are barely *of* age, Sergeant."

"Yes, sir, but before my five-year term is up and I am able to marry, I will be old, indeed."

He walked with me to the jeep and told me to drive it to Kugy's house.

On the short drive I thought of all I would tell her. I had been made a sergeant and decorated, and even though she was not in sympathy with my fighting, she would be happy about my honors. When I reached her

165

house, I was out of the jeep almost before it stopped rolling. "Kugy!" I shouted.

I ran toward her house, but suddenly I stopped. The house was dark, and it seemed strangely still. "Kugy," I said quietly, feeling out the night.

I went closer to the house. Her father was standing in the doorway, watching me, saying nothing.

"What's the matter here?" I said.

"Eddy," he said. "Come in, my son, Eddy." He pushed open the door for me.

I entered, looked about, expecting Kugy to appear. "Where is she?"

"She and some other girls were taking supplies to her brother, Eddy."

"Well, has she come back?"

"Eddy, she's dead. The French have killed her."

13

FOR DAYS I cursed the French. I cursed the French in the barracks, in the compounds, in the jungle. I could not say a word except it be cursing the French. She had been my closest friend, she had been beautiful and clever, and now she had been killed by the French.

My life had been cut off with her death, all my plans had gone with her. There was no future left for me. I could think of nothing except what I had lost because of the French.

You are fighting for the French, I told myself, and I began to look for a chance to desert.

Two weeks after her death, my chance came. We were ordered into trucks to make a long journey. In the northern province of Tonkin, the rebels, who were even stronger than in the south, had broken their truce with the French. In late November, the French had turned artillery and planes against the city of Haophong, killing many Vietnamese. Some estimated 6000, some as high as 20,000, natives dead. So, open war now flared in north Viet Nam, too. On December 19, 1946, Vietnamese turned

167

on the French in Hanoi, attacking with machine guns, mortar, and artillery.

I saw in Lieutenant Pilsoner's face the same harried expression I had seen in the officers in the final days of the war on the Eastern Front. "Hukov, we have to win," he told me, "or France will lose all her colonies, even North Africa. France cannot be a great power in the world, unless we win here in Viet Nam."

"You cannot win," I told him.

He looked at me sharply, but said nothing.

The fort we were to occupy was Dien Bien Phu in north Viet Nam. Our company's convoy, numbering ten trucks, began the journey shortly before Christmas, while Frenchmen still were fighting in the streets of Hanoi. On Christmas Eve, we stopped not far from Stung Treng.

We got drunk that night, and I grew depressed, thinking about my life, wondering when I would get home again or where my home was to be. Two years before on Christmas I had huddled near the tanks on the Western Front. Now I was in even worse shape in far-off Asia. Somehow I had to escape, not only the Legion but the fate which hounded me. I had to have a new chance.

At midnight we fired our guns to celebrate Christ's birth.

The celebration continued. Everybody was dead drunk, including a German from the Second Company who came over to me and shook hands. "Hukov, wish me luck," he said.

"All right. But for what?"

"A long journey."

"What kind of journey?"

"Two hundred fifty kilometers to the west is Thailand, a free country; and from there ships sail to all parts of the world. My journey is going to take me out of the Legion, Hukov."

168

I moved back to the truck where the whisky was kept. "Here," I called to him, "let's have a drink for your long trip."

We drank to his success, each one taking a drink from the bottle.

"You are going alone?" I asked him.

"No, there are several of us. You want to come along?"

"Not now, I'm drunk."

We shook hands, and I watched him as he stumbled away toward his company.

The next morning at eight o'clock a man told me the company commander wanted to see all sergeants and corporals. "Several men have deserted," he said excitedly. I crawled out from under a truck, where I had slept, and walked down the road to company headquarters. Already it was stifling hot.

About fifteen noncoms took places before the captain. He told us that seven men from the Second Company had deserted on the night before and that they had not yet been picked up. "To the west of us is a jungle," he said. "The villages are inhabited by savages, or people little better, and they will shoot Legionnaires. Even if the Legion fails to capture the deserters, the natives or the jungle will kill them. So see to it that every man under you knows the danger facing anybody who deserts."

A mumble acknowledged the order.

"Also, the colonel has heard about this, and he has decided to address all our men at 10:00 A.M."

We returned to our platoons and got the men out of bed. Almost everybody had a hangover, and there was considerable grumbling. But by ten o'clock the company was assembled, standing in three neat lines, when the colonel arrived. He was of the regular French Army, and not of the Legion. With him he brought fifteen tanks and a platoon of troops.

169

Our company commander called us to attention and saluted him. The colonel returned the salute and gave us "at ease." We relaxed and for a moment there was the clanking of rifles, bazookas, and grenades.

The colonel waited for complete silence. Finally he said, "You damned German swine. Last night seven German Legionnaires deserted from the Second Company leaving the Legion in a desperate hour. France is fighting for her life. We need every man who can fight, and I want to tell every German in the Legion that if he wants to desert he can desert at this moment." He pointed toward the tanks. "Desert now and we will blow you to bits!"

The guns of the tanks turned slowly toward us.

I was so angry I could hardly breathe. Here was a French officer condemning Germans for not wanting to die for the glory of France.

"Any of you German swine want to desert?" the colonel shouted.

The Germans in ranks began to whisper angrily. Someone shouted, "Frenchman, you better go home to your own troops and leave the Legion alone!"

Our entire company began to shout and whistle. Rifle shots were fired into the air, and the colonel realized for the first time the dangerous position he was in. A man near me loaded a bazooka shell into its chamber. Other men stuck anti-tank grenades on their rifle attachment. Our company commander ran to the colonel and began to talk frantically.

The colonel turned from him and hurried toward the tanks. Only when he and his tanks had moved down the road in a cloud of dust did order return to the company.

Our captain's voice quivered as he tried to talk to us. "It is only that he is angry because seven men deserted," he said. "You must forget what he said. The rebels have

170

increased their activity so it is a bad time for him. Forget what he said." His whole body was trembling as he tried to decide what else to say to us. "Now, it is Christmas, so we will stay here until nightfall. Just clean your guns, and that will be all the duty for today."

He called us to attention, then dismissed the company.

Immediately I went to the two strongest men in my squad, both Germans. I told them that I planned to desert the Legion that day and that I hoped they would come with me.

"Desert in the daytime?" one of them said. "Desert after that speech?"

"I will desert today," I said. "I have been hounded through all Europe, North Africa, and Viet Nam. I have lost my family and my closest friends, and now I am through with this. I am going to go my own way from this moment on."

They could not quite get up courage enough to go with me, so they started drinking whisky by glassfuls. After the second glass still neither of them had courage enough to go. They drank two more glasses each, then they did not recognize me when I spoke to them.

Angrily I left them and sought out other Legionnaires, trying to find somebody interested in going to Thailand. I soon found two, both good friends. One of them was Reinhold Turkart, who had fought beside me in the prison in France. The other was Gustav Romman. Both knew I had been in the SS and had faith that I could lead them to Thailand.

At noon we received our food, but I could not eat. I went to the truck where my squad's machine gun was kept and ordered a man to clean it. Then I went to the man who tended the infirmary and told him I was deserting. He gave me medicine and bandages.

171

I went to the lieutenant's truck and stole his map. I saw on the map that the highway we were following would take us to Pakse, which was very close to the Thai border, and it occurred to me that we should wait until the next day. But there was the chance the captain would not stop the trucks there, or anywhere else, once they came near Thailand.

I decided that it was better to go on with my plans.

In midafternoon I went to the man cleaning the light machine gun and took it from him, leaving the tripod.

It was four o'clock when I joined Reinhold and Gustav. Reinhold had a Garand rifle with a tank-grenade attachment, and Gustav had a sub-machine gun. Together we walked away from the convoy, moving down the road to the south. Nobody seemed to notice us. But when we were only an hour away, Reinhold called out to me, "Look, Hukov!"

A truck loaded with Legionnaires was coming toward us, and behind it was a French tank. Gustav whirled on me. "Let's go back. It'll not be hard with us if we go back now."

"Never will I go back," I said.

The truck began slowing down. The three of us jumped to one side of the road and ran down a path. We crossed a narrow swamp, where Gustav and I both lost our shoes. We ran for our lives.

But soon we came to the Mekong River. Only one boat was in sight, and that was quite far away.

"We will not surrender," I said.

Reinhold said, "We'll die, but not surrender. That's just as well."

Desperately we called toward the boat, and an old man started rowing toward us. Gustav opened fire, hoping to delay the French, until the old man reached us.

When his boat was within reach, we leaped in and Reinhold grabbed the paddle. He paddled for the opposite bank, but the French sighted us before we reached it, and they opened fire. We left the boat and splashed through the water to shore, then dashed into the jungle.

14

WE STOPPED at midnight to rest, and at dawn we began marching again. The rainy season had passed but the fields were still swampy. We kept going, swatting at the mosquitoes, so big they could be squashed between the fingers like beetles, pushing through densely-grown thickets that only rats had been through before. Sometimes we cut our way with a machete, hacking down the growth, as insects swarmed up and small animals' nests were exposed. Since neither Gustav nor I had shoes, we had to proceed carefully.

"Are there no roads near here, Hukov?" Gustav asked.

"Yes, but the French control them and keep them patrolled."

"Well, are there no trails?"

"They're patrolled by Cambodian rebels."

"Well, where the hell are we?" he said.

"On the map this land is marked as being held by neither. We're between two flames of fire."

At noon we came to a marshland, thickly covered with reeds and plants, stretching to the horizon. None of us said anything for a while, but we stood shoulder to shoulder and peered out at that impassable country.

"How will we get around this?" Reinhold said.

I took out the map and studied it, seeing that this was a huge swamp that went for many miles. "There's no way around it."

Reinhold peered out at the horizon. "No way through it, either."

"But it's safer through it," I said, rolling up the map and sticking it inside my shirt. I hoisted the heavy gun to my shoulder and set the belt of ammo around my neck. Then I stepped off into the marsh and started hacking a way.

As we moved deeper into the marshland the water came higher around our legs. As night began to fall the water was at our knees, and there was not a place where we could lie down to sleep. The insects attacked us. In the moonlight, I could see that Gustav's shirt was covered with them. Even his head was covered, so that he was a moving mass of insects, following Reinhold, who was hacking at the brush, making a path for us.

"Hukov," Gustav said, choking on his anger and pain, "we have got to get out of here. My God——"

"No," I said sharply, feeling the same rising panic. "Now, we have to pass the big test."

Reinhold brought the machete fiercely against the growth of reeds. "By God," he said, "let's talk about having a room in Bangkok and calling for some girls and whisky."

"Yes," I said, "that's a nice thought. I tell you, boys, all this is a place of testing. It's here that we are cleansed of all our sins, and we will come out on the other side better men."

"Good God," Gustav said in disgust, then stumbled and fell face forward into the water. He pushed himself back to his feet and started swatting frantically at the insects; but he soon wearied of that and again turned to follow

Reinhold, who, patiently and steadily, had moved on ahead.

That night we proceeded, each man in his own nightmare, and in the morning as the sun rose behind us, we stood on tiptoes to see as far as we could, expecting to see some land out there.

"I don't see a thing," Reinhold said.

"It's too early yet. There's not enough light."

"Hukov, don't be a fool. I can see the horizon line. There's nothing but this marsh."

"No," I said, "there has to be high land soon."

But as the sun rose I had to admit that, no matter how I tried to peer into the mist before us, there was not one sign of land ahead, and when I looked back, there was not a sign of land behind us, either. The three of us were the only shapes rising above the vegetation of that whole swamp.

Every half hour or so we would change off. The man in front would hand the knife to the man behind him and stand aside, spent and quivering from exhaustion, as the other two moved past him. Of the three, I had the hardest time, because as I swished the knife through the air, I had to balance the light machine gun on my shoulder, and the metal of the gun grew hot in the sun and the knobs on the gun dented my shoulder and bruised my muscles so that every swish brought a live, quivering pain.

"Hukov, you were crazy to bring that gun," Gustav said.

"Throw it away, Eddy," Reinhold said. "Just let it splash into the water with that belt of ammunition and don't worry about it. We have two guns and some grenades besides."

"Later," I said.

"You only punish yourself with it."

"Well, I have many sins," I said.

177

That day the water rose to our waists. In one place we saw some crocodiles, a few of them two meters long, and we proceeded very slowly through the dark, murky water, which swirled with surface insects breeding and catching their food.

"They like to go to sleep about twilight," Reinhold said. "We must be more careful now, or we'll step on one of them."

"Hukov, I don't think I can stand another night out here," Gustav said. "Let's turn back, men, for God's sake."

"If we turn back we'll have to spend a night out here, also," I said.

"Well, Jesus, Jesus, where the hell is land?"

"Not far," Reinhold said. "Isn't this swamp on the map, Eddy?"

"Yes, but it's not this size on the map. Now it's swollen with rains."

"I can't spend another night out here, I tell you," Gustav said. "I feel my body already crawling with insects."

Reinhold said, "There's nothing to do but . . ." and he said nothing more, for out of the water, brushing against him, rose a crocodile, taking a leap, splitting the water around him. We fell over each other getting back, and Gustav, hot-tempered as always, suddenly lobbed a grenade toward the place the crocodile had been, so that all of us had to fall down into the water and pray for safety for ourselves. The grenade went off under the water. A small wave circled out through the weeds and crossed over us, and when we looked at the place where our path had stopped, we saw several dead fish and two dead baby crocodiles rise to the surface.

Gustav ran to the spot and took up a fish. With his knife he ripped it down the middle and then began to chew on it. Reinhold watched him with disgust, as did I,

178

but our bodies also needed strength, so we joined Gustav and each ate a fish.

That night I wept as I walked. My feet were like bruised clubs without feeling, swollen, and cut. Gustav also was in severe pain because of his feet. My shoulders bent forward under the weight of the gun and my neck ached at the back, so that each time my head moved, my eyes squinted in anguish. The insects swarmed at us and began to crawl in our noses and ears; there was no defense against them. All we had was our hope. All we could think of was the morning when we would see land ahead. We told each other it meant nothing that the water was still sloshing around our waists. Soon we would come to a steep bank and climb up to dry land.

Morning came and we saw before us, to each side and behind, the same flat land, water-soaked and reed-coated. In gasps we breathed the air, thanked God for the warm sun rays, which were drying out our shirts; but as the day went on, the sun began to blister our foreheads with its heat.

Gustav, shivering with fear and pain, stopped in the path in early afternoon and turned to face me. "You God damned bastard, get me out of here or I'll kill you."

My throat was so clogged with my own fear I could hardly speak. "God will—take care of us," I whispered.

"God damn that! This is the end of the world! Don't you know we're two days out in a water grave? Do you think we could go back those two days' distance and get to dry land? Do you think we'd make it?" Gustav's head was quivering in his rage.

"We'll make it," Reinhold whispered. He looked up at the blue, clear sky. "We'll make it."

Night came creeping in as we pleaded with the horizon to show us one tree, one sign of hope for that whole night.

179

The insects, always worse at night, came again to feed on us. "Gustav, do you have a piece of fish?"

Cursing, he handed me half a fish from the supply he kept in his pocket. I chewed on the meat, careless about the bones, chewing and spitting out what my throat would not swallow.

A wind rose. It cooled my cheeks as it grew stronger. The insects buzzed angrily.

Gustav said, "Listen, I tell you, we have to do something very quick and very sure, or we are dead men." His hand grasped my arm. "Hukov, please, for God's sake, do something."

"Listen," I said, "I tell you, think only of Bangkok and a clean bed."

"God!" Gustav shouted in exasperation. He slugged me in the face. I and my gun went down into the water. I came up out of the water, and was about to club him when Reinhold grabbed my arm.

"No, Eddy, stop, you hear me?" In the darkness, so dark I could not see his face, he said, "Let's think of nothing. That's the best thought. Turn off our minds and walk."

He started on, and we heard his knife hack some weeds blocking our path, so we followed.

The next morning I did not have enough courage to look ahead, even to lift my head in hope, to see if land was before us. All I did was walk toward the west, like a man possessed. I could think of nothing. I could move the knife up and down in a swing, but if I wanted to speak, I had to force myself to think. I would stop in the path and try to settle on some word in German that might mean "tomorrow," or whatever was my thought; and sometimes I could not think of the word in German, but would think of it in Polish or Russian, and if not those, then perhaps in English or French, and if not those, then in Vietnamese.

"Tomorrow," I would say at last, and the other two men would stop in the path and stand like mummies as their minds took hold of the word.

That night I did not look high enough to see a single star. We stumbled on, the water at our belts, no lower and no higher. The vast swamp would settle for that until we fell and could not stand up again.

The next day, the fifth day in water, we moved slowly. The machine gun was now a part of my body, so that I no longer thought of throwing it away, any more than I would think of throwing my arm away. I wondered if I had lost the ammunition, or if it was still with me. But I did not have the presence of mind to think to find out, nor did I know how to go about it.

At noon that day, we stopped. Reinhold took a grenade off his belt and lobbed it as far ahead of us as he could. We stood like statues as it exploded in the reeds; then we made our way to that spot and tore open fish with our mouths and then threw the flesh up from our stomachs, then ate some more and swallowed it and threw it up, so that I settled for just chewing on the fish and letting the strong juice go down my throat.

When we had some strength, we moved on again. I fell and Gustav helped me up, but as I rose, I saw under the water one of his feet and the skin was white as a fish's belly and was wrinkled like a man's a thousand years old. "No," I said, meaning it for myself, a spoken prayer that my own feet and legs would not be in the same condition. But I did not know how to see my own, so I stuck my head once more under the water and stared at Gustav's feet, until he caught me by the hair and pulled my head out of the water.

We moved on until twilight, when a bird began to

circle above us, coming very low. It was a small bird and we had no fear of it, and then I decided it thought we were trees and wanted to light on us and roost for the night. I laughed, a chuckle that hardly seemed to come from me at all, and Gustav and Reinhold laughed, also, but the laughter did not come from them, but from a distance, way beyond where we were or could see. Somebody was laughing at us from far off.

So night came again, and we could not sit down, much less lie down, and nobody could go to sleep. We staggered like men long drunk, but knowing that if we lost consciousness we were dead. "I once loved a woman in . . ." Reinhold suddenly said in a loud voice, then stopped. "Huh, hell, I dunno," he mumbled.

I took some air into my lungs and clenched my fists. I was about to speak, but with my mouth open, I realized I had no words to say.

I heard Gustav weeping, or was I weeping? One of us was weeping. I wanted to know which one, but how do you tell who's weeping?

So we came to the sixth day. That day I could see myself clearly, but not from inside. I could see myself from twenty feet away, walking through water that was sloshing at my belt, and I was proud of myself as I watched, for I took even steps, and my head was steady on my neck, although bent down, and my shoulders, although humped, were still part of the machine gun. I was part of the machine gun as it moved on.

Then suddenly a flurry of shots went off and I stopped, stunned, and looked up as Gustav lowered his gun. Ahead of us two birds fell from the sky into the water.

Crazily I tore through the brush to get a bird. Reinhold was behind me and Gustav ahead of me, but Gustav fell. The machine gun beat against the side of my head as I ran, but I was the first man to reach the place the birds

182

had landed. I was where I knew the birds fell, but there was nothing there. I parted the thickets to either side, then began to beat at the thickets, but there were no birds. Reinhold and Gustav were also beating the thickets. We stood there, as I watched myself, and beat at the thickets until it was dark and we could see nothing. So I faded from my own sight.

On the seventh day, with the sun drying us, I heard Reinhold whisper in a hoarse voice, "See!" He was pointing at his thighs. I stared at his thigh and saw nothing, except how the cloth was falling away from the seams; but he ran his hand down over his thigh and then Gustav began to chuckle inside his throat. I understood then and felt my own thighs, drying in the sun.

I stumbled forward, grabbed the knife from Gustav and began to hack a path, moving faster, and as we moved the water fell some more, so that an hour later we were only knee deep in water. Then we sank down and sat in the cold mud and splashed in the water. We laughed to be off our feet.

We got up and began to run, stumbling along, and when we were exhausted, we stopped, still not in sight of land. We looked at one another and at the horizon, as if it were a nasty trick for God to play on decent men, to hide our land. Then we stumbled forward, not clearing a path now, but pushing through.

When the sun was directly overhead I stopped. I dangled the knife before me and let it drop. Gustav picked it up from the mud and began chopping at a cane. I sat down and held the machine gun in my arms and rocked it like a baby. "Lene," I said to it, "my pretty Lene."

Reinhold came up to me and hovered about unsteadily. He leaned over and put his hand on my shoulder, bracing himself. "Come along, Eddy."

183

I shook off his hand, grabbed his belt and tried to rise, but his belt broke in my hand and I fell back, stretched out. I rolled over and pushed myself to my knees. I got up and then saw my gun in the water. I knelt back down and got the gun and put it on my shoulder, then I staggered to my feet and started forward, not sure which direction was which now, for there was no shadow to show where the sun was.

But the water fell some more so that it washed our shins. We pushed through brush for hours until trees rose ahead of us. I did not know where Reinhold was, or Gustav either; but I could not stop my stumbling forward. I heard a splash behind me, but I kept on running. Each man must carry himself to the trees. And soon I realized there was no water.

With a cry I raised the machine gun above my head and hurled it aside. I fell to my knees and bent over and dug my face into the soft earth. I rolled over on my side, feeling clean and spent, as sleep came over me.

When I awoke it was just dawn, and so I decided it was the next day. Gustav was sitting under a big tree, staring at his raw feet as if they could not be understood. Beyond him I saw the sprawled out, sleeping form of Reinhold, now so closely a part of the earth and leaves that he looked as if he had been formed there.

I lay back, my hands clenched behind my head, and stared up through the cool covering of leaves where monkeys flitted about, noisily announcing to one another that the water had produced strange fruit. I lay there soaking into my body the simple fact that I was on land, not water, that the test was over and I was alive, that no more would I have to walk with insects covering me.

Gustav suddenly put his hands over his face, then wiped them hard down over his skin, as if to release his mind from a horrible thought. He peered over at me. Reinhold turned over on the ground and sat up. He stared ahead for a moment, then he saw Gustav and then he saw me. A big grin came to his face.

I got up and hobbled over to him. I knelt down beside him and patted his face with one hand. "Big walk's over," I said.

"Yes," he said, laughing. Then we looked out over the broad marsh that we would never cross again.

"Well," I said, rising, "I'm a hungry man. I think I'll find some dinner." I picked up my machine gun and loaded it and started into the jungle. Behind me Gustav and Reinhold, holding onto each other for support, followed.

I walked for a kilometer and saw nothing except monkeys in the trees, chattering and following us overhead. We kept moving on, but there was nothing. My stomach felt like a small ball, no larger than a fist.

Then I heard the shattering sound of gun fire and spun around to see Gustav firing away at the monkeys. Some of them fell around us, their bodies plopping onto the soft ground. Instantly Gustav was on his knees, ripping one apart with his knife.

I turned away and tried to vomit, but there was nothing in my stomach. I sat down and throaty sounds came out of me as I saw the little monkeys, dead and wounded, and heard the chattering of their families overhead. I reached out and took a dead monkey and held it in my hands as if it were a hairy, cotton-stuffed puppy.

I took out a small box of matches and tried to strike one, so that I could light a fire, but the ends broke off. I tried four or five and realized they would not work because of the wet crossing.

I laid some of them out on a rock to dry. As the sun began to set, I moved my matches into the final rays of

185

light, and when they were almost gone I tried to light the matches, but it was no use.

Reinhold brought his monkey over and sat down beside me. We took out our knives and began to eat the raw flesh.

With the fresh monkey meat in us, we gained strength, and with some moonlight to see by, we started toward the west; but two or three hours later Reinhold grabbed his stomach and fell to the ground, crying out in the throes of a grippe. Quickly I gave him some Brooklex, to clean out his stomach, and anticholera pills. Then the sickness hit me, and then it hit Gustav, so that all three of us were lying on the ground, doubled up in fierce pains.

I forced my fingers into my throat as far as they would go and vomited up the monkey meat. Almost immediately I felt better. Reinhold and Gustav did the same, and we soon were well, but very weak.

"We have to walk," I said, my words coming out slowly.

The three of us got up and stumbled off toward the west.

At morning we came to a river. There was little hope that we could cross it with no more strength than we had, and we sat down on its bank and stared at the flowing water. Then on the other bank we heard dogs barking, and immediately we knew there was a village over there. We stood up, nobody speaking, and waded out into the stream, our eyes gleaming with the thought of food.

The water came up to our shoulders, and then I stepped off over my head. I swam and walked and fought my way across the deep part, carrying the gun, until my feet touched the rocky bottom again. I went on to the other bank. There I started toward where the dogs were barking.

"French troops could be in the village, Hukov," Reinhold called out to me.

186

I moved on. Let one Frenchman stand between me and food and I would cut him in two with my gun.

"Or rebels," Gustav said.

I did not care about rebels, either. I would cut them in two.

The barking grew louder, and as we emerged from the jungle into the village clearing, the barking changed to nervous yelps. The villagers stopped their work of preparing a meal and stared at us, three heavily bearded men, our clothing half torn from our bodies, armed like inhabitants of another planet. As we approached, the natives fell back, then began to run. Gustav, Reinhold, and I entered a bamboo house, where we found rice and fried fish.

We ate all the food there and, still desperate, moved down the village street, searching for more. We went into another of the houses, and there found cold rice. We ate that. We went on down the street to another house and went into that. And when we had eaten all we could hold, our stomachs rumbling and coughing in protest, we stuffed our pockets full of rice and dried fish. Also we got some matches.

We came out of the house to see, standing before us, some thirty natives, the women half naked. They had jungle knives with which to kill us. Also two old men had French rifles, which could only be loaded from the end of the barrel and were good for one shot at a load.

Our weapons were in our hands ready for use. Gustav raised his, but Reinhold reached out and slapped the barrel. "Put it down," he said. Then he turned to me. "What shall we do?"

I was thinking of the time I helped the German farmers win back their village, and now here these poor farmers were facing our invasion. It had taken more than a little courage for them to return. I wanted to explain to them

187

that we meant no harm, but we were armed and they were armed, so there was immediate danger.

I raised my machine gun and pointed it into the air. I squeezed off five or six shots. The rapid fire shocked the air. The faces before us seemed to melt with fear. Women suddenly dropped their knives and grabbed their children as they ran away. The two old men threw their French rifles aside in their haste, and the whole population fled down the street.

That day we got our strength back and our laughter returned. That night we made a fire to keep back the mosquitoes and tigers, and stretched out our legs, resting back on the ground. "Now, this," Reinhold said, "is the real life. It was a fine idea, this little trip, Hukov."

"Well, I thought a walk through the jungle would do us good, boys."

"It's very refreshing," Reinhold said.

Gustav grunted disapproval of our conversation, but we paid no attention to him. "Gustav won't be happy until Germany wins the war," Reinhold said.

"That's right," Gustav said angrily.

I stared at him, unable to grasp a concept of another war between Germany and the world.

"Gustav is a good Nazi," Reinhold said, "even in the jungle. It's hard to be a good Nazi in a jungle, Eddy."

"I'm very much impressed," I said. I reached out and caught Gustav's arm. "But you stay with us, Nazi. We need you, boy, on this trip."

That night we slept like children, and the next morning, refreshed and content, we warmed ourselves in the sun. Not until midday did Reinhold begin to get restless. "Let's not forget our walk for the day," he said. "We must have our exercise."

"Hell," Gustav said, aggravated by any attempt at hu-

188

mor. "How much farther is that damn country, Hukov?"

I took out the map and studied it, but I had less faith in it now than I had back in the Legion camp. "Well, since we are lost, I don't know how far it is," I said, "unless we are not lost but are right here." I made all the calculations I knew and decided that that point could very well be where we were. "In that case, from here, we could be there in a very little time if we were to fly in an airplane."

Gustav let out a stream of obscenity and broke a club against a tree. Reinhold yawned sleepily. "How far if we decide to walk?"

I folded up the map. "About 180 kilometers."

Reinhold nodded, still yawning, and peered off into the jungle. "I suppose the direction is still westward?"

"If you want the shortest route," I said.

"Let's take the shortest route," he said. "Once we get there we can plan other jungle trips, as we please."

Gustav was now so furious he was red in the face, and Reinhold and I decided we had better move on and say no more at that time.

We had assumed that we would find many native villages in the jungle and that food would not be a problem, but we found no others for several days. Also we saw no game to shoot, except a few birds, that we could shoot with Gustav's sub-machine gun. In the damp jungle, bothered by the slow progress we could make, never certain that we would not be set upon by rebels or wild animals, we grew despondent. A dizziness came to my head, so that sometimes I could not judge distance, even as to where my foot would fall, and I would stumble. The dizziness grew until I had to stop every ten minutes or so, but since Reinhold and Gustav were also weak from hunger and exertion, they thought that these were only normal rest stops on our trip. I told myself I had a jungle fever that would pass over, as jungle fevers do; but I be-

189

gan taking quinine, in case it was malaria. That did no good.

Finally, one afternoon, I fell and was surprised to find I did not have enough strength to get back on my feet. Reinhold tried to help me, but he was almost at the end of his strength, too, and so he stumbled around ineffectually.

I lay back on the ground, tears in my eyes, for never before had I been ill. For the first time in my whole life, I felt absolutely helpless.

Reinhold touched my forehead with his hand.

"What's the temperature?" I asked.

"It's—it's a hot temperature for a man, Eddy."

His face blurred. "Well, look, you do what I ask. You take the map out of my shirt, and the compass, and the medicine. You and Gustav go on as far as you can, and maybe you'll find food."

"Oh," he said, a small smile on his face, "no, Eddy. You have the wrong man."

"Now, damn it, Reinhold, you do what I ask."

He laughed and went aside to where Gustav was waiting and sat down. The two of them began to make ready to stay there for the night. Gustav gathered wood for a fire.

"No," I said angrily, but my eyes blurred and suddenly my mind began to fall, as if through a distance.

When I awoke, it was still light, though dim, and Gustav and Reinhold were sitting by the fire, both of them making deep, moaning sounds in their misery. I tried to sit up but could not, so I called Reinhold over to me. I got one hand inside my shirt, found the map, and dropped it on the ground at his feet. I tried to get a hand into my one good pocket, where I kept the compass, but I had no strength, so Reinhold got it out for me. I tried to speak,

190

but could not, and then he nodded, tears in his eyes. "Eddy, good God, Eddy . . ."

He turned away and went back to Gustav, and they had a conversation. Then he sat down beside Gustav, and they sat there until it was night. I tried to sit up again and failing that, made a gurgling sound in my throat, so that Reinhold came over to me.

"You—go now," I whispered.

He knelt beside me and felt my forehead. I felt the cold touch of his fingers on my skin as I lost consciousness.

15

WHEN I AWOKE the fire was low and Gustav and Reinhold were gone. Still beside me were the map, the compass and the chest of medicine, but the chest was open, and some of the medicine was gone.

Through the tall trees I saw the stars and thought of my helplessness. "God Almighty, did You forget about me?" I said. "If not, where are Your angels?"

I began to pray to God and Jesus, to my dead father, and my sister Lene. "Lene, you came to me on that day when I didn't need help, but now I need help, and you are not here. Lene, I want to see you."

I waited, but she did not appear.

"God, I want to see Lene," I said.

I prayed until morning. I lay motionless on the ground and looked at the rising sun. I thought of my life as a path behind me, then I went to sleep and dreamed of the swamp.

I woke up with a cry.

I looked around at the tall trees and wondered how many shapes life takes.

So this is death, I thought. It is easy. No wonder I have no fear of death.

The sun was high. I began to feel lazy. You should rise from your bed and get walking, I told myself, even though I knew I could not rise to my feet.

The sun cut through the trees and blinded me, so I closed my eyes. The sun began to bake my face, so I tried to turn over and found, to my surprise, that I had strength enough to do it easily.

I pushed myself up on one elbow. I pushed myself to a kneeling position, then stood up. I felt my forehead and there was no fever, only the warmth left by the sun.

I picked up my machine gun. I could lift it with little effort. I leaped up and down and laughed at the jungle and at the idea that I would ever die. I kissed the machine gun. "Boy, you are a dear friend, sir," I told it. I began to sing a German marching song, and with the supplies crammed into my pockets, started walking, still singing.

I walked for hours, happy with my new strength, unwilling to stop for fear it would go away in rest as stealthily as it had come. The jungle disease had had its night; now I was well again, and I would not give it another chance at me.

In late afternoon I heard a voice behind me. I whirled around.

"Hukov, don't shoot. Hukov, it's Reinhold."

He parted the undergrowth and peered out. I sank to the ground, laughing.

"Eddy, you are a ghost," Reinhold said. He and Gustav approached cautiously.

"How the hell did you two get behind me?" I said. "I was sleeping the whole night, while you were marching. I thought you would already be in Bangkok having your lunch."

They began to laugh and Reinhold to weep.

"Why the hell are you crying?" I asked him.

194

"Well, I am happy to meet you again. You are my brother and I didn't want to leave you alone in the jungle, but I thought you were dead, Eddy."

Happily we marched the whole day. Just before nightfall we stopped to study the map. "Boys," I said, "we are nearing a road and probably will cross it tonight. It goes from Sisophon to Battambang, and the French might patrol it."

We checked our guns. They were in good condition.

At ten o'clock, we reached the road. Before crossing it, we waited for several minutes, listening. There was nothing. Then, just as we started across, headlights appeared far down the highway. We ran off the road and hid in the grass behind some trees.

The truck approached, decreasing speed. It stopped directly in front of us and about a dozen French soldiers jumped off and came into the bushes toward us. I heard Reinhold click off the safety of his rifle.

Then I realized that they did not know we were there, that they intended to use the bushes as a lavatory. Still it was a dangerous situation; the soldiers were directly in front of us and only ten feet away.

Suddenly Gustav's gun went off.

The French soldiers leaped up; everything was confusion. "Natives!" "Rebels!" they shouted. Men grabbed their pants with one hand and their rifles with the other. They started back to the truck, some of them before they had their pants up. They climbed over one another getting into the truck, and the driver started down the road while three of them were still not aboard. Two of these were pulled in over the tail gate, but the last of them, a sergeant, ran along behind, one hand holding his pants and the other his rifle, bellowing out orders for the truck to stop. The last we saw of him he was not yet aboard.

I could not help laughing. Gustav laughed, too, but

195

Reinhold was in a rage. "Why did your gun go off?" he demanded of Gustav. "They weren't doing anything to us and wouldn't have seen us."

"Yes, you could have gotten us in trouble," I said to him. "What would you think if Reinhold and I should open fire on the French, get all three of us involved, maybe cost us our lives?"

Gustav listened to all this attentively, but there was a big grin on his face.

The next morning we studied the map. In our area were numerous crosses and other marks made with a red pencil, which indicated guerrillas. But we selected a nearby village and headed for it. There we fed ourselves, taking what we wanted, and ignoring the natives, who seemed to be afraid of us. We saw not one armed man, yet on the map the village was marked in red as a dangerous place.

Once away from the village, we stopped for a rest. Gustav began to talk at long length about what he would do to the women when he got to Bangkok, but we did not care much about his exploits at that point.

I said, "What I want to do is get on a ship leaving Asia."

"I want to go to Latin America again," Reinhold said, "and maybe once more to the United States."

"What? You've been there?" I said.

"Yes, when I was in the German Merchant Marine."

"What's that country like?" Gustav asked suspiciously.

"New York City is as much of it as I saw, and it's a rich place. The buildings are high, and it is big, with people from every country living there. And the harbor is good."

"What about the girls?" Gustav said.

"Yes, there are girls there," Reinhold said, winking at me.

"Well, I know that," Gustav said, "but what do they look like?"

196

"Like girls from all the countries. You see every possible kind of human being in New York City. If you take a cab from the docks and get off at Times Square at 42nd Street, you can stand there and see girls that look like French, German, Latvian, English, Spanish, African, Chinese . . ."

"I will have to see it," I said, rising from the ground. "I'm on my way there now."

"But first we must get to Bangkok," Gustav said in a sad voice.

"Come on," I said, "and no more talk. It's eighty kilometers to Thailand, and from the border we must get to the city, and from the city to the ships. We have a long way to go yet."

Gustav and Reinhold pushed themselves up from the ground, and we started out. "I don't know which would be better, to go to the United States or Latin America," Reinhold said to us. "I like warm blood in a person. There is too much cold-bloodedness in the northern European and in most Americans."

"Well, we will have to think about that," I said. "We'll talk more when we get back to Bangkok and see what ships are available. The important thing is to get to Bangkok and get to the docks, then——"

Rifle shots rang out. Instantly we hit the ground.

We lay there, each man trembling, the three of us spread out like spokes of a wheel. Reinhold put a rifle grenade on the tip of his Garand. Gustav and I put hand grenades by our right hands, ready to pull the pins and throw.

"They have disappeared," Gustav whispered. "There's not a sound."

"Yes," I said, "they're out there though, moving up."

"But why did they fire rifles so soon and warn us?" Reinhold asked.

197

"Nobody can answer such questions," I said. "It's usually a native's mistake that saves the white man."

Suddenly there was a cry, "Banzai, banzai, Isara, Isara." I got to my knees, braced my machine gun at my hip and opened fire, spraying bullets in a half-circle which tore off low limbs of trees above the guerrillas. Gustav's automatic also fired in short bursts, and Reinhold fired a rifle grenade that went off against a tree, splattering shrapnel in a singing, swishing wave.

I swung around and fired over Reinhold's head, my bullets cutting through the leaves. Reinhold set another anti-tank grenade on the tip of his rifle barrel and exploded it against another tree. The tree broke at the trunk and fell.

"Go back," I shouted at the natives. "Get back or we'll have to kill all of you." I felt pride in their courage as they came on against our heavy arms, carrying only knives and outdated rifles. But their courage had been shaken by our automatic weapons, by the grenades and the anti-tank shells, which had terrified them. Momentarily, they were deafened and frightened, and when I shouted at them and waved them back, many turned and ran away.

Reinhold lobbed a grenade into the jungle. Gustav and I did the same. I opened up with a long burst of machine gun fire, splattering the bullets into the trees. The rest of the natives broke order and fled.

Reinhold sank back on the ground, ran his hands over his bloody face. I crawled over to him to see if he was all right. There was not a wound on him, except where broken tree limbs had cut his face and body, as they had mine.

I rolled back to my gun and got up, moved several yards into the jungle, and far off down an animal trail I saw two natives fleeing. I called to Gustav and Reinhold, and we began to run in the opposite direction. We ran until we dropped, and lay on the ground gasping for breath and asking God to spare us another attack.

We lay there for half an hour, then pushed on. That night two men stood guard while one man slept, and at dawn we started again. Late that afternoon we heard dogs barking, so we knew we were near another village. Our stomachs were growling from hunger, and still we had at least two days more of walking before we could reach Thailand.

But Reinhold advised that we not enter this village. "We have almost no ammunition, Hukov. Gustav has three grenades and only fifteen shots, and you have only a few rounds, also."

"I have twenty-five," I said.

"Which is not enough for a long fight. I think we should keep walking and not go near a native."

"I don't know," I said. "All the villagers have left us alone, except these last ones."

Gustav, nursing his gun, said, "Hukov is right. Our matches are gone, and it's the only way to get safe food."

Reinhold consented, and the three of us followed the sound of the barking dogs until we saw the bamboo houses. Then we moved into the open street, acting as if we were not afraid.

It was a larger village than the others, and here not one villager showed fear of us. They looked up, curious, and they called to each other to look at us; but not one woman grabbed her baby, not one man reached for a gun or a knife.

"What the hell?" Gustav said, more nonplussed even than I.

We went down the street to the largest house, which sat high on bamboo poles. I went inside, Reinhold waiting with Gustav who could not be trusted alone, as he might fire his gun. Inside the house the natives stared at

199

me, but not one of them seemed to be afraid. "Food," I said in Vietnamese, and made motions of eating.

No one moved.

Seeing nothing to eat, I went back outside. About fifty natives had gathered at the house. A few of the men were armed.

Gustav said, "Let's send a couple of shots into the air, Hukov."

"No," I said, "these are good people." I took my machine gun off my shoulder and studied the group. A stocky, well-made man of about forty, one of the older men there, seemed to be a leader. I approached him, moving slowly, holding the machine gun out as a gift.

A mumble started among the natives and grew in excitement. The native leader stared at the gun, then he touched it. Instantly, the mumble stopped. He laid his hands on top of the gun, then put his hands around it. He juggled the gun up and down, and indicated that it was heavy. I nodded in agreement.

The other natives moved in closer. Some of the men laid one finger on the gun, some ran their hands over it, some grasped it firmly; but the leader did not relinquish it to anybody.

I saw the natives never would finish looking at the machine gun, so I interrupted by saying in Vietnamese, "We are friends."

A hush came over the group. Three or four other older men moved up to stand beside the leader. Once more I spoke, this time to all of the older men. "We are friends and mean no harm."

The leaders peered at each other, then back at me.

"We go from the Legion," I said. I pointed to the west. "We go to Thailand."

The man with the machine gun was concentrating on

200

my words. The flicker of a smile came to his face. "Muang Thai?" he asked.

I stared back at him. "Muang Thai?"

He nodded, then said, "Indothin?"

Reinhold said to me, "Maybe Indothin is Indochina." Gustav shrugged. He was nursing his sub-machine gun, looking stern and suspicious.

The natives were awaiting our answer. I picked up a piece of charcoal and drew a straight line in the dirt. Pointing to one side I said, "Indothin," and pointing to the other I said, "Muang Thai."

All the natives nodded excitedly.

I pointed to Reinhold, Gustav and myself and said, "Muang Thai."

Happily the leader turned to the assembly and began making a loud speech. Everybody nodded and laughed, and some of the women ran back to the houses. They returned with food, which they set down in bowls before us on the ground, fried chicken, rice, boiled chicken eggs, bananas and other fruits.

Gustav forgot his fear of the natives. His appetite was fully awakened. The three of us ate so rapidly the natives became fascinated with us.

We finished dinner, then leaned back against the supporting poles of a house, more than satisfied. Gustav and Reinhold were permitted to doze off, but the natives wanted to see my machine gun in operation. I led them to the main street, there loaded the weapon, and pointed to a towering tree at the end of the street, indicating its trunk as my target. I braced the gun against my hip and squeezed off a short burst.

Instantly Gustav was on his feet, ready for what he believed to be an attack. The natives were at first startled, then insulted. An awkward pause followed. I knew of nothing to do except laugh, which I did; and fortunately,

201

laughter was a language everybody understood. All the natives laughed at poor Gustav until he retreated angrily back to his shady spot and sat down.

I unloaded my gun and gave it back to the young men, then went over to sit beside him. He was so angry with me he would not answer any question I asked. "Look," I said, "you are too anxious to show you can't be fooled by anybody's kindness. These are our friends now. If we had tried to frighten them, we would have made enemies. Our big mistake was made in the first village where I fired off shots to frighten the natives. Even there we could have had a good time with them and maybe gotten help."

Gustav patted the stock of his sub-machine gun and peered suspiciously at the happy natives.

Reinhold said, "You're right, Eddy. It's a big lesson for us."

Gustav spat in the dirt. "The natives will kill both of you soon."

Reinhold and I stared at Gustav angrily, but I recalled incidents in the Legion when natives had guided us into traps.

We rested in the shade until our meal was settled, then we made ready to leave. Seeing this, two Buddhist monks came toward us, each carrying a jug of water and a pouch, probably full of food. "Muang Thai," they said.

"My Lord," Reinhold said, "they're going to guide us."

Once more the people gathered, now to say good-by. We had a short period of parting. My machine gun was passed around so everybody could lay his hand on it for a final time. We said good-by to their friendly leader and to the other older men and followed the two guides out of the village.

"This is enough to make a man cry," Reinhold said to me.

"Yes, it's strange about people," I said.

202

It was a good day for traveling, and we knew soon we would finish our journey. We would have done what most men had thought impossible. We walked for an hour through the dry, parched jungle before I remembered to take a compass reading.

I was stunned to see that we were traveling not toward Thailand, but toward the East. "Reinhold," I said, calling to him. Gustav also left the guides and the two of them peered at the compass.

"I told you the danger," Gustav said angrily. "They are taking us back into Indochina."

"No, I still trust those two," Reinhold said.

"I trust them, too," I said.

Gustav complained heatedly about the danger we were leading him into, until finally we asked him to be quiet so as not to displease the guides. Still he grumbled. "I came from the Legion to be a free man," he said, "not a slave to you."

Even when he quieted down, he kept alert, expecting an attack from every bush.

Just at sundown, the guides changed their direction to the south. We camped for the night by a clear creek. Along each bank was a wide marsh, as in the swamp, which in the rainy season perhaps would be covered when the creek rose still higher. At sunrise the next morning we started out, still moving to the south. But toward midday we turned west. Before us, although far off, were two mountain peaks. We walked toward them.

That night when we made camp, they seemed to be only slightly closer. The next day we started again and soon came to the bank of a river. Our guides stopped there. One of them stepped toward us, then made a sweeping motion toward the land on the other side. "Muang Thai," he said.

Reinhold and I embraced each of the guides and, al-

203

though they were not sure exactly what to conclude from our doing this, they realized we meant only kindness. Quickly we made ready to enter the river. But Gustav stopped; then turned to the monks, laid his sub-machine gun aside and embraced each of them, also.

After which the three of us waded into the river, and so came at last, after a journey of twenty-one days, to Thailand, where we could be free.

Part III

16

THE TRAIN MOVED through hilly country, where open fields occupied the valleys, and trees covered the slopes. Occasionally we would pass a cart drawn by an ox, a farmer walking alongside, negotiating the treacherous, narrow paths that ran beside the train track. The people were of medium height, bronze-skinned —about the same as the Vietnamese, darker than the Chinese.

In the distance were isolated mountain peaks.

Now the train entered a jungle area. "Why is this land not farmed?" I asked one of the two Thai train guards. They were seated across from Gustav and Reinhold.

The older one, whose teeth were black from chewing betel, said, "There is no need. We are not crowded."

The other guard said, "No, it is because the land cannot be irrigated, therefore rice cannot be grown. Everybody grows rice and nothing else. Also the water buffalo would do poorly here. They must stay near water, because if their skin dries out, they go mad."

The first guard said, "No, it is chiefly because we Siamese are not crowded."

The train roared out of the jungle and again overlooked

207

a long, lean valley, now gray and deserted, asleep until the rainy season. No doubt in two months water buffalo would be dragging the wooden plows over the soil, breaking the baked crust, making it ready for the rains. Then the barefoot, stoop-shouldered women would move through the shallow water, planting each plant separately.

Gustav, Reinhold, and I said little to one another. On the border we had surrendered our weapons to a young Thai officer. He had three bars on his uniform, so we decided he was a captain. He had assured us that the Thai would never turn us over to their enemy, the French. He had arranged our passage on the train, explaining that we would have to go to Bangkok to answer questions and receive papers. Now we were on our way to that great Siamese city.

Only one other westerner, an Englishman, was in our section of the car. Twice I tried to start a conversation with him, but he remained aloof, giving me only sullen glances. I suspected he resented our torn clothes and ragged beards, and he verified this when his anger grew too much for him and he came to my seat. "All westerners should be clean and appear prosperous," he said. "There are too many of you in Bangkok who think it doesn't matter what you do or how you live. It hurts all of us for any westerner to live like a beggar."

I held out my hand to him, palm up. Muttering mild profanities, such as gentlemen use, he selected a coin and placed it on my open palm. When he turned toward his seat, Reinhold and Gustav also asked him for a coin, so it was an expensive lecture for him.

At Chachoengsao we had a three-hour wait, so we found a barber and had our beards shaved off. The border officer had given both Gustav and me rubber shoes, and we had washed our clothes at his place near Aranyaprathet; only in shaving had we had a problem, because the

Thai pluck their whiskers, and there were only two razors at the border-patrol post, both dull.

After we had shaved, a Thai officer invited us to have lunch with him. He ordered fried fish and a bottle of Mekong, a whisky which tasted like gasoline. He was an extremely pleasant man. Already we began to learn that a chief characteristic of the Thai was their cheerfulness. This officer, as well as the Thai we had seen on the train, were happy; everyone of them seemed at peace with the world. They laughed and chatted endlessly. It was as if they had found a solution for the problems of life, one which they all knew and kept as a big secret from westerners.

The officer said good-by to us, and we boarded the train to go on to Bangkok.

"First our country was called Siam," the older of our guards told us, "then in 1939, when the Japanese were in charge, it was changed to Thailand. Then in 1945, it was once more Siam. Now it is changing back to Thailand again. But I like Siam better."

"No, Thailand is better," the younger guard said. The younger guard had a small mustache which he frequently felt with his fingers, as if he were polishing it.

Thai dogs were running along beside our train now. They were small and brown. About nine of them were in this pack, and all were barking as if they wanted to pounce on us and get a meal.

Off in the fields huge water buffalo were bathing in the klongs, coating their bodies with the slimy mud. "Why is it the children are allowed to play around the water buffalo?" I asked the older guard. "It's a wonder they do not get a horn stuck through them."

"They never hurt anybody," he said fondly. Some of the klongs were almost covered with flowers, and buffalo

209

heads poked up from among the white and pink lilies. "They are big, harmless clowns."

"Do you have elephants in this country?" Reinhold asked.

"Yes," the older guard answered, "but they are more serious beasts."

We were on a wide, cleared plain now, stretching to the horizon on both sides of us. The vegetation was dying out, the last tips of green fading. "How does one farmer know his field from another's?" Reinhold asked the older guard.

"The banks separate the paddies. The banks enclose the individual fields, and the fields will be flooded in May."

We saw a group of Buddhist priests walking in a line along the side of a dirt road, each one dressed in yellow and carrying a red umbrella. "In Thailand every man is supposed to be a priest for a while," the older guard said. "For some it is only a few months, for others many years; but every man should be a priest for a time and serve in the temples."

"How long were you a priest?" Gustav asked him.

"Ten months," he said, "and that was long enough." He laughed, a quaint, kind laugh that seemed to irritate his younger comrade.

We were traveling south and the afternoon sun shone directly on my face and shoulders. "I've traveled many trains," I said lazily in German. "I've spent important days of my life on trains. It's a good place to think, for the sound of the wheels calms the mind." Even now the rumble of the wheels brought back past days and old thoughts. "Reinhold, I was thinking that all our punishment is from God, that He is angry because we Germans lost the war to the Communists."

Reinhold smiled. "God is not punishing all Germany with jungles and swamps. Why should He single us out?"

210

"We are symbols," I said. "We are selected to take the punishment."

He idly chewed at his lower lip and studied me, then turned his gaze back to the passing countryside. Down in a stream women were washing clothes. Nearby, children played in the water.

"I wonder what my country is," I said. "Reinhold, what if they ask me in Bangkok? I suppose I'm a Pole, but all the Poles would do with me is hang me from a street lamp for being a German."

"You were born without a country, Hukov," he said. "You had a home, but never a country. And because of the country you never had, you lost your home."

"No, it was American bombs which killed my parents, not German," I said correcting him.

"American bombs in Lvov?"

"Well, they were not German, in any event."

The train pulled heavily. The younger guard stretched his short legs out before him. "In the war, Japan occupied our country," he said. "We told them they could cross through and attack Burma. But once they arrived, they took charge here, too, and taught us a great deal. It was a bad time in the war, however, with the Americans bombing our factories."

"Did the Americans bomb the whole world?" I asked.

"They bombed our factories and the railroad line," the guard said. "So now we have fewer trains. It is not as fast a service as it used to be."

Reinhold shifted, seemingly annoyed with the comments. "Tell me, what will happen to us in Bangkok?" he asked. "How long will it take to get our papers?"

The younger guard shrugged and shook his head.

"Well, when we get papers, can we find jobs and earn enough money to get to Europe?"

The guard considered that for a while. "I don't know.

211

You are westerners. If you were Thai, it would take many years to earn enough to take even a short voyage on a steamship. But westerners are sometimes rich in this country, in which case they spend much money and blow their car horns loud at the Thai and Chinese. Others are poor, and for a westerner to be poor in Siam is bad for them, because it is not like their country. In some bars are found westerners who beg from other westerners for food and drink, and some of them do crimes."

"Well, we are not afraid of them," I said casually. "How long until we are in Bangkok?"

"Even now." The guard nodded toward the window. We turned to watch the city appear, sprawling and sparkling, a crowded mixture of European and Asian architecture. The people moved in seething throngs, but there seemed to be no pattern to their movements. With quick steps many of them were darting across streets, squeezing between trams and cars, rickshaws and carts. Car horns honked continuously. Loud-speakers blared out Thai music and speeches from open windows.

I was attracted to the noisy, bawling city; here it would be easy to lose ourselves.

At the train station the guards directed us onto a bus. It was crowded with people, many of whom were carrying bundles. One lady had a small wooden log, which she was trying to get inside the door of the vehicle.

"Where are we going?" I asked the younger guard.

"To the C.I.D."

"What is that?"

"The Criminal Intelligence Division."

The C.I.D. headquarters was only four or five blocks from the train station, it also being located in the eastern part of the city. Reinhold, Gustav, and I were ushered into the office of an officer, who took our names and directed the old guards to return to their regular duties. We

212

said good-by to them, then new guards took us to a barracks a hundred feet behind the main building.

On the first floor lived the police, but we were led upstairs. It did not seem that we were taken to a jail, or even a place of detention, until we were led into a long room, where some fifteen other men were lying on the floor, and the door closed behind us, the lock shot into place.

"What the hell!" I said.

A few of the other men turned over lazily. One of them, speaking in French, asked where we were from.

"Germany," Reinhold said. "We just escaped from the French Legion."

A big-bodied man jumped up with one bound. "Hukov!" he said. He ran to me and shook my hand. All of us recognized him at once as a Czech from our own Legion battalion.

"What are you doing here, Carl?" I asked him.

"I also escaped from the Legion," he said. "That fellow over there, the Dane, and I stowed away aboard an English ship at Saigon and were put off here."

"Did you just arrive?" I asked.

"We have been here for some time."

"But you were just detained for questioning, then you should be released."

"We've been here three months."

Reinhold, Gustav, and I went to one side and talked about our problem. The young border lieutenant had assured us we would be freed immediately, but he was stationed many miles from the city and might not be well informed. Still, we had no reason to doubt him yet. Perhaps there was a difference between the cases of these other men and ours.

The Czech came over to us. "I tell you, men, I've been thinking about escaping from here."

"Don't speak of escaping to me," I said.

213

"No, nor me, either," Reinhold said, turning away.

A young Thai boy was the attendant for the cell, and at 6:00 P.M. he brought us dinner. It was a big pot of rice with a few pieces of vegetables and salted fish. When the boy came near me, he must have thought I was about to strike him, for he backed off in fear.

"It's all right," I said to him in Vietnamese.

He peered at me suspiciously. "I don't speak French," he said with a thick French accent.

"Do you speak German?" I asked him in that language.

"I don't speak English, either," he said in English.

I couldn't help but grin at him, this little kid, no more than fourteen years old, holding a pot of food for the prisoners. "You," I said, pointing to him, "teach me to speak Siamese?"

A grin came over his face. He nodded and began talking swiftly. So, while Reinhold, Gustav, and the others were discussing why we should or should not escape, this kid and I started to teach each other languages.

We stayed in the barracks three days before the guard finally called our names. Slowly, with deep resentment forming inside us, we made our way to the door. Reinhold said to him, "Now I hope we will get our release from here."

He motioned us to go down the stairs. On the first floor of the C.I.D. he directed me to the office of a young lieutenant, perhaps only twenty-five, who wore thick-lensed glasses.

I took my place before his desk. He removed his glasses, studied me as if I were a problem he must master, then wearily pulled out a piece of paper. "What is your name?"

"Eddy Hukov."

He put on his glasses and wrote out my name. "Nationality?"

"German."

214

"What town in Germany are you from?"

"I was born at Lvov, Poland."

He stopped writing, took off his glasses, and peered at me. "I thought you said you were German."

"Yes. My father was a German born in Poland, and I am German, too."

"No, if you were born in Poland, you are Polish and nothing else, do you understand?"

"I leave everything to you," I said.

He put on his glasses, crossed out "German" and wrote in "Polish." "Now, Hukov, on what date were you born?"

"May 21, 1924," I said.

He asked many questions about my family, about my schooling, my war record. All that day he questioned me, then I was taken back to the barracks.

The next day the questioning continued. "Why did you want to leave the French Legion?" the officer asked me. "Didn't you like it there?"

"No, I didn't care much for it," I said.

"What makes you think living in Bangkok will be better?"

"I'm just here for a few days, Lieutenant, then I am going to Europe."

On and on the questioning went, until finally in late afternoon he seemed to be satisfied. "Now, if you have someone in Thailand who can guarantee for you, a property owner who will assure us you will have lodging and food, you will be released tomorrow morning. If not, we will have to hold you under arrest until you find such a person. That will be all."

I did not move.

"That will be all, Hukov."

I still did not move.

He took off his glasses and peered at me. "Well?"

215

"How am I to find a guarantor in your jail?" I asked.

"Perhaps somebody will come around and offer to stand good for you at a fee."

"Two Legionnaires upstairs have been here for three months. Other prisoners have been here longer. When does this angel come around? When I surrendered, I was told I would be free. I was given the word of a Thai officer."

"Mr. Hukov, we must have a guarantee. You have no money, and finding a job in Bangkok for a westerner without a passport is impossible. You are better off in jail."

"Sir, nobody can live in a jail."

"Yes, perhaps so. If I can find some way to help you, I will. Now I can only tell you the truth."

When I came out of his office, a guard led me to the barracks, where I stretched out on my mat. Soon Reinhold came back also and lay down. Later Gustav came back and began pacing up and down the room. "Give me back my gun," he said. "If only I had my gun."

Reinhold, Gustav, Carl, and I talked every day about escape. Most of the other prisoners were uninterested in any idea, the place having won them over—feeding them twice a day, offering them protection while they slept, relieving them of the painful problem of survival in a world which had rejected them. Of all the others, only Carl and, to a lesser degree, his friend the Dane were also interested in escape.

When we were not discussing how this was to be done and the inadvisability of doing it without some friend or other protector on the outside, I spent my time talking with the boy attendant, learning Thai and teaching him German. He learned quickly, much quicker than I learned Thai, a language which has thirty-three vowels, forty-four consonants, and five tones. A word spoken in a high

216

pitch might mean something different from the same word spoken in a low pitch or a medium pitch. This characteristic alone made the language three times as hard to learn, and, in fact, made it almost impossible for me to learn, because I could not hear some of the distinctions the boy insisted on.

But he was patient, as I tried to be, even when he persistently made the same mistake, that of pronouncing "R" as if it were "L."

One day, after we had been in the prison for three months, Reinhold grew impatient with our conversation. "Ask that kid something that makes sense," he said. "Ask him if we could get on a ship if we got out of here."

I asked the boy.

"No, sir," he answered in German.

"He's a little liar," Gustav said. "Ask him again, Hukov."

"You ask him yourself if you want him asked. He says no, and how would he know about such a subject, anyway?"

"That's right," Reinhold said. "If he said no he doesn't know anything about it. I'm sure it can be done without even asking. If you find a Panamanian ship, anybody can get aboard."

The little boy spoke up on his own. "The ships are watched, because they do not want stowaways. It is hard now."

"What did he say?" Reinhold said.

"He said nothing. Only that it's hard to do."

"No, he doesn't know anything about it," Reinhold said.

"Damned liar," Gustav said. "Little boy liar."

The boy paid no attention to their harsh voices so long as I was there to protect him, and I was always there. There was no other room for me to enter, no place for me to go. I stayed in that bare room and talked with him and listened to the men discuss escape, and I wondered to

217

myself how I had come halfway around the world to a prison in Bangkok and when it would end, when the bad dream would end and I would once more be a boy in Poland.

On the walls and ceiling of our detention barracks were four lizards, or geckos. They were pets, kept in the room to kill flies and mosquitoes, and I got to know them well in the months we were there together. I had never cared much for lizards before, but these four had interesting personalities.

One was a sad lizard, and at the same time he was lucky. He would stay at one spot on the wall, and flies would come to him. Out would flip his tongue, in would go tongue and fly; nothing else moved. But he never seemed to be pleased because of this. He was the grumpiest lizard in Asia.

Another lizard was anxious for food and was always scurrying about, his feet flicking over the wooden walls. "Tut tut," he said, "tut tut." He reminded me of a locomotive which had lost its train and was seeking it out in a hurry. "Tut tut," and here he would come slithering along the wall, the insects and mosquitoes rising before him and escaping.

Also we had a shy lizard. He was the most successful of the four, because he planned his campaigns carefully and carried them out to perfection; but each success seemed to bring him a fresh wave of embarrassment. He had done so well it shamed him.

The last of the lizards Reinhold called "the Nazi," because he was so proud. He goose-stepped, or so it appeared sometimes, and if insects did not want to be caught by him but preferred one of the others, that only showed their stupidity. He was a very fine lizard, although arrogant.

218

Each time Reinhold would call him "Nazi," Gustav would puff up in anger. "Making fun of the Nazis only shows how stupid Reinhold is," he said.

"When I go back to Europe, I'm going to take a gecko with me," I told Carl, the Czech. "They are good pets and are practical."

"When are you going back? When are we going to escape?"

"We might have to do it soon," I said, "but first I must learn the language and more about the city. For a time yet I will study and question the boy and watch the geckos."

One day, however, I told the men I would take action. From a guard I borrowed a piece of paper and a pencil, and I put my mind to considering what I would write.

"Who's the letter to, Eddy?" Gustav said.

"Never mind," I told him. I wrote:

To the Director of the C.I.D.
Dear Sir:

The humble undersigned Edward Hukov begs your kind and considerate attention to my petition, as I am a deserter from the French Foreign Legion, and I entered your country with guns, which I turned over voluntarily, and as I was told at that time by one of your officers that I would be a free man in Thailand when I turned over my guns as I did; and now I am detained for five months and maybe for the rest of my life.

Dear Sir, if you do not pay attention to my calling on you, I will have to escape from here.

Awaiting your early and favorable reply, I am, sir, your obedient servant,

E. Hukov

I read the letter over, then called a guard. "You give this to the commander of this barracks," I said.

The other men began to mumble among themselves about what could have been in my letter, but I would not tell anybody. Also they began to tell me that no letter ever written could bring us freedom in Thailand.

For one long week I did not receive an answer. Then late one afternoon a wide-eyed young lieutenant came to our door, the letter in his hand. "Hukov," he shouted.

I got up slowly and went to the door.

"Are you Eddy Hukov?"

"Exactly right, sir."

"You wrote this letter?"

"Yes, sir."

He stared at me as if he could not make out what to say, then shook his head and signaled for a policeman to approach the door. "Hukov, the commander of the C.I.D. has ordered me to give you a policeman to go with you."

"And what use have I for a policeman?"

"He will show you Bangkok, will take you to any consulate or company in which you want to find a job or guaranty."

"I understand," I said. "And I tell you, Lieutenant, this is a fine day for me. I appreciate your courtesy. But what of these other men?"

For a moment he studied the anxious faces of Reinhold, the Czech, and some of the others, and the glowering, resentful face of Gustav. "First let's find out how successful you are, Mr. Hukov," he said, "then we will see about the others."

17

THERE WAS NO German consulate in Thailand, so I asked my policeman to take me to the Americans. Their embassy was close by, on Wireless Road, a large and nicely furnished building, and the people were kind to me from the first minute I entered. They noticed I had a guard tagging along, and no doubt they knew he was a policeman, although he wore plain clothes; but they acted as if he were not present. When I told a receptionist I wanted to see an official, she arranged it at once.

I was shown into the office of a vice-consul, who offered me a soft chair, then sat back behind his broad desk. "What is it, sir?" he said.

Not in some time had anybody called me "sir," and I thought perhaps he was joking with me. But when I looked up, I saw that he was serious.

"Well, sir," I said, "I was born in Lvov, Poland, and I fought with the German Storm Troopers. Since that day, I have been trying to get established and have had poor success. Six months ago I fled the French Legion, so now I'm in jail here in Thailand. They locked me up and now say I can't be released without a guaranty."

He nodded. "Yes, I know about that regulation."

221

"Sir, I want the United States to guarantee for me."

He produced two cigars from his coat and offered me one, which I accepted. "Mr. Hukov, we're pleased you thought of us as being friendly to you, but this is the United States Consulate. The United States cannot very well stand good for a Polish citizen."

"Sir, America is supposed to help all people who are in danger. The only time I ever got any help it was from an American captain. That one time was all."

"I'm glad he was able to help you. How was that?"

"He helped me escape from an American prisoner-of-war camp, sir."

The vice-consul got a wisp of smoke in his lungs. He coughed it out and went back to studying me. "I don't believe I can be of similar help at this time."

"Sir, I want a chance to get out."

"Yes, I understand, and I can sympathize with you in that. But I don't see that the United States Consulate can do much in that regard. You are a Pole."

"Sir, many Poles are now American citizens, but all I'm asking is that you guarantee for me."

"Well, Mr. Hukov, do you have a job or can you get a job?"

"No, sir, I have none. This is the first place I've stopped."

"Even if you were free, you would have to make a living."

"Well, I tell you, sir, if I get out I plan to leave this country."

He peered at me through the tobacco smoke. "How's that?"

"I plan to stow away aboard a ship, sir."

His expression clouded. "You want the United States to guarantee for you when you plan to try to stow away?"

"Yes, sir."

222

"Well, where do you plan to go?"

"I am thinking about going to the United States."

He swung out of his swivel chair and began pacing the floor. "Mr. Hukov, are you being serious with me?"

"Sir, I'm being honest with you. I am trying to work out this problem the best way I can, and if you can think of a better solution than to stow away aboard an American ship, I wish you would tell me."

"Sir, I have not one suggestion in the world."

"Well, what am I to do? Stay in jail and rot there?"

He shook his head as if in pain, but slowly a big grin came on his face and he peered over at me, then he shook his head again. He returned to his desk and sat down. "Mr. Hukov, I think I'll tell the boys in Washington about you."

I grinned back at him. "What will they do for me, sir?"

"Not a damn thing." From a desk drawer he took out a bill, which he pushed over the desk to me. "Take this, and the best wishes of the United States go with it."

It was a bill for 100 baht, about five United States dollars. "I thank the United States," I said.

"I'm sorry," he said. "But you were in the SS and that marks you. Also you have deserted a recognized army. I can offer you little hope." He showed me to the door, where my policeman was waiting.

Unfortunately I still had the 100 baht in my hand when I came out, so the policeman saw it; and when we left the consulate, he asked me for half of it as his part. "I'm not paid much in my job," he explained.

At a coffee shop, I ordered Coca-Cola for each of us, and there gave him fifty baht.

That day we went to several European and American businesses, but I was not well received by the receptionists. Whenever a secretary did make an appointment, the executive came to his office door and talked with me in

223

the hall. Under such circumstances I could not get far. Also my policeman, since he suspected I might receive another 100 baht, stood so close to me everybody thought I was dangerous.

There was not a job open in all Bangkok, to hear the Europeans tell it. Even the German business men shrugged off my pleas. "You have no passport, so even if we had a job open, we would hire another man."

"Sir, I am a German, just like you. My clothes are torn and I've been in jail for six months, but I'm German, too, and fought with the Storm Troopers."

But none of them would give me work.

"It's difficult," the policeman said to me. "I tell you, there are no jobs for westerners here, unless you are sent from Europe. All the men who work here are hired in Europe or America and sent over by ship. Nobody hires anybody who is already here."

Reinhold said to me that night, "We are out of luck, Hukov, and will have to escape."

"No," I said. "Not yet. I will get a job."

By the afternoon of the fourth day, however, I was tired and discouraged. When my guard and I went into a coffee shop to rest, I told him that the next day I would stay in the jail.

"It's very bad," he said. "It's rough on westerners."

"Yes, well I think tomorrow I'll just take a day of rest."

We drank Coca-Cola and talked about how strange life was. "When I go back to prison, it may be that I will learn to like it there and will stay till I die. Some of the others are satisfied. What does it matter where a man lives or where he's buried?"

"When a man dies," he said, "he is often soon forgotten. So death doesn't matter so much, but being alive matters."

We talked for a long while, perhaps two hours, and then the day was over. I was miserable. I could not go

224

back to jail and face Reinhold and the others. "There is bound to be some last hope," I told the policeman. "I don't want to die in jail."

"Maybe they will help you." He nodded toward three westerners who had come into the place and taken seats two tables away. They were speaking loud enough for me to recognize that they were Russian.

"I don't like Russians," I said.

"Well, do you like the jail?" he asked.

I listened to them talk a while longer. Maybe they would help me after all, I thought. But I hesitated to approach their table since I was not a beggar yet, so instead I began to speak in Russian, in order to be overheard.

The poor policeman did not know what I was doing and immediately became excited. "What is the matter with you?" he demanded. "What are you saying?"

I spoke a few more words in Russian, commenting on the weather, then one of the Russians came over to me. We accepted his invitation to come to his table. There the three men told me they were White Russians. When they asked who I was, I told them briefly about my life and my predicament. A Mr. Kasharin, who had fled Russia in 1917, showed particular interest and asked several questions, which I answered.

After a while he said, "Mr. Hukov, I am a businessman. I am willing to guarantee for you tomorrow morning, but only on a business basis. You can return me a reasonable rate of interest on the sum of the guaranty."

"Sir, I ——" I was almost unable to speak. "I will pay you any interest you ask. If you get me out of jail, Mr. Kasharin——"

"Yes, yes," he said quickly, for he was also embarrassed. "You can stay at my apartment for a while. There's room, and my wife will not mind. So let's decide it that way."

225

I left the coffee shop and on our way to the barracks I thanked God and all angels, and I thought what kind, good-hearted people lived on this earth. This man had known me only an hour, and already he was willing to take a risk on me.

That night I promised Reinhold and Gustav I would work to find jobs for them, as well as for myself, and I promised Carl, too. The man from Denmark, however, showed little interest, and I feared that the jail had won him over.

Reinhold told me, "If you find a ship, take it. Don't wait for us."

"No, I'm not leaving alone. Also I must pay Mr. Kasharin."

"Mail him the money from Berlin," Gustav said.

At 9:00 A.M. Mr. Kasharin came to the C.I.D. headquarters. We took a taxi to his apartment, where his wife gave me clean clothes, and he brought me a pair of shoes, socks, and several handkerchiefs. In a beautifully tiled bathroom, I stripped off my rags and rubbed my naked body with Lux soap. Then I dipped cold water from the corner china vase, using the small silver bowl which was provided, and splashed water over myself. Soon I was suds all over.

When I had rinsed and dried, I put on the clean clothes. Lunch was ready, so we ate, servants waiting on us; and immediately after lunch I went out to find a job.

Now I was clean and no guard was with me, so I got in to see more people. The result, however, was no different. "If I give you a job," an Englishman said, "I will lose profits. In Bangkok we operate on a narrow margin."

"I will work for native wages. You don't have to pay me like the Europeans."

"Oh, Mr. Hukov, we couldn't do that."

226

"Sir, I had rather do that than have nothing at all."

"No, we couldn't. Once that word got out, my company would lose prestige. A company gains reputation by hiring Europeans, but to hire a European at native wages——"

"Sir, it will be a secret between you and me."

"But I will have a European employee living like a native. No, Mr. Hukov."

"I will be living worse than a native without any money at all."

"But you won't be working for me. I have my business to think of. In Bangkok every man is a businessman, Mr. Hukov."

That first day when I dropped by the jail, I found that several Germans who lived in Bangkok, people I had talked with at their offices, had come by and had promised to find guarantees for all the Germans there, of which there was only one other beside Gustav and Reinhold. The other German was almost resentful that they had come, and expended much effort pacing the room, explaining to the rest of us how difficult it would be for him in the outside world, for he had never learned a trade of any kind, and had never worked much. Also he had a deep cough in his chest, he said. And once he did cough, but it was not deep and it was not a cough that I had heard from him before that day.

It made little difference about him, however, compared to Reinhold and Gustav, who were feeling hopeful; and I felt that if I should succeed, good would come of it for the others. I spent all my time looking for work. Each morning I started out with new determination. I lay awake nights thinking up approaches which might not have been tried. Sometimes one of the managers would tell me he would consider me for a job, and I kept notes on every man who said that and checked by once each day. But I found nothing, no work at all.

227

Mr. Kasharin told me not to worry so much. "It will ruin your mind," he said. He told me he was glad for me to live in his apartment and eat at his table. But as the second week went by and I had nothing to give him, not a single baht, I began to feel like a beggar.

"No, Eddy, don't you worry," he said. "Here, tonight we will go out on the town and you will forget your problems."

Always he wanted me to forget. He could not stand for anybody to worry, and sometimes he would take me to dinner, or to see an American movie, or sometimes in the afternoon we would go to the fights at the stadium, where two or three thousand Thai and a few westerners would watch Thai boxers kick and slug each other. The boxers could use their feet in regular Siamese boxing, although each man had his sex organs protected with an aluminum shield. Even so, the stomach and kidneys were unprotected, and the sex organs were not protected well enough, I felt. The Thai boxed to music and only one tune was used during the actual fighting. This steady rhythm almost hypnotized the boxers and the audience, carrying them to frenzied participation. Most matches ended in a knockout, and more than half of those knocked out were carried from the ring on a stretcher.

Also the Thai had international boxing, that is, western boxing with three-minute rounds, but even western boxing was more colorful in Thailand than it had been in Europe. For one thing the fighters usually had descriptive names, such as "The Jaw Breaker," and for another, the audience was extremely vocal and partisan.

Mr. Kasharin saw to it that I visited all the sights of Bangkok. He showed me the Royal Palace, a walled town a square mile in size, filled with temples, beautiful buildings, and statues of dragons, paved with tiled walks and covered with colored, tiered roofs. Here also was a marble

228

palace for the King, and the Wat Phra Keo, where we took off our shoes and walked between the statues of two demons to stand before the Emerald Buddha. It was a small image, a sitting Buddha about two feet high, carved from translucent jasper. It was dressed in the finest raiment, with much gold and many jewels, and Mr. Kasharin told me that the Buddha's clothes were changed at the beginning of each season, in a ceremony which the king himself attended. I could see that if one liked statues, one could grow quite fond of the Emerald Buddha.

One morning Mr. Kasharin hired a launch and, while the water in the klongs was high, we moved past the floating markets, where hundreds of boats were laden with colorful merchandise. We passed communities where families lived on boats tied along the banks of the Menam Chao Phya, which cuts a wide swath through Bangkok.

Another time he took me to the Wat Po, the biggest temple in the city, where lies the Sleeping Buddha. This image was over one hundred sixty feet long and was stretched out, with its head resting in one hand. The whole image was covered with gold leaf, and the floor of the temple was inlaid with animals and flowers in colored tile.

Always around the temples was the sound of tinkling bells, and this combined with the flashing beauty of the many bright colors to add another dimension to the mystery of the Thai people.

Mr. Kasharin showed me the sights with pride. Yet I noticed he spoke of *these* people, not *our* people; of *their* country, not *my* country. He had lived in Bangkok for decades and respected the Thai, but Thailand was not his home. Nor was Bangkok the home of many westerners; and for some it was a city which wrecked their hopes as well as their bodies. Often we would see westerners who evidently had no money, no jobs, but who lived by beg-

229

ging from other westerners. They had been cast ashore at Bangkok, like refuse, just as I; and they had concluded that it was hopeless to struggle. They were to me as pitiful as the Chinese bodies stacked in tiers in the opium dens.

More than ever I determined to escape to Europe or America.

In the third week, I overheard Mrs. Kasharin tell her husband she wished I would not live in their apartment any longer. He told her he had tried to find me a job and could not, and that I had tried everywhere. She only said she wanted her room back.

I had sympathy for her, but I had no intention of returning to jail. That night I left her place. I walked northwest toward the center of town, seeking out the Chinese quarter, the one place I had not tried. At Yawaraj Road, the center of the section, the road was lighted with thousands of electric lamps, and the Chinese hotels and shops were beckoning to the people. There were no Thai there and no other westerners; I felt so much out of place that I hesitated even to ask for a job, but I did ask at two shops and at two large hotels. The Chinese managers smiled at me in their secretive, all-knowing way and offered me nothing.

I walked down Rama IV Road to Lumbini Park. There I sat down and tried to decide what to do. All night I sat there.

The next morning I washed my face in the klong water and went once more into the streets, seeking a job. I walked that day without food, then returned to the park, where I fell asleep.

The next morning, sick and hungry, I started through the streets again. Now I looked like a bum and everybody peered at me suspiciously. I tried to think of an idea that would save me, even if just for that day.

230

I thought of nothing. I asked God to take me to one place that would give me a job. I asked Him to give me help, so I would not have to go back to jail. Even then I had no doubt the police were looking for me.

I started walking, praying to God for a sign. I had walked for only five minutes when I had my sign. It was posted on the boxing stadium.

The dressing room area was a shambles of litter. I made my way through a dark passage, and by questioning the attendants found the manager, a hefty Thai who wore a white western suit. When I told him I wanted to fight, he laughed and called his friends to look at me, a westerner who thought he could beat a Thai. "We have the best fighters in the world," he said to me. "No westerner can stay in the ring with a Thai boxer."

"Well, I need money," I said, "and will take my chances."

"Have you experience?"

"No, except in the army. And a few fights as a boy."

"Then you will not last one round with a Thai. We have the best in the world, do you know that?"

"I heard you say that before, and I am still willing to fight, if you will pay me."

The manager laughed at me as if I were crazy, but I could tell his mind was working on an idea. "What country are you from?" he said.

"Germany."

He nodded, still thinking.

Everybody was staring at me. My clothes were dirty, and I was in need of a shave. Seeing a westerner in such a state seemed to give a few of them a great deal of pleasure.

"I tell you," the manager said. "I have an idea and

maybe it will work out. You get a shave and come back. I want to take a picture of you."

"I have no money for a shave."

Now he had a good laugh. "Then we will give you one."

He gave orders so fast I could not follow them, and attendants started running around, chattering away to one another. Within five minutes they had me soaped up and were scraping away my whiskers. All the while the manager waited anxiously, and when they were through he stared at me, walked part way around me and back. "You are a young man," he said.

"I'm not so old," I said.

"Yes, you will do. Come back tomorrow at four o'clock, weigh in and let me take your picture. You will fight the Black Tiger Sunday."

He started away, but I ran after him. "I have no money, no place to eat. Could you advance me money?"

"Ah," he said, his eyebrows arching, "so that you won't be here to fight, is that it? No, I do not loan money."

"Only a small percentage. How much will I get if I win?"

"Well, this is your first fight, so you'll receive 30 baht."

I was stunned. "That's not enough to—to buy a day's food."

"If you want to fight, that's your fee. In the second fight, you'll go up to a better one. As for an advance, there's no chance of that."

Nothing was left for me except to go back to the C.I.D. barracks. There I would be fed and have a place to stay. Also I could talk to Reinhold and Gustav.

I made my way down Kashem Road to Rama I, walking the whole distance. Many peddy carts—tricycle-type rickshaws—went by, the men who peddled them barking out offers to me, but I had no money for the fare.

At the prison the lieutenant who had sent me out with

232

a policeman shoved aside his work and frowned at me. "Hukov, I thought you would make it. I didn't know how you could, but I had hopes because of your gift of talking so much."

"Well," I said, "my tongue is dry."

He motioned for me to sit down, then gave me a cigarette. "We received word from Mr. Kasharin that you disappeared. I suspected you had gone into the north country."

"No," I said, "I have been looking for work, and at last I found a job; I'm to box in the stadium on Sunday."

"A westerner boxing?" he asked in surprise.

"I'm to weigh in tomorrow afternoon at four. Let me tell you, not since I was a small boy have I ever lost a fight; but now I'm weak from little food. Also I don't understand why the promoter wants my picture. He wouldn't agree to my boxing until he had had my face shaved and he could get a good look at me."

The lieutenant began to drum the top of the desk with his fingers. "Perhaps he's going to play this up. He thinks you will lose, and he's going to tell all Bangkok that a westerner will fight a Thai Sunday afternoon, so that he will sell all his tickets."

I realized he was right, and now I saw too how low it was to be broke in Bangkok, to have to crawl, disgracing all Europe and America for 30 baht. "He offered me 30 baht if I won," I said with a laugh. "The Americans gave me 100 just for dropping by."

The lieutenant stood up abruptly. "You come with me, Hukov."

I thought he was going to lock me up, but he led me to the main door. We went outside and he hailed a taxi. "Get in," he said.

I got inside, believing we were going back to the boxing arena where he would talk to the promoter, but after

233

half a kilometer or so, we stopped at a small house, set in the Platoo-nan market.

"Where—where are we?" I said.

"This is my home," he said. "I will give you a place to sleep and eat until Sunday, so you can win the fight."

That day was Wednesday, and after a large dinner, I went to the C.I.D. to tell Reinhold and Gustav the news about what the lieutenant had done for me. Everybody said he was a better officer than they had thought.

But when they began asking for details about the fight, I began to grow depressed again. Every time I thought of getting into the ring with three thousand Thai watching, I grew shaky. "I'm out of training," I said, "I haven't a chance."

"Stop such talk," Reinhold said. "Get up from the mat right now, and let's see how strong you are." He picked up a mat and put it across his body. "See how hard you can hit me."

"Reinhold, you're not a punching bag."

"Well, we don't have a punching bag. Go ahead."

I tapped the bag.

"Hit it. You have to win. All of Europe is being represented by you. Now hit the mat."

I punched it. Then I hit it hard. I kept knocking him back until he was at the other end of the room and against the wall. He returned to his original place and took his stance again, but Gustav jerked the mat out of his hands.

"Let's go, Hukov," he said. "You knocked Reinhold back there in seventeen blows. You'll not have so easy a time with me."

With Gustav it took twenty-two, so Reinhold insisted on another try. He found he had to wait in line, however, because Carl wanted a try. Nothing would do but that I knock him and then the Dane back to the wall, which took eighteen blows each. This angered Reinhold, be-

234

cause his score was only seventeen, so he put up such a resistance when his turn came, that I had to give him twenty-five blows before his shoulders struck the wall.

Our training period continued for two hours. The next morning I was so sore I could hardly move, but I exercised and got limbered up; then I went down to the boxing arena and weighed in at 172 pounds. The manager had a photographer take several pictures as I posed guarding myself with my gloves. Already there was much talk about my fight on Sunday.

When I left the stadium, I went back to the jail and worked out with the boys until the lieutenant came upstairs and told me it was time to go home to eat.

That night I went to bed early, feeling sick. I knew I was working my body too hard.

My picture came out in the papers. It was a poor picture, I felt, but almost always pictures of me were poor. On Sunday morning I showed it to Reinhold and the others, and the boy attendant translated the news story. It played up the fight as being a Thai-western bout. I was a professional boxer with an excellent record who had just arrived from Berlin.

"Well, I don't think I can win," I told the boys.

"Here," Reinhold said, springing up and pulling a mat in front of him. "Come on, Hukov."

I refused. I was so tired I could not hit anybody. But he insisted, so I tried to knock him back to the wall, and it took me almost thirty blows.

Everybody made a big joke about how much stronger Reinhold was than a few nights before. Then Gustav got the mat, and it took me twenty-five blows for him. I tried with two other men, and each time it was harder than it had been on the previous Wednesday night, before my half-week of training.

A deep gloom settled over all of us. "I tell you, boys," I said, "I'm going to lose for the first time in my life."

I went to the lieutenant's office and thanked him for his kindness and told him I would lose.

That afternoon at four o'clock, I walked to the boxing stadium. There I saw thousands of people waiting for the bouts to begin. In the dressing rooms, as I undressed, I heard the attendants and other boxers laugh about my white skin, and also about how easily a Thai could beat a westerner.

When a Thai came over to feel my muscles, I chased him away. This made him angry and he spat on me.

I just kept quiet and did nothing. That was the best thing I did.

When I was through putting on my trunks and hanging up my clothes, I sat down on a bench and listened to the Thai talking. I told myself that if I let them make me quite angry, I could win, no matter who was fighting me, or under what conditions. But at the same time I felt weak. I knew I would lose. I knew the Thai would be happy when I lost, and I told myself that I would make three thousand men happy in person, and everybody else could read about it in the paper.

When the promoter called me, I moved out into the arena and made my way to the ring. A few of the Thai were rowdy, but they let me through. As I climbed eight feet of steps into the high ring, several men made threatening gestures with knives.

The referee told us in Thai that the rounds would be three minutes long, and that we were fighting international style. I kept my eyes on my opponent, the Black Tiger. He was of medium height, with broad, thick shoulders, and the glistening, olive skin of the Thai. His nose was broad and flat, his face wide, his lips full. As he

236

walked back to his corner, there was grace in his movements.

I went back to my corner and told myself it soon would be over. I looked out over the audience, most of which was standing. Then I saw a strange thing. Somebody waved at me. It was Reinhold. Reinhold was out there, and beside him was Gustav, and beside him were Carl and the police lieutenant. Now they all waved at me and somebody said in German, "Kill him, Hukov." Then I saw the boy attendant who had taught me the Thai language.

I wanted to cry. Now I knew I was going to tear the Black Tiger limb from limb. Also, I thought, somewhere in the audience was Mr. Kasharin, pulling for me. These were my friends, and all of them were out there, wishing me luck.

When the first round began, I moved in confidently, caught up with my new-found strength, but at once the Black Tiger struck me a flurry of sharp blows. I was thrown off guard. He landed blows on me in volleys, and each time the people screamed. Everybody was standing now, yelling at him, while I was trying to protect myself.

When I did regain my balance and tried to land a blow, I would miss or my glove would glance off his body, so that I did him little damage. He was fast and as agile as a cat.

I managed to stay on my feet until the bell, then made my way to my corner. A Thai climbed into the ring and started rubbing a cotton cloth over me. I cared nothing about that. I cared nothing about my friends who had come to see me fight, either. All I wanted was to go off somewhere and forget who I was.

Then I heard a German voice. "Hukov, you're letting him punch hell out of you. What's the matter with you?"

237

It was Reinhold, part way up the ladder to the ring. Somebody was trying to pull him down, but he was holding his place. "Hukov, how many of his blows can you stand in this next round? Can you take five of his blows before you go down?"

I nodded dumbly, hardly aware of what he had asked.

"Then move in on him. Give yourself five blows to take, and in that time, land blows, no matter what. He can't take one of your punches, Hukov. Get in there, damn you!"

Two Thai grabbed him and pulled him off the ladder. They almost had a fight on their hands, too, but the bell sounded for round two. All attention once more was focused on the ring.

As I started in, the Black Tiger hit me twice in succession, and the Thai started in their roar, anticipating the blow that would knock me unconscious; but at the tag end of his third blow, I hit him once, and the roar cut short. I hit him one more time while he was still dazed. I hit him with a left and a right, and he dropped his guard entirely.

A rumble rose from the three thousand Thai, but Reinhold was once more halfway up the ladder, screaming encouragement. I hit the Black Tiger a solid blow, and his eyes fluttered. Blood flowed from a cut on his forehead.

He backed off, danced away. He tried to stay back from me now, but I pressed him hard. I hit the wound on his forehead. I hit it again and blood began to stream down his forehead and into his eyes.

The audience was in a frenzy. I hit the forehead again.

The referee moved between us, pushed me off. He stopped the fight to wipe off the Black Tiger's face, and

238

the ring doctor put a plaster on the wound. The referee moved out of the way.

A nervous hum stirred among the crowd. The Black Tiger moved toward me. He hit me twice, but his power was gone. I hit his forehead, and the plaster flew off. I hit him twice more, and his eyes closed. I pounded blows into his face, when the referee pulled me back. He raised my arm to stop the fight. I had won.

The crowd was in a storm; their roar grew. But Reinhold was shouting jubilantly. I could not help but smile because of that fool Reinhold, halfway up the ladder, laughing as the crowd roared at me.

When I got my 30 baht, I asked the manager how he had liked the fight.

"Well, I lost money," he said grimly. "I tell you, it didn't go the way I had hoped."

"How much did you pay the Black Tiger?"

He turned away, as if he had not heard me, so I followed him. When he recognized me again, I asked the question a second time. "I gave him 50 baht," he said.

"I get 30 for winning and he gets 50 for losing?"

"He got 15 for losing. The rest is for medicine." He turned away, still gloomy, and went out to watch another bout.

I went to the dressing room and changed into my street clothes. Not a word was said to me. Everybody was unhappy; they were throwing the damp towels around angrily.

About seven-thirty, as I was leaving the arena, the manager caught my arm. "Hukov, I'll pay you more if you'll give a Thai boxer another chance."

"No," I said, "I'm not in proper training. It's a mistake for me to fight when I'm not strong."

239

He thought I was joking. "Hukov, I'll give you 600 baht if you win."

I started away, but I stopped almost immediately. With 600 baht I would have enough money to work out a real plan. It was not a large sum, but it might be enough to get aboard a ship. "When would I fight?" I said.

"Sunday afternoon. One week from today."

I knew once more he would slant his publicity—a European against a Thai. I resented the idea of another fight, but I needed money. "Yes," I said, "I'll do it for 600 baht."

"If you win. Otherwise 250."

I agreed to that.

Outside the stadium a crowd of Thai awaited me. Some of them taunted me, simply to have a good time and take part in the sport of the moment, while a few were angry. But another group stood aside, evidently resenting the words of their countrymen.

Two young men struck out at me, perhaps to see if I was as tough as I had seemed to be, but their blows glanced off, and I did not return them. I forced my way through the crowd.

Nobody followed.

I started toward the C.I.D., but a deep weariness settled on me. After the excitement and confusion of the stadium, the comparable quiet of the city lulled me into depression. When I came to a small Siamese hotel, I went into its restaurant and ordered fried rice.

While I was eating, a dancing girl came to my table. She seemed to like me and wanted me to like her, so I agreed. It would be well to be with her, I decided, and to avoid talking about the fight, even with my friends.

The next morning, however, I went to the C.I.D. and everybody congratulated me, as if I were champion of the world. Then, that afternoon, I went back to the room of the dancing girl and stayed there with her for that week.

On the next Sunday, I went to the arena and fought a large, fast Thai boxer. In the third round I knocked him out and collected my 600 baht.

18

THAT SAME NIGHT I told Reinhold
and Gustav what I planned to do with the money, and
they encouraged me to go ahead. All three of us wept.
It was not easy to say good-by, not for three men who
had been in the Legion together and crossed the swamp,
who had lived six months in the same bare room.

I told them I would soon send money to them at the
C.I.D., as well as to Mr. Kasharin.

I left them at eight o'clock and caught a bus for Kohsichang, the island harbor 150 kilometers south of the city,
where the boy attendant told me the big ships lay. There
I went up and down the road to see what ships were in.
I came to a large ship and asked her country.

A sailor, heavy-set and over six feet in height, came
over to me. "The United States, mister, that's her country."

"Is she—going home?"

"Tomorrow morning. Why? You want a ride to the
States?"

I was struck by the thinness of his voice and the small-
ness of his features, which hardly seemed to belong to

a man of his huge size. He kept his tiny eyes intently focused on me.

I pulled out my 600 baht. "Yes, I would like to go along."

He counted by money eagerly, but his happy look of anticipation soon vanished. "This is only thirty dollars. How do you expect help for that?"

"Well, it's all I have."

"Thirty dollars is all you have?" He counted the money once more. "Well, there are crates in the second hold, and among them are hiding places. I might get you in there, but we'll be two weeks crossing, unless we stop off at Manila, and in that case longer. Can you get by on damn near no food for that period?"

"Of course."

"I can't bring you much food. Let's give it a try, what do you say?"

"For the 600 baht?"

"That's right." He shoved the money into his pocket.

"Look," I said quickly, "I'll pay you part now and part later."

He took out the roll of bills and handed it to me. "You don't trust American sailors?"

"Yes, but . . ."

"I was trying to do you a favor, then I get insulted."

"No—I——" My body was damp with perspiration. "To get that money I had to do much work."

His tiny eyes peered at me, his tiny mouth smiled.

"I—I trust you," I said.

"Hell, I don't care one way or another, you know." He took the money and shoved it back in his pocket. "Come along. I'll show you a place to hide."

On board the vessel, he led me down to the second hold, where the hatch cover was off. We moved inside

244

and made our way to a tiny niche, no more than two by three feet in size.

"You get in there," he said.

I squeezed into the space, pulling my legs up under me. He scrambled back to the deck.

I prayed to God Almighty. I said He should let me stay on that ship. I told Him this was right, and that I would go all the way to America without food. Just let me stay.

Perspiration was dripping from my face; my clothes were damp from sweat. Already my body was aching because of the cramped quarters. I dared not move or make a single sound, and when a sound was made elsewhere on the ship, it startled me. I was tense, waiting for a sound.

For the rest of the night I waited. My muscles ached. But I had a hope, a great hope. Two weeks of hell would not be too much to pay for getting to the States.

At dawn the engine of the ship turned over; the ship vibrated. An officer ordered that the holds be covered. I heard heavy sounds and the tramping of feet. Now I welcomed sound. The men were up above me at the number two cover. I was waiting to hear them close the hatch, and so cover me up and leave me safe.

"Hey, you," somebody said in English. "Hey you, down there, come on out, the game's over."

I remained silent and motionless.

"Hey, mister, come out of that hold or we'll come down and drag you out."

I said not a word.

I heard footsteps on the crates. They came closer. Two sailors came into view and walked directly to me. They motioned for me to come out.

I had so many tears in my eyes, I could hardly find my way to the deck. I said nothing to the American officer, or to any crewman. I did not see the big sailor who had taken my money. Now he would not have to feed me, I knew, and maybe he had gotten a reward for reporting a stowaway to his captain.

I did not want to see him. He was not worth despising, this American who had grown up in that rich country and would steal from me, who had only 600 baht.

Once away from the ship, I went off to myself for a while. When I was more relaxed, I went to the big bar at Kohsichang; but I had not a baht with which to buy a drink, and I would not beg from anybody.

I had no money to pay for bus transportation back to Bangkok either, so I tried to find a truck that was driving that way, but was out of luck.

I had no place to stay, until a girl asked me to her room. She gave me food and wine. I stayed with her two days, and then another American ship came into port.

The boys from the ship were soon filling the bar, and some of them invited me to drink, so I had a few drinks with them. When they asked who I was, I told them I was an escapee from the French Legion. They asked many questions, and I answered them all honestly. I hoped one of them would agree to stow me aboard, but when I mentioned it to a man from Washington, he said it was difficult for an American seaman to help me. "Hukov, on an American ship, everything is strict. Also an American seaman has a high salary and steady advancement. What you need is a ship where the sailors need money, and where they don't lose much even if they get fired. Rather than American, I would suggest any other country's ship."

So I was left when they sailed, and many of the sailors waved good-by to me and I waved back. In my pocket, I had forty U.S. dollars they had given me and so many cigarettes that, when I got back to Bangkok that afternoon, I sold them for 200 baht.

Some of the money I spent on a present for Mr. and Mrs. Kasharin. When I had told them about my experiences, Mr. Kasharin said, "Hukov, I tell you, I never saw anybody who could have as many experiences as you. I have lived a long life and nothing has happened to me." Then he said quickly, "Well, I got married and I have had some happy experiences, but I have not had any boxing matches or been a stowaway or anything like that. Hukov, you are always in action."

"It's not so easy to keep still when you are sitting on a hornet," I said.

He laughed and brought out a bottle of whisky. We had a drink.

Then I changed to the best clothes the sailors had given me and went down to one of the exclusive bars, hoping to meet a westerner who would help me out with a job. The doorman looked at me suspiciously, but he did not try to keep me out.

Inside there were several groups, but none of them was interested in me until a Mr. Baron, a Scotchman, and his wife arrived. We started talking and soon were sitting at the same table. We talked about Bangkok, about the many years he had lived there. I mentioned I was out of work and would take almost anything.

"I have no work for anybody," he said. "My chauffeur is no good and perhaps I should replace him with another Thai, but . . ."

"How much does your chauffeur make?" I asked.

"Only ten baht a day and his room."

"I would—I would like to have that job," I told him.

He laughed at the idea of a westerner being his chauffeur, but he was pleased with the idea, too, I could tell, and after a few more drinks he went outside and fired his

247

chauffeur. Later that night I drove him and his wife home.

My room was in the gatehouse, upstairs, and had a soft bed and a chair as well as a chest for my few items of clothing. Also it had an electric light, so it was a good place for me. The salary, however, did not permit me to save money.

But no other place offered me so much, except perhaps fighting. And the more fights I won, the less willing the manager would be to schedule me.

I worried about this, seeing that I was probably to be stuck in Asia for some years. And I worried about Reinhold and Gustav, still in prison. Three nights a week I would walk downtown and visit them. They had been in the C.I.D. now for eight months.

"We are planning to escape," Gustav told me one night. "Next time you come we won't be here, Hukov. We will be down on that island, where you say the big ships are anchored."

"No, first we must meet, so that we can go there together," I said.

"Well, we will be in the nearest bar then," Gustav said. "We will be waiting for you there."

But the next time I went, they were still in jail. Sometimes I tried to give them money, but only occasionally would they take it; although when I brought candy or cakes they would accept them, as would the other prisoners.

"You come with us when we escape from Thailand, Hukov," Reinhold said to me one night.

"Yes, all right. But where are we going? I have only one move left. Then I'll have lost my chances. The more I think of it, the more I would like to go to America, because I have met American sailors, and their names are from all different countries, but there's no politics between them. All of Europe went to America and became

248

good friends, and I think I'll go there for my last move."

"I had rather go home to Germany," Gustav said. "It's still the best country."

"Go to Argentina," Reinhold said dreamily. "The women paid me, can you imagine it? They paid me in Argentina."

"You're a big liar," Gustav said.

"It's true. I supported myself on it."

"How much did they pay?"

"None of your damn business."

"Come on. Would it amount to 10 baht?"

"Hell," Reinhold said, "that's only half a U.S. dollar."

"Well, I'm trying to find out how much you're worth," Gustav said.

Reinhold peered about uncomfortably. Everybody was listening to him now. "They paid me—hell, I don't know —it was five times that for each time."

"Ahhh," Gustav said, "how could you live on two and a half dollars a month?"

Reinhold's mouth fell open, but no words came out; then he leaped at Gustav and they rolled to the floor. It was a friendly fight, a good way to break the monotony of the evening.

For three months I visited them, but one night in November when I arrived, they were gone. The Czech told me a German had guaranteed for them that afternoon.

With a yell I ran down the steps and into the street. I went from one bar to another, but they were not to be found. Finally I went home, planning to search at Kohsichang on the following day; and there, sitting on the lawn in front of Mr. Baron's house, was Reinhold, as drunk as he had been the night we decided to escape the Legion.

We raced to each other and beat on each other's backs,

249

then he came with me to my room to talk about our future plans.

"Where's Gustav?" I asked him.

"Drunk and crazy. The last I saw of him he was running down the street chasing two Chinese girls. I don't know where he is."

"He's a good boy," I said, "but he has a great deal to learn."

Reinhold stretched out on my bed and stared up at the naked light bulb, which was burning that night. Sometimes it did not work. He said, "Hukov, I want to ask you how I can find a soft life like you have, so I can get lazy like you." He yawned and stretched his long arms above his head.

He looked much older, I saw, than he had looked in the Legion. Lines were deeper on his face, and his eyes were set far in, so that they seemed to peer out from a distance. I wondered if the same was not true with me.

"Here you have everything a man needs," he said.

"No," I said, "I just have a place to die."

He yawned again. "I tell you, Hukov, we must become like these rich westerners, get started in business, big business. We will have to become Asian millionaires, so that we can buy our way safely. I have no confidence in stowing away, for the ship's captain would only put us off at another Asian port, should he find us at sea. But nobody who is a millionaire has to worry."

I laughed at the idea of our gaining riches in that country. "You tell me what business we can start with a few baht, and we will do that. I've not one idea in my head."

He squinted at me, then peered about craftily. "How did your father make a living?"

"As an engineer in the Prazownik steel mill."

"That's no help here in Thailand. What about your grandfather?"

"I never knew him, but I think he was an engineer, too, although he had something to do for a time with medicines."

"Medicines," Reinhold said thoughtfully. His face slowly lit up. "Hukov, this town needs a good supply of medicines."

"I have no medicines."

"Listen, no Oriental city is going to keep us prisoners. Now, how many medicines do you know the recipes for?"

I tried to think. "I don't know of any. My grandfather didn't have any secret recipes. What he would do is make salt water and sell it on the streets for eye medicine."

"Good!" Reinhold said. "That's a simple recipe, one we can always remember. Tomorrow morning . . ."

"Look, who will buy salt water from us when they can make it for themselves?"

"Ours will look professional. Now go ahead with what your grandfather would do."

I tried to think of other stories I had heard about him, but none came to mind. "On the Eastern Front," I said, "some of the boys would mix talcum powder, Lysol, and motor oil for a skin salve."

"Good," Reinhold said. He took out a stub of a pencil and marked down powder, Lysol, motor oil.

"Now," I said, "you name some recipes."

He peered at me critically. "Hukov, I don't know anything about medicines. My field is business. I know only that many a man has made a fortune by starting out with a few bottles of salt water, and you listen to me, I can see us getting rich enough to leave this country in style. What do you say?"

I also began to see hope, so I shook hands with my new business partner and the next morning told Mr. Baron I was leaving his place, that Reinhold and I had a job at our own risk.

251

Mr. Baron was interested in what I planned, so I told him about the new company.

"Hukov, take care now," he said. "To sell medicine on the street, you either must be doctors or the medicine must be registered in the Government laboratory."

"Well, we have a third way," I said. "When we see the police, we'll run like hell."

The next morning I moved with Reinhold to a hotel for Thai and we began our company. We bought eighty small bottles, a pound of salt, four tins of baby powder, four jars of Lysol, and two quarts of motor oil. Reinhold had asked an old Thai at the hotel what she used for skin ointment and she had recommended alcohol and glycerin. Nothing would do, therefore, but that we buy those ingredients too.

Out under a tree in the park, we prepared the mixtures. We worked quickly and laughed often, making jokes about our new-born company. "I am going to write Erika for the first time," I told Reinhold, "and tell her I'm an important Asian businessman and will send her presents from the Orient soon."

"By this late date you had better send presents for her children. She has forgotten about you, Hukov."

"When she finds out how rich I've become, she will remember me again."

We prepared the eye solution first, because it required little experience. Then we went to work on the other two. "Reinhold, we're going to have two skin medicines," I pointed out.

He looked up from his work, surprised, then he realized I was right. "But one is liquid, and one is salve," he said.

"Well, why do we need two?"

He set the motor oil can aside and gave the matter thought. "The liquid solution is a holy water ointment, and after it's used, the salve is put on."

"Very good," I said. "I just wanted to know, in case I was asked."

We mixed up the skin medicines and stacked those fifty bottles with the thirty bottles of eye wash. The skin medicines looked quite good, but the eye wash appeared to be only water, and nothing more.

"Your grandfather sell much of this, Hukov?"

"I don't know."

"Maybe we should add another ingredient." We looked over our supply of chemicals but decided Lysol, motor oil, and alcohol might not be good for the eyes. So we bought yellow coloring and colored the salt water until it looked professional.

This took only an hour, but the tension left both of us spent. "If this gamble doesn't succeed, we'll be in trouble," I said.

"It ought to succeed, Hukov," Reinhold said with a grin. "We've done careful measuring."

We gathered up the remains of our ingredients and put them in the oil can, which we dropped in a klong; then with our precious bottles, we went to the market. There, in a café, we borrowed a chair so we could display the medicine.

"Reinhold, you do the talking and I'll collect the money," I said.

"No, Hukov, I don't speak Thai."

"Then get the people buying by speaking German. I don't know anything about making a speech."

Reinhold shifted nervously before the gaze of the two or three Thai who had already stopped to peer at our merchandise. Suddenly, he took in a deep breath and in a loud, clear voice began to shout like a carnival barker.

He rolled along in the German language, which only I could understand. "Come right up, ladies and gentlemen, and see our new medicines, made especially for skin dis-

253

orders, and our eye wash, manufactured by Europeans in a big laboratory. Step right up to the best little pharmacy in Thailand, where you can be assured of only the finest product, made after old family recipes. Come on and buy a dozen bottles for your own and your families' use. Buy our medicine for presents. No homes should be without our skin ointments, one made of holy water——"

I grinned at the damn fool and could hardly keep from laughing, but by such talk he collected forty or fifty people around us in exactly one minute. Then he asked me to explain further. "Hurry, Hukov," he whispered. "We might get arrested."

I told briefly what our medicines would do. "Now I see many of you have your five baht out and are trying to push your way through—let the people through, please ——" Two kind people in the back, who thought they were good judges of medicines, started forward. "That's right, everybody come up and get medicine for his family, so everybody can get over his eye troubles and skin itches. Be sure to keep a bottle of our medicine with you at all times——"

They came pushing up to buy, and our medicines began to sell like crazy. We became so happy taking in baht that neither of us could keep from laughing, but we remained serious enough to keep an eye out for police, should they appear.

We sold our entire stock and when the sale was over we had collected 400 baht.

That night we mixed another supply. Before starting out the next morning, however, we made a spot-check of our customers to see if it was safe to continue. Several customers greeted us warmly, and we soon realized that the Thai and Chinese were crazy about our medicines. Some told us that their eyes were getting better, some that their wounds were healing. Only one man wanted

254

to beat us up because we had sold such a damn skin salve, but we talked him into trying our skin ointment.

That day we did only 200 baht in business, however, and only 180 on the day following. Both days we had to close our sale when police approached. The fourth day we did better, selling 400 baht worth of medicine, but Gustav helped us, so the money had to be split three ways.

This was the last time we permitted him to sell with us. We found he insisted people buy the medicines whether they wanted them or not. He took it as an affront to be refused; and Reinhold and I had to keep an eye on him, so that we could intercede before a fight started.

Our first week was mildly successful, and Reinhold and I called a business meeting in one of the Thai coffee shops. We ate our rice and fish dinner, then each of us produced all the money he had in his pockets, and we counted it. After deducting expenses, we found that we had saved 260 baht.

We celebrated by spending 30 baht on a bottle of wine. We drank that and were feeling quite prosperous, until we tried to figure out how long we must sell medicine before saving enough money to make a sure escape. Reinhold contended that we would need at least 10,000 baht, or 250 United States dollars each, if we were to have any hope of reaching Europe or America, and that we should have considerably more than that.

We divided our week's profit into the amount needed and found that we would have to continue our business over a year; and if we wanted to continue until we were wealthy Orientals, we would have to work longer than we would be alive.

We had done very well, but we had not made much money.

During our second week, the police became troublesome. Frequently we had to stop our sales, and sometimes we had to flee. Our first month ended with only a small profit of 600 baht. The second month was not so profitable. Some days we sold only forty baht worth of medicine.

We stayed in Bangkok for two or three months, then we widened our territory—we started into the north country, where police were not so plentiful.

19

ONLY A SMALL PART of Thailand
was cleared and planted. The rest was covered in teak,
oak, chestnut, and pine. In these jungle areas were tigers,
leopards, rhinoceros, elephants, wild pigs, bears, monkeys.
There were snakes and crocodiles, and many birds.

In the north we found steep, high mountains, which
rose as much as 4000 feet above narrow, troughlike valleys, where rice, tobacco, and sugar were planted. It was
rich earth, even after many generations of farming, and
sometimes two crops of rice were planted in a single
season.

The people were well fed, and they were friendly to
us. Only occasionally was it evident that any of them
resented westerners. However, of greater importance to
Reinhold and me at the time was the fact that they bought
medicines. We made high profits in the north. Everywhere we went we sold eighty to one hundred bottles a
day, sometimes for as much as twenty baht a bottle.

And we added a fourth medicine to our stock: alcohol
and ether for toothache. Presents were given to us for that
one.

For four weeks we did an excellent business. When we

reached Chieng Mai, the chief city of the far north, it was more than we could do to keep medicine prepared for the buyers. We were saving money and living well; soon we would have enough money to insure success in making our escape.

But on the afternoon of the sixth day in Chieng Mai, the hotel keeper reported that a prosperous-looking Thai had been searching for us. "He has been to your room five times this afternoon," he told us, "and he asked me about you and if there had been complaints concerning the medicines."

Reinhold and I hurried to our room and began to pack. We threw our few possessions into our worn, leather bag and were ready to open the door and flee, when the door shook with knocks from the hall side. We held our breaths. The knocks came again and again.

After a while, I set down the bag and opened the door.

An excited man of about fifty, wearing a white suit, came into the room. "Pardon me," he said in Thai, "but I must talk with you about a serious matter." He was looking at me, ignoring Reinhold. "First, what is your name, please?"

I hesitated. "Eddy," I said finally.

"Dr. Eddy, I heard you were selling medicine in Chieng Mai, and that you have special eye drops."

From my pocket I took one of our bottles of salt water. "I have this fine medicine."

He asked for the bottle, and I handed it to him. He smelled the contents, then screwed the cap back on. I glanced at Reinhold. Neither of us knew what to do. If he were a high official of the government, there was no escape, unless we could talk our way to freedom, or perhaps offer him money.

"Dr. Eddy, perhaps you will be kind enough to come with me. And your friend also, if he is a doctor."

"No, he is not a doctor," I said.

"Very well. My car is downstairs."

I expected his driver to take us to the city jail. Instead he drove into the suburbs and stopped at a lavishly appointed house, built in western style. I began to feel hopeful again. It seemed unlikely that this was a government official, under these circumstances. And I began to hope that actually any money involved might be coming to Reinhold and me.

We entered into a wide hall. He led me down the hall to a sitting room.

At the door I stopped, a chill striking through me. Before us, sitting in a wooden chair, sunlight falling on her face through the curtained window, was a girl whose eyes were running sores. Her eyes peered at me from between pussed lids.

"Did she use my medicine?" I muttered. "Just tell me that?" I had never thought salt water would hurt anyone's eyes. I thought it would be good for the eyes, but now I was looking at these running sores through which the tiny, brown pupils peered, and I felt that God Himself must certainly damn me for eternity, considering what I had done to her.

An elderly lady came into the room. She was introduced by my host as his wife and the girl's mother. "Dr. Eddy," he said, "we have not tried your medicine. That's why I have come to you."

Immediately I felt relieved. Now I could take my eyes off the girl's face. "What can I do for you?" I asked.

"Sir, cure my daughter. All the doctors in this part of the country have tried, and nobody has helped her. So when I heard that a western doctor was in town selling medicine, I knew I had to see you. I thought perhaps you would know how she might be cured."

259

I glanced at the girl. "Yes, but it would take time for an examination and——"

"Please help her, Doctor," the mother said.

"Yes, Dr. Eddy," the man repeated. "I will pay you well. I have made much money in teakwood, and in situations like this money is easy to part with. What does it mean, compared with her eyes?"

I realized the truth of what he said, for even I could not think of the money, but only of the eyes of the girl. I was asking myself, what if I were she and my father brought in a Legionnaire who had never studied medicine, and such a crook should prepare salt water and color it and use it on my sick eyes, what of that?

I went closer to the girl. All the time the pupils, like prisoners, peered out from between the swollen lids, focused on me. She said nothing.

I turned to her father. "Sir, I tell you the truth; whenever I see this particular disease, which is not one of the common eye diseases in Thailand, I always send the patient to the Chulalongkorn hospital in Bangkok, where several European specialists are at work. I would take her there right away, if I were you. Also I would not use any of my medicine on her eyes, because it's not made for this disease and might make the condition worse.

"Doctor, you have given me hope," he said. "But can these men in Bangkok cure this disease half the time, three-quarters of the time——"

I looked at the young girl. "No, they cure it always," I said.

Then she smiled, a nice warm smile, and I smiled at her in return.

The incident was soon over, but because of it I came to see myself in a new light. I decided that, even though we were in desperate circumstances, what we were doing was

260

a poor excuse for a business. So I told Reinhold I wanted to stop selling medicine.

Instantly he became angry. He cried out that in Chieng Mai we were saving 100 baht a day. But I held to my stand. Even then we had 2500 baht, which would give us some hope of escaping on a ship.

"Only ten more weeks, Hukov," Reinhold pleaded.

But I could not do it. And when I failed to find work in Chieng Mai, we agreed to return to Bangkok. Together we bought train tickets for the one thousand kilometer journey.

On the train we discussed going straight to Kohsichang and gambling the money we had left on escape, but we decided to stop at Bangkok to see Carl and Gustav.

Carl was still in the C.I.D. barracks, and Gustav we could not find. We moved into a small hotel for the night, hoping to locate him the next morning, but when morning came Reinhold insisted that we sell medicine for a few hours. "The train tickets were expensive, Eddy, and for five days in Chieng Mai you did nothing except look for work. Now we have only 2000 baht, so sell for this one morning."

I agreed, and we were both selling medicine near the Wat Spaket when the police came up from behind and arrested us.

We had to pay 1000 baht to the police and a Thai doctor. Both Reinhold and I were furious, angry at our fate, which was set against us. We drank Mekong and talked about Germany. Then we went out to find Gustav and found him looking for us. We drank more Mekong. Gustav told us he would sacrifice one arm and one leg if he could get back to Germany. We talked about that. Reinhold said he would rather sacrifice both legs and keep his two arms, but he was drunk and did not know what he was saying. I said I would not sacrifice any of my limbs,

261

which had served me so well, but that I was going to Europe or America soon.

"We can go to Kohsichang tonight," I said. "If a British ship is in, do we have enough money to buy our way to Europe?"

"We have only the equivalent of ten pounds each."

We drank more Mekong. "We need to do something very smart," I said.

Gustav came out of his drunken daze for a moment. "Go to Burma. Burma is owned by the British and is a much better place for westerners."

"How far it is?" Reinhold asked.

"I don't know," Gustav said.

We drank whisky until we did not care how far it was, but we still talked about Burma, going over and over the one or two rumors which Gustav had heard months before.

When morning came, Reinhold and I dashed cold water on our faces and went out to buy two American-type khaki uniforms. We sought out Gustav, who was still at the bar, and asked him to come with us, but he said he would never enter a jungle, or go on any other kind of trip, with the two of us again. We had a final drink together, then Reinhold and I took two peddy carts to the train station. "To hell with Bangkok and all of Thailand," I said.

At Phitsanulak, 400 kilometers north of Bangkok, we left the train and started walking to the west. Three days later we entered mountainous country. We kept walking west, avoiding the road, and when we crossed a small river, we knew we were in Burma.

We took off our torn, ragged clothing and put on the clean American uniforms.

"Now," I said, "we are on English soil. This is better; these people will understand our problem and help us."

262

20

IN RANGOON there was a great pagoda shaped like a cone called the Shwe Dagon. It sat on a hill far above the level of the city, and the pagoda was over 350 feet high. All of it was covered with pure gold.

Surrounding the pagoda was a large open space for worship, a circular platform. Under the pagoda were gardens, and from there one could look out over a lake and other gardens.

We had come to Rangoon by bus, and we wandered about for a few hours, seeing the sights while we waited for sunset, when we planned to go to the docks. Then, if we found it difficult to find a ship, we planned to go to the British and ask for the help of the government.

About six o'clock we selected a nice restaurant. The waiter brought our food, and we ate in proper style, trying not to appear greedy. Many others were in the restaurant, most of them natives, including two policemen. Reinhold and I finished our meal with a toast to our coming success, and we rose to leave.

It was then that the two policemen approached us and asked to see our papers.

"We are American soldiers," I said in English, and have no passports."

"Let me see your papers as American soldiers."

"But American soldiers can go anywhere," I said heatedly.

The policemen smiled knowingly. One of them, a bald man of greater height than most Burmese, told us to come with him to the police station for questioning.

We walked along with them, concerned now but sure the British would help us. After passing several impressive buildings, we reached the police headquarters. There native police officers questioned us and had us taken to the C.I.D. headquarters. "Where are the English?" I demanded over and over. I saw only a few, and they avoided answering questions. The Burmese seemed to be making the decisions.

We were taken before a court and sentenced to six months. Still we were not sure what was going on. "What crime did we do?" I demanded of a Burmese C.I.D. official following our trial. "We came into your country, paid for a bus ride to Rangoon and ate dinner in a restaurant, and for this we are given six months?"

"That is correct," he said. "You did not have papers."

"Where are the English?" I demanded.

"They cannot help you now. In January we inaugurated our own president, Sao Shwe Thaik, and Burma became a free country. Several weeks ago the English might have taken charge of your problems, but now we Burmese are in charge, and we are against white people."

Reinhold and I were taken to a large room, which we shared with twenty-eight other prisoners, all of them Burmese. In the mornings the others were taken out and worked, but Reinhold and I were left alone. In the evening the others came back, worn out by prison labor. The door locked the thirty of us in.

264

At first Reinhold and I stayed awake at night, ready at all times to protect ourselves from the natives. But the hatred of the white man, that we had been told was universal in Burma, did not exist in our cell. Perhaps it was not strong enough to turn prisoners against their fellow prisoners.

Soon Reinhold and I made a few friends; then a few more. Many of the Burmese prisoners were from fine families, and a few were rich. "Everywhere the natives want to rule themselves," one prisoner, whose father had been closely associated with the English, told me. "Everybody thinks he is free now, and that this means he owes no taxes and can do as he pleases. This is a bloody time to be alive."

I counted the days I was in prison. I counted, at least, until I reached 150 days, where I stopped. I did not care any longer; the jail had deadened my hopes through inactivity. Reinhold went on counting, he told me later, but for me it was a surprise one morning when we were released.

We were brought before a buglike Burmese officer. He insisted that we stand before him while he stared at us. Our clothes were now rags, our faces needed shaves, our eyes were sunken. We had prison pallor, and from prison food we had lost weight. There was little fight left in either of us.

"Now," he said, "you have served your terms. Remember the welcome you received in Burma, should you ever want to visit us again."

Guards grabbed hold of us and pulled us outside. The sun was brilliant, and I had to cover my eyes with my hands. The guards kept pushing us along the street, so we were moving like blind men.

We were shoved into a near-empty bus. "Where are you taking us?" I asked the guards in English.

265

They ordered me to be quiet. They insisted that we stand. The bus moved for several hours, and the roads were bad. Burmese passengers kept getting on and off. I thought I could not stand up much longer. "Why it is that only the prisoners are friendly?" I asked one of the guards.

"Shut up," he said.

"Ah, listen," I said, "where do you come by that kind of talk? Who are you? You think you have a right to tell another person to shut up?"

He leaped from the seat and swung his fist at me, but I ducked the blow. With one left to his stomach I doubled him up. I tapped the back of his neck and he collapsed on the floor. Then something struck the back of my head, and I lost consciousness.

When I came to, I was lying on the floor of the bus; the bus was still bumping down the road. I looked around. Reinhold was standing not far away. The two guards were sitting nearby, and the seven or eight Burmese passengers had moved to the back of the bus, where they huddled silently.

I got up. The guard who had tried to hit me had blood coming out the side of his mouth, so he must have struck his mouth as he fell. I said nothing to him or he to me.

At last the bus stopped and the guards ordered us to get off. They told us where to walk, directing us into thick woods. I whispered to Reinhold that they might kill us and who would know the difference?

We came to a small river and the guards pointed across it, toward the east. "Now go," one of them said. "Remember we are Burmese; we hate white people. Now go! Go! Go!"

Reinhold and I splashed into the water. We swam and crawled to the other side, pulled ourselves up the opposite bank and stumbled into the deep jungle.

266

21

THREE WEEKS LATER I was back at Kohsichang Island, while Reinhold was in Bangkok, still staking his hopes on saving money from selling medicine. At the harbor I stayed with a dancing girl, who said she loved me and told me there was nobody in the world who was as fine as I, which were words I liked to hear. So in the nighttime she helped me forget my worries, and in the daytime, I looked for work on the ships. But I could not be hired, not officially, since I had no papers, so I had to find sailors who would hire me to do their work for them. This was sometimes possible, but it was never easy, and the work was not continuous.

When I did get on for a day, I would work hard. I would lift twice as much as any other man in the harbor, and I was a steady worker. Whenever the sailors asked me a question, I answered it, but did not fall into conversation. In my mind now was a bitterness toward all western people who had no troubles, and toward myself for having ended up in Asia without papers. Even so, I was working, making my way. And I had this girl who every evening told me that she loved me best of all.

After a time I moved out of her room to a Thai hotel.

There Gustav came to tell me Reinhold had been arrested.

"Already I've been to the police station to pay the fine," he said, "but they say there is no fine. It is four months in jail, and no way out unless a medical authority should decide that the medicine he was selling is good medicine."

"Never in this world will we find such a doctor." I thought to myself that here was the difference between the way Reinhold had chosen and mine. I had worked in the shipyard and had my own room, while he was in jail without hope.

"We will have to save him," I told Gustav. "It is up to us. Somehow we have to get him out of jail."

We talked about how to do it. He had the idea of getting arrested himself then breaking out with Reinhold; but this was not a sound plan. I had a notion in my own mind, but it was not a sound plan, either. It was so farfetched, in fact, I would not tell Gustav what it was for fear he would laugh at me; but the next morning, having no better idea, I rented from the owner of the hotel a white suit. It was too small for me in the shoulders and the seat of the pants, but it did very well so long as I did not sit down.

When Gustav and I took a bus to Bangkok, I stood up all the way, since I could not chance sitting down. We walked the distance to the jail.

Inside I told a guard I wanted to see the chief.

"Your name, sir?" he asked me.

"Dr. Eddy," I said.

Gustav gave me a slight flicker of a smile, but the guard did not see him.

"You'll never pull it off, Hukov," Gustav whispered to me.

"Probably not," I said, "but I have nothing to lose. And four months in this jail, after what Reinhold went through in Burma, might mean the end for him."

The guard returned and told me the chief would see

me. I went down a hall, following the guard, and so was admitted to the small, private office of the official of this station. He got up from behind his desk.

"Sit down, Doctor," he said. "It's a pleasure to meet you."

"Yes, sir," I said, "but if I may, I would prefer to stand."

He had been about to sit down, and my answer came as a surprise to him. Looking rather uncomfortable, he leaned on his desk. "Well, what can I do for you, Doctor?"

"Sir, a young man is in your prison for selling medicine. I know about his medicines; they are very fine. I recommend them to my patients."

Perspiration came through the collar of my shirt. It was difficult to think, standing there, with the chief standing also, and having this lie to tell. "I sent several patients to buy medicine this morning, and they couldn't find this young man, and I was told he was arrested, so I have come to ask you to let him go free."

The chief gave me a curt, puzzled nod. "I see." He peered around the room as if trying to decide where he was. "Won't you sit down, Doctor, so we can discuss this." Once more he started to sit down.

"No, sir, I prefer to stand," I said.

He was halfway into his chair this time, but he straightened up once more, giving me a baffled look.

"The reason is I haven't been able to sit down for a few days now. I have some sores that bother me."

"Well," he said, suddenly brightening, "have you tried the skin salve made by this young man?" He picked up a bottle which I recognized instantly. "In here, Doctor, is a mixture of Lysol, baby powder, and motor oil which might be excellent for you."

"Yes, sir," I said.

269

"It's just the thing, all right. It'll scorch the skin right off you."

"Yes. Well, Chief, sometimes we doctors like to scorch the skin to get a cure for sores."

"I'm sure you do, Dr. Eddy. Now, sir, let me have more information about you for my record." He sat down, took out a piece of paper and a fountain pen. "Your name is Eddy. Now, where did you study medicine?"

"In Vienna," I said.

He nodded approvingly. "And did you practice in Vienna?"

"I—I practiced in Lvov, Poland, for many years," I said. "Also I have done work in the northern part of this very country, in Chieng Mai."

He wrote it down. "Now, you say that this medicine is good for skin ailments. And the other medicines, the medicine for toothache is excellent, also?"

"Yes," I said.

"Very well." He finished writing. "Dr. Eddy, we will give proper consideration to your request." Now he was grinning, however, so I knew I had not helped Reinhold.

Also I knew the best thing I could do was leave his office as fast as I could; but I could not do it. "Sir, I'll tell you the truth. In all honesty, I'm not a doctor from Lvov."

He erupted into laughter which grew so loud guards rushed in. He chased them out and finally got control of himself again. He peered at me, serious now. "What's your name?"

"Hukov," I said.

He stared at the paper for a minute, then tore it down the middle and threw it away. "What do you want?"

"Sir, my friend was recently in jail in Burma for several months. He has been through all the prisons he can stand, and now he is in your jail for four months. I ask you to release him."

270

The chief glanced up. "Will you guarantee for him? You appear to be a man of substance."

I wondered if the chief had guessed that my suit was borrowed. "I would sign any papers to get Mr. Reinhold out of prison," I said, "even if I had to lie."

The chief's eyes narrowed. "You lie, Mr. Hukov?" he said. He took out an American cigarette and lit it, sat back in his chair smoking.

I had only 200 baht to offer him, but he refused the bribe. "No, I know what it's like with you men," he said gruffly. He called in a guard and told him to bring Reinhold.

Reinhold was surprised to see me, especially dressed up and looking prosperous. The chief told him he could go free, provided he would sell no more medicine.

Reinhold promised him that, and the two of us jubilantly went out to the lobby, where Gustav joined us for a celebration.

22 WORKING AROUND the docks, Reinhold and I came to know many sailors, and we got to work on the different ships. But usually the Thai took what jobs there were, and the pay was poor; so we could not save money. Often we were hungry.

But there were girls there, and although Reinhold was always jealous when I got prettier ones than he, we both enjoyed their companionship. Sometimes we argued about women, but more often about escaping to Malaya. Now that we had found Burma was not a decent place for a human being, he had Malaya on his mind, and not a day passed but that he told me what some sailor had told him about the wonderful country of Malaya.

But we did not have money even to get to the border, and there was no reason, so far as I could tell, to believe the British would send us on to Europe. "Let's give ourselves a few more months here," I would tell him. "Something will come up in our favor if we stay at work with the sailors."

At last, in November, something did. I got a job working for the engineer in the engine room of the S.S. *Minnesotan*. I spent fourteen hours a day in that hot place, and did so

273

well that my work was called to the attention of the captain, who invited me to his cabin. There we had a long talk and some American whisky. He seemed to like me, as I liked him, and before the afternoon was over he wrote a letter in my behalf to the consul of the United States in Bangkok.

"Now, Hukov, you take this to the consulate. You go up there tomorrow and see this official. Can you read English?"

"I can make it out, sir."

His letter requested that the United States give me papers so that I could get a job at Kohsichang. Captain Griffin told the American consul that I had proved myself to be able, and that he wanted to help me. He said he would consider it an official and personal courtesy if the consul would give me a recommendation.

When I tried to thank him for the letter, all my English escaped me. I did say a few words in German, but he did not understand German. He did, however, understand what I meant, how deep in my heart went my gratitude.

That night Reinhold and I talked over his problem. If the American consul gave me papers, I promised I would go to the captain and tell him that Reinhold also needed a letter. Then we could easily find jobs at the harbor.

That night we took a bus to Bangkok. I could not wait until morning, sleep would have been impossible for me. When the American consulate opened, we were on the steps, waiting to get in.

Immediately I was shown into the office of the vice-consul, who remembered me. He read my letter twice before laying it down on his desk. He stared at his desk top for a long while, then picked up the letter. "Mr. Hukov, there's no way I can do this. I'm sorry. Please tell the captain of the *Minnesotan* that I can do nothing for you."

When I went out, tears were streaming down my face.

I did not have to tell Reinhold that we had been turned down.

That afternoon I reported to Captain Griffin and told him the American vice-consul had done all he could, but without results. The captain seemed to be truly sorry. "Hukov, all I can say is to go on doing your best work, and God help you." We shook hands, and I left his cabin and went back to the engine room.

Before leaving Kahsichang, the crew gave me clothing and an envelope in which I found sixty United States dollars.

Reinhold was drunk when I reached our room, so I got drunk, too. We told each other we had not really had a chance of getting a job in Thailand, that never would we get help.

"Malaya," Reinhold kept saying. "Malaya is British."

"I'm not going there, Reinhold. First I want to try other ideas. We've not tried the tin mines."

"The Chinese work the tin mines. But nobody has said one word against Malaya. It's the only country touching Thailand we haven't tried. In Malaya we can be free men. They will give us papers."

"To hell with papers," I said. "We can't live anywhere in the whole world because we don't have papers. Even when an American has a ship and wants to hire us to work for him, he can't do it. What the hell are papers, Reinhold? I wasn't born with any damn papers! Why are they more important than human beings?"

"In Malaya, Eddy——"

"Damn Malaya! Damn all countries."

"No, Eddy. Listen, will you come with me to Malaya? Will you at least try Malaya, Eddy?"

I glared at him. "Well, why not?" I said. "Why the hell not try Malaya?"

"That's right, Eddy. Everything will work out well in Malaya."

In Bangkok we bought train tickets for Haad Yai, Thailand, near the border. There we entered the Wattana hotel and took a room. It was hot and stuffy, so we left the door open, even though we took off most of our clothes to cool off. I was lying on the bed, and Reinhold was sitting on a chair talking about the wonders of Malaya, when a girl walked by our door, stopped for an instant, then went on. Reinhold called out to her.

She came back, a beautiful girl with golden skin, small features, and an extremely nice body. I saw right off she had the build to be a star in Hollywood.

"Come in," Reinhold said in Thai.

She came in, and she sat down on the bed beside me. Reinhold got up from his chair and came over to us. He sat down on the other side of the girl, because I did not see him when he motioned for me to move over so he could sit between us. When he sat down, he said, "What country are you from?"

"Viet Nam. I'm a refugee."

When she said that my heart went out to her. "We're from Germany," I said, "but we've been in your country, Star."

She smiled. "Star?"

"That's your name because you should be in Hollywood."

"Star," she said softly, fondly considering it.

"That's a beautiful name for you. My name is Eddy."

Reinhold cleared his throat to try to gain her attention. "How long have you been in this country?" he asked.

"Only a few months," she answered.

"How do you make a living?" he said.

"How do you think?"

I said, "Well, you must go on your way then, because

276

we have no money, and tomorrow we will be in jail anyway. I can't pay you."

"I have money," she said, smiling at me, "and I like you
for being honest with me. Also I like to be called Star."

Suddenly Reinhold stood up and took out all the money
he had. "Well, I have money. I have seven hundred baht
right here, and I will give you three hundred baht if you'll
stay with me for the night."

Immediately I said to him in German, "Reinhold, this
girl has shown a preference for me, and now you have
made a fantastic offer and will spend all our money. If
you go through with this, we're through as friends."

He ignored me. "You come out in the hall a minute,
Star, and let's talk. I can't talk to anybody in here."

She hesitated, but went out into the hall with him. A
minute later, she came back and sat down beside me. "He
offers me four hundred baht," she said. "What shall I do?"

Reinhold was a nice-looking boy; always he had had
women around him, and now I was not sure why he was
having to pay four hundred baht to get a girl for one
night. I knew the value of four hundred baht to this girl,
but it hurt me to tell her to go with Reinhold when I
knew if I said "no" she would stay with me. Also I liked
her. She had a baby face, and always I liked a baby face
on a woman.

"Eddy, you tell me what you want me to do."

"I want you to stay with me. But also I would like to
know if this friend of mine will go through with his
scheme. I tell you, go with him, get his four hundred baht
and, as soon as you can, come back to me."

She thought about that for a moment, then got up
rather primly and went out, closing the door after her.

I listened to their footsteps fade away, then locked the
door and stretched out on the bed.

I was awakened by knocks at the door. I opened it to

277

find Star there. She came in, and I closed the door. As I turned around, she immediately threw her arms around my neck and kissed me. She pressed against me and hardly was able to get out of her clothes for kissing me and holding me. I gave up trying to undress after a while, for this was the best girl I had ever met in any place I had ever been in the world. Her small hands were all over me, and she would kiss me all over, until I did not know what in the world had happened to keep me away from this girl, and I did not give a damn for Reinhold and Malaya or the whole damned politics of the West and the East.

When the sun came up, I was lying in the bed as happy as if I had citizenship papers to seven countries. I was very thankful for this girl, for nobody else could have made me feel half so good; and still she was beside me, snuggling up to me and making me think that any man who did not marry a Viet Nam girl was making a mistake.

Then she bounced out of bed and fumbled with her clothes. I was afraid she was going to dress and leave, in which case I would be at a loss; but instead she got Reinhold's four hundred baht out of her dress. She gave me Reinhold's money and then plopped beside me in the bed.

I was so happy about her giving me that man's money that I had some more happy minutes with her before I finally got up and pulled on my pants. "You stay right there," I said. I ran down the hall and called for beers and a breakfast for two.

I ran back to the room and told Star we would have a nice party. A few minutes later a boy came running in with the beers, and I took those and chased him out to bring us breakfast. Soon he was back, and then Star got out of bed, draped a sheet around herself, and we sat down on the floor and ate. We were eating and laughing

278

together when Reinhold came in through the door of my room. "My Lord," he said, "what's this?"

"We are having beers and food with part of your four hundred baht," I said.

He sat down on my bed, all the color drained out of his face. "With my money?"

"That's the way the world turns, Reinhold. It's always hard on the losers, but thank all angels, I'm not the loser this time."

"Well, hell, aren't you coming to Malaya with me?"

"Malaya?" I said. "No, I'm not leaving this room until I've spent all your four hundred baht, then I'm not going anywhere with you."

Reinhold was jealous and sorry at the same time. "Eddy, now you are coming to Malaya with me, aren't you, Eddy?"

"No, you go ahead without me. I'm going to stay here with Star and celebrate your departure."

"Eddy, are you angry with me because I took this girl away from you?"

Star and I looked at him, our mouths full of food. "Took her away from me?" I said.

"Well, are you angry because I took her away last night for a few hours? Eddy, you have no right to be angry with me for that, because I couldn't help it. Star is the most beautiful girl I've ever seen."

"She is a beautiful kid," I said, grinning at her. "So I will stay here."

"Look," Reinhold said in agony. "I tell you what, I'll go to my room and wait there all day and night, and tomorrow we'll go to Malaya."

I winked at Star, and she winked back at me. She had the cutest face I had ever seen on any woman anywhere. She was absolutely the last word in women on earth.

Reinhold stared down at us for a while, but we went

279

on with our breakfast. "Eddy, I tell you, I'll go on back to Bangkok, but when you get back to Bangkok, you look me up, will you, Eddy?"

"Okay," I said. "I'll stop by to see how you're doing."

He stared down at us for a while longer, then went out, closing the door softly behind him. For the first time, I was sorry for the way I had treated him and started to get up and call him back; but when I saw Star's dark eyes looking at me and the smile on her happy face, I decided I had been right in every word I had said and that Reinhold would be very much in my way in the hotel.

So instead of calling him back, I moved over to her side of the "table" where I could be close to her.

We had the happiest days of our lives, staying together for three weeks. I asked her a hundred times to marry me, but she would only say, "Where would we live, and where would you get a job?" Often I left the hotel and went through town, begging for a job, but Haad Yai was even worse than Bangkok. There was not a glimmer of a chance of work for me.

So when I had not another cent for food, and when Star admitted she had spent almost all her money, too, I told her the only thing I could do was go back to Bangkok and find a job in a hurry. She smiled at me when I said that, a very old smile for a young kid, because she knew I had already looked in every street in that huge city.

She gave me money to buy a train ticket and more baht to spend on the way. She came with me to the station, her pretty face smiling as if she did not see anything wrong with the world, yet in her eyes I saw tears forming. All I could think of was that I loved her more than I loved my own life, but now I must take a train for Bangkok.

"Star, you come with me."

"No. First, you go. I have friends here. There are several Viet Nam families in Haad Yai."

280

As the train rang its bell for leaving, she pressed more money into my hand, but I gave it back to her. "My darling Star," I said, "I'll write for you soon."

"Yes, Eddy. Good-by, dear Eddy. I have had three happy weeks with you. Good-by, precious Eddy."

I ran after the train and got aboard, but I did not look back because I knew she was crying now. She would not want me to see her crying.

The trip to Bangkok was full of sorrow for me, but when I got in, what did I see the first minute but Reinhold, standing by a chair selling medicine. I sneaked around behind him and clapped him on the shoulder. He swung around, expecting to see a policeman, and when he saw me his face opened up with a big smile. "Hukov, boy, where have you been so long?"

"You know where I've been."

"Not for three weeks, Eddy!"

"Well, my money ran out so I had to come back."

He started laughing. Suddenly he turned and kicked his medicine bottles all over the street, so that the Chinese and Thai began to laugh at him. "Come on, Eddy, let's go somewhere and have a conversation."

We went to a coffee shop, and he ordered tea and cakes. "Well, so you and Star got along well." He had a pleasant smile on his face, and I could tell he was thinking about her himself.

"So well I would marry her, if I could, and take her to Europe with us. I tell you, Reinhold, I am desperate to find money for her and me."

That day we went down to Kohsichang Island. There we found one day's work on a Greek ship, but for four days after that we found nothing. I wrote Star, asking her to write me at my hotel.

Reinhold and I continued to look for jobs. Occasionally we found day labor. We made enough to live on, but not decently. As time went on, however, we began to meet old friends about the docks; business picked up, and we were able to pay our back hotel bills. I decided that in a few months I would send for Star.

However, one night when I came in from working in the engine room of a Swedish ship, Reinhold said he had a letter for me. I tore it open; it was from Star.

Dear Eddy:
I love you, but I have accepted the proposal of a young man who is also a fugitive from Viet Nam. He is a good man, and you two would be friends together. He knows about you, and is helping me to write this letter, because I do not know much about how to write a letter, so he is putting down the words on paper. Please, Eddy, you will see that this is best for you. Eddy, it is best for him and me.

Star

For several hours I was completely lost in grief. Late that night I left the hotel and walked down to the docks. I came to a ship which nobody was around. I did not know what ship it was or where it was going.

I crawled aboard and sneaked across her deck. I made my way below deck and hid myself deep in the engine room. When day came, I pressed myself tightly into my hiding place and did not move a muscle.

That night and the next day I stayed in my hiding place. That afternoon the engine was turned over. I heard orders on deck, spoken in English. I gathered that our destination was San Francisco.

I hardly breathed, for fear of being found.

Soon the ship was vibrating heavily, as if it were moving across the harbor. Later I felt the rock of the ship, the gentle sway as it entered the ocean.

We were at sea. Relief swept through me. I had done

282

it. Thanks to Star and my bitterness, I had taken the chance. My only regret was that I had left Reinhold and Gustav behind.

Ten miles at sea the chief engineer passed the place where I was hiding and saw me. He ran down through the room and disappeared down the hall. A minute later, the engines cut down to a low speed. Several men came into the room and ordered me on deck.

The captain was in a rage. He stormed out at me for getting aboard his ship. "Take him ashore," he shouted.

The ship turned back and I was put ashore and given to the customs officials, who threw me into prison.

23

FOUR MONTHS LATER, when I got out of jail, I could not find Reinhold and Gustav. They were not at the C.I.D., not in any of the more likely hotels. All one day and night I looked, then the next day, anxious to find them, at last to see faces of friends.

That night I slept in the park, and the next day I went to one of the busier corners of the city and waited, hoping to see somebody I knew. I stood there for two or three hours. Then an ex-Legionnaire, who was staggering from whisky, came along.

I stopped him. "Reinhold and Gustav, where are they?" I asked.

"You don't know? They're not here."

I stared at him, baffled and frightened. "Where are they?"

"Gone to Greece. Caught a Panamanian ship three months ago."

He went on down the street, but I stood there on the sidewalk, not seeing any face or person, loneliness gripping me, covering me, so heavy and full that I knew I would never shake it off.

A policeman came up to me. "What's the matter with you?"

I shook my head angrily. "What does it matter?" I quickly crossed the street and lost myself in the crowd.

That night I lay in the park. It rained and by dawn I was quite ill. Two little boys called the police, and they took me to the C.I.D. headquarters. The young lieutenant bought me tea at the canteen and gave me the first food I had had in three days.

"If your friends are gone, I will mark their names off our list," he said.

"I was out of detention long before they," I said. "But I have not made it yet. I was in the SS and should have managed to escape first."

"You will find a solution for your problem soon."

"I'm no closer than I was two years ago. Twice I tried to stowaway, and both times I failed."

"Don't try again, either, Hukov, unless you are sure you can make it. This last time you got four months. Next time you will get a long sentence."

"Yes, time is closing in on me," I said. "And now I have been ordered to stay away from Kohsichang. It was the only place I could find any work at all."

He nodded slowly. "You want to stay in the barracks tonight?"

"Yes," I said.

Going up the stairs we saw the boy attendant and he came with us. I spoke to him in German. "Are you surprised to see me back again?"

"One never knows, sir," he said, "the way the world is."

"A few new men arrived," the lieutenant said. "But they are out on guaranty. Some of your old friends are here, however."

When we entered, the men glanced at us. Some of them said hello. Carl got up slowly from a mat and came to me.

286

"Eddy, I haven't been here all this time," he said apologetically.

I shrugged. "I just returned to Bangkok, myself. Reinhold and Gustav got away."

"That's good. That's good, Eddy," Carl said.

The lieutenant went downstairs. When I had found a place to sleep, the Thai boy crept close by and sat down. He asked a few questions in German, mostly about where I had been.

"I taught you to speak a language," I said to him. "That is one thing I have done."

The next day Carl told me about his trials outside the barracks. He had tried to stowaway, but had been put off the ships before they sailed. Then he had been ordered to leave Kohsichang Island, and nowhere else could he find any work at all. He had almost starved before coming back to the C.I.D. He had been hungry and afraid, that was the worst of his experiences. "I was out for almost two months, Hukov."

"Two months can be a long time," I said.

That morning the boy attendant brought me my rice and salt fish. That afternoon I thought about asking the lieutenant to let me go, but the time went by. I watched the geckos and rested. It was a dry room, the food was brought to us, and there was no danger.

That night I slept well for the first time since I left the prison. The next morning I thought about calling for the lieutenant, but Carl asked me to wait until later and perhaps he would come with me.

That afternoon, however, he told me he was not going to leave the detention center, just then, and perhaps not until he had papers and could get a job. He sat on the floor, trembling, and told me he was afraid to go out again. "I almost starved, Eddy. And there are no jobs."

I went to the door and called for the lieutenant. The

287

guards told me he was out, that he would be back later. So I paced up and down the room, peering at the sleeping bodies of the others.

The Dane propped himself up on one elbow and glared at me at one point, perhaps because I was interfering with his rest, then he lay back down.

At the far window I looked out over a tree-shaded street. People were down there, going about in peace and safety. They were very fortunate. I thought of all the people on earth who were safe, who had no worries like mine, who knew their citizenship and had homes. I thought how lucky they were, every one of them.

At six my boy attendant brought me rice and fish. I ate and we talked for a while. He said he hoped to get a job someday with the C.I.D. and asked me what I thought. I told him it was a good organization. "They have been kind to me," I said. "But until some country gives me citizenship, I cannot be helped by anybody."

"You can get a Polish passport," the boy said.

"And be sent back to Poland, yes," I said. "No, some other country will have to give me papers."

About seven, the lieutenant came to the room. "Hukov, do you want to leave or stay?"

A few of the other prisoners heard him. Carl turned over on his mat and stared up at me. In his face I saw that he would not leave the prison with me. He had grown a part of his bed; the room was his home. There was about him already the pale skin of death.

"I want to go," I said.

A quick smile flashed on the lieutenant's face. "Yes, I knew you would. I knew you would not be beaten." He smiled and tapped me on the shoulder. "Don't let them beat you, Hukov."

"No," I said.

He, the boy and I went down the steps and walked to

288

the exit of the building. We stood there staring out at the street.

"It's a cool night," the lieutenant said.

He offered me a cigarette, then one to the boy, and the three of us smoked. "Do you have any ideas, Hukov?"

"No," I said. "But sometimes I get an idea while I'm walking uptown."

"You have a place to sleep tonight?"

"No."

"Perhaps it would be better for you to leave tomorrow morning."

"No. This is a good time for me," I said. "You watch your Rs," I told the boy.

Then I left them and started up the street.

24

I WALKED AWAY from the barracks
that night in 1949 to begin nine years of lonely struggle.
Only this year, 1957, have I finally gotten my feet on the
ground. Now I have some perspective on these past years,
but I cannot see their struggle objectively, of course, for
much of their pain, as well as happiness, clings to me.

I am still in Bangkok, still have no passport; I am a man
without a country, and this is even more dangerous now,
for each year it becomes more difficult for the white man
in Asia. The effects of Communist propagandists, as well
as Asian nationalists, are increasingly felt.

If the Communists gain power in Thailand in some future year, I will most likely be killed. I have fought them
for a long time—in Europe, in Viet Nam, and even in
Bangkok. Here, three years ago, I was the bodyguard of a
German named Gottlieb, who had been born in Russia
and reared in China. Four Russians were after him in
Thailand, he said. I heard one of them threaten him, tell
him that they had failed to get him in China but that they
would succeed in Thailand. It was my job for a few
months to see that they did not, and repeatedly I stepped

in to protect him. Before Gottlieb left Thailand, two of their four I sent to the hospital for treatment.

The Communists do not like me for that. I think it was the Communists who made me leave the tin mines, too, where I had a job for seven months in 1950, working as a wenchman under an American named Hare. One night I was in my bungalow, which was off to itself in the jungle, when knocks sounded at the door. I opened it to find a Chinaman holding a gun on me. Behind him were three other men.

The Chinaman came inside and handed me a letter. It was written in Russian and told me to return to Bangkok at once where, every day between 1:00 and 5:00 P.M., a man would give me instructions. I would receive good pay for carrying them out.

I slipped the letter into my pocket, but the Chinaman demanded its return, so I gave it to him.

"If you do not leave this place," he said, "you will be killed."

The next day I returned to Bangkok and immediately went to the United States military attaché and told him what had happened. He got me on a plane at once, which took me to a military training camp, where I was kept for two weeks. Then I was taken back to Bangkok and let go.

Since then I have had no messages from the Russians and, of course, this one might have been a trick. Living in Asia in my circumstances, even jests are desperate. But it was quite possible the Communists engineered it, for one reason or another; it is difficult to overestimate their thoroughness, and when they seek revenge, they usually find it. Some night in Bangkok, for example, a single blow or the flash of a knife and life would be over for me.

Even so, the fear of the Communists is sometimes overdone, at least by the British. I know this from experience. Back in 1948, soon after I found Reinhold and Gustav

292

were gone—in fact, the same night I left the detention barracks—I went to two of the tourist hotels, the Princess and the Oriental, and begged money from westerners. Then I went by train to Malaya, hoping there to find a way to Europe or America, but the British arrested me and threw me into the prison at Alor Star, where I stayed for two weeks.

Then, for questioning they took me to the C.I.D. headquarters at Kuala Lumpur. For two days I answered questions, and only near the end of the questioning did I determine what they were getting at, and, when I did, I became furious. They thought I was a Communist spy. Evidently they could not imagine any reason for a person to leave Thailand and come to Malaya unless he was working for Communists. Looking back I see some humor in this incident, but it was not funny while it was going on.

The British returned me to Alor Star prison, and nobody told me how long I was to be kept there or for what crime. They locked me in a cell alone. In the months to follow I came to know that cell quite well, even to its measurements. It was six feet wide and twelve feet long; the floor was concrete; the walls were light gray and there was one window, placed very high in the wall. Over the window were iron bars.

Sometimes I heard screaming from beyond the window, but I could see nothing except the sky, so I did not know what was going on. One morning, however, while a man was crying his heart out, I leaped high into the air and managed to grab a bar with one hand. I pulled myself up until I could see out. I saw a police "beater" laying stripes on a Malayan prisoner.

In days that followed, I watched many other beatings. The prisoner's hands always were bound with leather and tied to a heavy bench, then their legs were tied to the

293

bench, too, so that they could do nothing to help ease the force of the whip. Always at the beatings, a doctor stood by. If a prisoner was to receive twenty-five "ropes" on his back, the doctor counted the twenty-five and saw to it that he received not one more. Also the doctor tended to the bleeding flesh.

The same doctor was present at the hangings, of which I witnessed two while in the prison. Both the hanged men were Malayan. I did not know their crimes.

There were about 350 prisoners at Alor Star, guarded by sixty guards, fifteen of whom were on duty at any given time. The prisoners worked long hours, farming, cooking, washing, welding, working in the blacksmith shop, repairing cars, and so forth. Also, every other day they had to take English lessons. They hated that most of all.

The English jailer did not order me to work or take lessons, and he had the guards bring me European food. But after four or five months, with no word of when I would be released, I decided I would have to try to break out, even at the risk of my life.

Late one night I bent the handle of my chamber pot into proper shape and squeezed it into the lock on my door. I twisted the lock and threw all my strength against the door, and it flew open.

The guard at the end of the corridor did not awaken, although the thirty Malayans in the cell opposite mine did. They beckoned to me to open their door, but there was a light near the door to their cell, and I dared not try to help them.

I made my way down the corridor toward the sleeping guard, planning to knock him out and take his rifle. I was only a few yards from him when a guard outside said, "Stay where you are. Any movement, and you are dead."

I stood still. The alarm system in the prison went off;

the sound beat at the walls around me. Guards shouted instructions to each other. "Call for the British soldiers," one of them kept shouting.

The guard who had been asleep was wide awake now. "The Legionnaire broke an iron door," he kept repeating. "Can you imagine that?"

They took me to another cell and locked the door with two locks and assigned two guards to watch me for the rest of the night.

Although unsuccessful, my prison break brought success, because the jailer Shaffer's report interested the High Commissioner of Malaya. When he investigated my case, he ordered that I be released.

The British turned me over to the Thai emigration authorities at Haad Yai, with the request that I be investigated to find out why I had come to Malaya. Still the only reason the British could figure out was that I was a Communist spy.

The Thai police chief at Haad Yai contacted the C.I.D. in Bangkok and was told to let me go free in Thailand. The chief then offered me some money, so that I could get back to Bangkok. He said to me, "Hukov, everybody is afraid of Communists now, and they think if they lock up everybody who is strange to them, they will lock up all the Communists; but it is not so easy."

Back in Bangkok I did not have a hope of a job or of escape. With assistance from a priest, I wrote the Pope in Rome, asking for help. When I did not receive a reply, I wrote Perón in Argentina, but he did not reply, either.

Then the war broke out in Korea, and immediately I wrote the U.N. Supreme Commander, General MacArthur, in Japan. I told him I was a German born in Poland, that between 1941 and 1945 I had served in the German Storm Troopers, that from 1945 to 1947 I had been in the French Foreign Legion, and that now I was in Thailand

295

with little hope for my future because Poland was held by the Communists. I asked him to let me fight the Communists in Korea.

In two weeks a letter came from Brigadier General Kenneth Bush, Adjutant General of the Far East Command. He told me he had received my letter and that the need for my services would be considered. He thanked me for my offer.

I read the letter once, I read it twice, I read it ten times and could not see any hope in it. So I went to the nearest dispensary and bought a large bottle of aspirin. I asked the pharmacist how many of them I should take for a bad headache.

"Two," he said.

"And if I take all of them?"

"All in that bottle? Then you die."

I went to my room and thought over the whole situation. Then I swallowed the contents of the bottle and fell into a coma.

I awoke in the Chulalongkorn hospital, where doctors were pumping out my stomach. The owner of my house was there, also. He demanded to know why I took "poison," but I told him nothing.

That night I tried to strangle myself. I pressed my thumbs into my windpipe until it was closed; but my mind blacked out, my hands released my throat and my lungs filled with air.

After two days in the hospital, I was released. Again I had no money, no place to go. Not even God would take you, I said to myself.

But walking through Lumbini Park, a strange notion struck me about God. I got to thinking about the whole business of killing myself, wondering what it was that had taken me through the wars and the swamp, through jungles in Indochina, Thailand, Malaya, Burma, which had taken me through prisons and adventures and had not allowed me to be injured once. Now it had even refused my will to die.

I got to thinking about my body and how perfect it was, and how it had taken punishment that no machine could have endured. I sat down in the park and considered the strength of my body and the strength beyond that, which was greater than I was, something that lay beyond myself, beyond the reach of my own will; and just thinking about who I was, and thinking about my body, which had been my only good possession for many years, I came for a few moments to feel the presence of a force which I supposed was God Almighty.

As I walked toward the major part of the city, I had greater confidence than before. Now I knew God was aware of all I did, and that He was permitting this punishment, perhaps had ordered it because of some wrong I had done. Or perhaps it was not punishment so much as it was a time of testing, to judge my strength. I knew He was aware of it, in either case, and that someday He would make me free again.

I still hold to that view confidently.

Other Legionnaires have killed themselves in Bangkok. One of them was a friend of mine; he died in 1954.

Two other Germans, Hainze and Loter, could not stand their lives here, and they worked out a scheme to escape to Europe. On a map of the world they plotted out a way to walk the whole distance. Their route lay through Burma, across India, Pakistan, Iran, Iraq, Syria, Turkey, and to Greece. From Greece they planned to get a fishing boat to take them to Italy, where they would hike north to Germany. Almost all the distance was through Asia, and it was while we were studying their map that I real-

297

ized Europe was only a tiny bit of land tacked onto the northwestern tip of the body of Asia. When I saw how small Europe was, compared to the massive continent to the East, I began to wonder what the future held for the world.

I did not go with Hainze and Loter on their trip, which is good, because they were shot at the Burmese border and died there. They did not get very far, and any westerner who starts today on such a march is not likely to get far, either, not in Asia.

So life goes with Legionnaires, of whom some twelve are now in Bangkok. Three years ago, the government of Free Germany opened a legation here, which gave a few of us hope. I went to them at once. They gave me money and promised me a passport. But then from Bonn they received word that in the future no one born outside of Germany itself would be given a passport. The ambassador himself talked with me, told me he was sorry. He said if I could reach West Germany, the Bonn Government would doubtless protect me, since I had fought for Germany, but that he could not give me papers. I knew then God was not yet satisfied with my punishment.

Then followed many months of near-starvation. But in September, 1956, I found a job. I was coming back from the north country, where I had been trying to sell medicine—even though it was the rainy season—and I met an American, Mr. Schneider of the U.S. Operations Mission. I told him my problems and that an American author was writing the story of my life. When we reached Bangkok he phoned his friend, also an American, who owned a chain of gasoline stations, the Caltex Company. And the owner, Mr. Reece, offered me a job starting the following month.

I had no idea what it would be or what the salary

298

would be. When the day came, I went to see Mr. Reece, and he gave me a job as a mechanic at 700 baht a month, or about $35. It was good to have work again.

I stayed with him only one month, however, because I received an offer to become assistant to a German engineer at the Belgo-Thai company, which handles Westinghouse air conditioners. There I received 3000 baht a month.

I worked for them eight months and then went with a larger company, as chief mechanic at a salary of 3500 baht. Opportunities were everywhere for me now. Suddenly after eleven years jobs were offered me. I knew then that God had forgiven me for my sins and had accepted me once more.

Also this book is a sign that my fate is changing. I believe this book will fall into the hands of some individual or agency which will help me find a permanent solution. That is one reason the book is so very important to me.

Beyond that it is important because I have had many experiences and must tell about them. Those who have seen the sun rise in foreign places must tell what they have seen. I have been through wars, through jungles, have spent time in Oriental prisons, have been hunted by the Russians, the Americans, the Poles, the French, the Vietnamese, the Cambodians, the Thai, the Burmese, the British.

I have crossed the Sahara to the Legion's prison, and have been through Suez on a Legion ship. I have loved many women and made love to many more. Nobody can have as many experiences as I without wanting to tell them.

My only fear in telling them is that some person will pity me. I seek no man's pity, unless he has known better men, has loved better women, has endured greater suffering, has fought harder battles. My life has caused me suffering, but it has left me strong.

I stand today as tall as I stood in Poland, when as a boy I went out to fight for my country, and so started my journey.

Appendix

Reproduction of some of the papers which support the story of Eddy Hukov.

Gesandtschaft
der

Bundesrepublik Deutschland

Bangkok

522-01 Tgb.Nr. 03711/54

Bangkok, 8. Dezember 1954

Herrn Eduard Hugo
Soi Prida 634/23
Bangkok-Bangkapi

In Ihrer Staatsangehörigkeitsangelegenheit werden Sie gebeten,
in den ersten Tagen der kommenden Woche vormittags in der Gesandtschaft
vorsprechen zu wollen.

Im Auftrag

Bangkok, 8 December 1954

German Embassy, Bangkok
Mr. Edward Hugo
Soi Prida 634/23
Bangkok
With reference to the matter of your citizenship, you are requested during the first
days of the following week in the morning to present yourself at the embassy.

Quittung

Beleg Nr.

330.- Tical = _____ DM

in Buchstaben : _Dreihundertdreissig Tical_____

(Landeswaehrung)

sind von __Herrn Eduard Hugo Bangkok_____

in Sachen _Rückzahlung erhaltener Bar - Unter-_

_stützung_____

an die Zahlstelle der Amtskasse in ___Bangkok___ gezahlt worden.

Umrechnungskurs :

_____ ___Bangkok___, den __7. 1.__ 195_5_

Zahlstelle der Amtskasse

d. Maack

Kons. 118
5000 6. 52

Z.B.E. - Nr. _____

Receipt for 330 ticals, which Hukov obtained January 7, 1955,
on repayment of a loan made to him for his support by the
German Embassy.

Der Geschäftsträger

der Bundesrepublik Deutschland

lädt Herrn Edward v. Hugo

herzlich zu einem thai-deutschen Abend mit
Abendessen und Tanz am Freitag, den 21.
Januar 1955, 20.00 Uhr, in der Gesandtschaft der Bundesrepublik Deutschland,
64 Petchburi Road, ein.

Tagesanzug

U. A. w. g.

An invitation to Edward Hugo to attend a dinner and formal dance at the German Embassy, January 21, 1955.

Mcc/pf.

บริษัท เบลโก-ไทย เอเยนซี่ส์ จำกัด
BELGO-THAI AGENCIES LIMITED.
7 SILOM ROAD
BANGKOK (THAILAND)
PHONE: 32132   CABLES: CATHEXCO

TO: The Manager,
Post Publishing Co. Ltd.,
Bangkok.

YOUR REF:
OUR REF:

BANGKOK   1st. June, 1957.

Dear Sir,

      Please insert the following advertisement for three
consecutive days in the classified columns of the Bangkok Post,
charge to our account, and send all replies to Mr. E. Hukov, at
this address.

    "European, thirtyfour years old, speaks fluent
    English, Thai and German, presently working as
    workshop supervisor, xxxxx will shortly be
    available to take up similar position, or other
    related work. Excellent references. Please
    reply to Box No........."

        Yours faithfully,

บริษัท เบลโก–ไทย เอเยนซีส์ จำกัด
BELGO-THAI AGENCIES LIMITED
7 SILOM ROAD
BANGKOK (THAILAND)

PHONE: 32850
CABLES: BELGENGINE BANGKOK
ENGINEERING & REFRIGERATION DEPT.

YOUR REF:
OUR REF:

Bangkok, June 29th, 1957.

TO WHOM IT MAY CONCERN

      The bearer of this note, Mr. Edward Hukov, was employed by this company in the capacity of Workshop Supervisor from October, 1956 until the present date. Mr. Hukov's work during this period was extremely satisfactory, and we can highly recommend him to any one requiring his services in a similar capacity.

      Mr. Hukov is leaving this company due to reorganization, and carries with him our best wishes for the future.

s/d M. C. Culley.

Orient Steam Navigation Company Limited

MANAGERS Anderson, Green & Co. Ltd., 9-11 BILLITER SQUARE LONDON EC3

RDA/HMP.   26th September, 1957.

J. Ehle Esq.,
Visiting Associate Professor,
New York University,
Communication Arts Group,
Washington Square,
New York 3,
N. Y.

Dear Sir,

      The Registrar General has passed to us a copy of
your letter of the 18th September together with a copy of
his reply, and we now write to confirm that the "ORMONDE"
carried a battalion of troops of the French Foreign Legion
from Tunisia to Saigon on her voyage in the spring of 1946.

               Yours faithfully,
      ORIENT STEAM NAVIGATION CO. LIMITED.,

                For the Managers.